The sociology of sovereignty

Manchester University Press

The sociology of sovereignty

Politics, social transformations and conceptual change

Terje Rasmussen

MANCHESTER UNIVERSITY PRESS

Published by Manchester University Press
Oxford Road, Manchester M13 9PL

www.manchesteruniversitypress.co.uk

British Library Cataloguing-in-Publication Data
A catalogue record for this book is available from the British Library

ISBN   978 1 5261 7081 1   hardback
ISBN   978 1 5261 9575 3   paperback

First published 2023
Paperback published 2026

EU authorised representative for GPSR:
Easy Access System Europe – Mustamäe tee 50,
10621 Tallinn, Estonia
gpsr.requests@easproject.com

Typeset
by New Best-set Typesetters Ltd

Contents

Preface   *page* vi

Introduction: a concept in action   1
1 A sociology of constitutions   19
2 Political uses of 'sovereignty': sociological methodologies   51
3 Paradox: early modern formulations of sovereignty   66
4 Differentiation: national sovereignty and the sovereign state   95
5 The political, politics and sociology   124
6 Constitutional symbolism   145
7 Human rights versus state sovereignty   164
8 Federal sovereignty?   184

Select bibliography   201
Index   216

Preface

The term 'sovereignty' is one of those terms that constitute a surprising shortcut between philosophers like Hobbes and Rousseau, and day-to-day politics on local democracy or the European Union. It is a philosophical term and a polemical sword for use in heated debates. It is also a key word for a sociological discussion on the current meaning of the term and how it has developed, that concerns democracy and the state. This book's intention is to provide a sociologically informed resonance for discussions that I think will only grow in intensity.

The book unfolded in a project based at the University of Oslo on the turbulent life of the Norwegian constitution, *Grunnloven*, from its inception in 1814 until 2024. For the first time, the history of Norwegian liberalism and democracy was examined by focusing on conceptual struggles, from the Treaty of Kiel in 1814 to current controversies concerning democracy and European integration. When the pandemic 'state of exception' surprised us all, I had the opportunity to delve more closely into the philosophical aspects of the question of sovereignty and its arguments. Along the way, I have benefited from meetings at the Centre for Political Communication in my department at the University of Oslo, and from activities at the project and working group *Voicing Democracy* funded by the University of Oslo (UiO Democracy).

Introduction: a concept in action

How is it that national democracy is celebrated as the highest ideal at the same time as it is placed at the centre of political struggle? What implications lie under key concepts like 'democracy' and 'sovereignty' that are mobilised in political conflict? In this book I argue that these are sociological questions, not merely philosophical and political ones. I present a sociological perspective on the historical dynamics of constitutional debate. The aim of the book is to clarify how societies draw on their constitutions in their political conflicts and transformations. At the centre of interest stands the contested and probably indispensable concept of sovereignty.

The sociological perspective presented here is historically informed. Asking questions of sovereignty there can be no doubt that history is the science of the past *and* present. History is one of the remedies we have against confusion, resentment and ultimately political instability. Accounting for the history of the idea of democracy and autonomy is a way to inform the present and its social and human sciences what the stakes are. The story of sovereignty goes beyond reason and will; it spans from *realpolitik* to utopianism as a response to structural transformations. I therefore revisit some classic positions on the topic to look for their underlying sociological strategy.

The long history of the idea and concept of sovereignty is integrated in processes of social change and political struggle. I argue that the history of the concept is in need of an elaborated understanding, particularly of a – broadly understood – sociological approach. This book examines a sociological approach to the study of the concept of sovereignty in modern public debate, where its political power is played out. The term is seen as intimately connected to its public performative and argumentative use. It is located on the boundaries of legal and political knowledge and in its performative use as a rhetorical resource. Its dominant version specifies constitutional form assumed by a political community.

I will confine the discussion to Europe. The idea to take the superior (*soveranus*) from the king to the people was a revolutionary idea, and guided constitutional development in America, France and my own Scandinavian region. However, the term 'popular sovereignty' itself was as much a rhetorical weapon in public debates as a statement in constitutions. It still suggests an idea of governing, while keeping its deeper meaning in the shadows grasped by theology and philosophy – and sociology. National and popular sovereignty as concepts and structural facts have been shaped by revolutions, distinctions and exclusions, state power, social inequality, human rights and transnational constitutionalism. At the outset 'sovereignty' refers to political and legal entities – its ambivalence and liminality derives from its complex position in the language of law and politics, applied by both courts and parliaments, referring to norms and facts. It refers to both people and nation, a duality that needs to be explored. I argue that 'sovereignty' more than anything is a social concept and suggests the basis of its liberating and troubling power.

This book presents political and sociological approaches to the debate on sovereignty. I should caution the reader at this point that I wish to present a general perspective, and I do not actually carry out this sort of analysis in detail here. The book operates primarily on the level of theory and methodology. It provides an overview of ways to handle the problem of sovereignty conceptually and analytically. Specifically, the entry of the semantics of 'sovereignty', in political history, its function and how it is assumed and constructed – in short, its historicity – is to be discussed discourse-contextually here. As the term today is so tied up with its past origins of interest, sociological research will need to account for social and historical transformations that encouraged sovereignty arguments.[1] I assume a contingent or loose linkage between concept and social reality, and in focus is the argumentative use of the term and concepts with which it shares a family resemblance, as a weapon in circulation on all sides in political-constitutional controversy.

The question in many quarters is how state autonomy and popular sovereignty can be secured in a transnational world.[2] The embeddedness of 'sovereignty' and related concepts is assumed to provide political debates on such issues with meaning. Constitutional democracy and governing are matters of communicative struggles over the distribution and appropriation of power among political and social groups. A sociological approach of the kind I am advocating claims that the concept of sovereignty, with its interpretations and reformulations since Jean Bodin, has been a semantic method to simplify conceptually European political society. It examines the context in which sovereignty-arguments occur, and to whom sovereignty-arguments are addressed. What norms are put into action to assess the legitimacy of a claim to sovereignty? What consequences follow from the acceptance or rejection of a sovereignty claim?[3] To quote Kalmo and Skinner, the approach engages in untangling 'the complex links between concepts, institutions, practices and doctrines – all of which have been seen as the true nature of sovereignty'.[4] Another way of stating the intent of the approach presented here is that it argues for examinations of *production of legitimacy* of constitutional politics.[5] I argue that production of legitimacy including interpretations of sovereignty continues to semantically negotiate and handle paradoxes of power inherent in liberal society. I elaborate on the sociological claim that the complexity of political society in the 1800s could only be handled by linking sovereignty to the conceptual tradition of rule of law and the nation-state. Again, I do not test specific arguments empirically here, but advance insights into what has been labelled a sociology of constitutions, or, more generally, to what I call a historical sociology of the political.

Contested and paradoxical concepts

The theme of this book is how to observe sociologically how societies differentiate themselves semantically and conceptually to handle the paradox of legitimate rule. Its credo is: follow the paradox! Because the paradox of authority is unavoidable, it runs as a constant theme in political thought and debate, from Machiavelli, Bodin and Hobbes to the present day. For example, Thomas Hobbes introduced the term 'authorisation' to argue that the representative of the state's sovereign power nevertheless is granted authority by the multitude in their state of nature as authors and in a sense act in the name of them. Despite their total submission, authors will have to take the consequences of the sovereign's actions. In this way Hobbes navigated between the propagators of the king's divine right and the revolutionary position of popular sovereignty held by 'democratic gentlemen', that in his opinion would result in civil war. He produced a theory of the legitimate absolutist state. The paradox of legitimacy was ingeniously stated and handled, but of course not solved. Inspired by Collingwood, Quentin Skinner regards theoretical texts like *Leviathan* as polemical responses to questions and as interventions into debates. This ground-breaking insight began to guide Skinner's work in the 1960s. I tend to consider intellectual and other political texts in a similar way but as *methodology* for a wider sociological approach. Theoretically I see such texts as political and conceptual 'tactics' to deal with contradictions and paradoxes produced by European rationalisation (the printing press, secularisation, urbanisation, industrialisation, social inequality, colonisation, militarisation, etc.). The difference between the 'Cambridge school' approach and the one presented here is primarily a matter of degree of generality. In both approaches constitutional and political debate produce discontinuities and new ways of understanding established and contested concepts, that carry political change. I believe this long path of theory and polemics throws light on how differently we have come to see these things today.

Normatively the book is in line with the argument that the concept and discourse of sovereignty grounds the debate on democracy. Its influence remains politically potent, and many congruent terms are constantly used as ammunition in debates. I suggest, however, to study normativity, not to depend on it. I will not operate within the framework of normative political theory that tends to place demands on political rationality, deliberation and representation based on moral theory. Such idealism tends to neglect reality beyond principles and formal procedural elements.[6] It ignores that history tends to perform as contingencies. In line with most historical sociology, I suggest that a) history provides political and judicial norms; b) politics is constitutive of conflict and its own normative language and yet reflective of political society; and c) central political concepts are moulded in political exchange and conflict over vital issues. I see concepts and stories as essential and legitimating resources for political positions in their historical contexts. As Pierre Rosanvallon points out: 'Political concepts (democracy, liberty, equality, and so forth) can be understood only through the historical work of their testing and the historical search for their clarification.'[7] When history reconstructs political conceptions, there is a chance that present contestations can find a firm and common ground as an antidote to identity-based struggles that sometimes turn bitter and deep. It may possibly permit a wider appreciation of political authority.

In short, I consider publicly articulated norms, arguments and claims as material for sociological analysis of political struggle with a paradoxical world. For this reason, I will not engage normatively with the substantive claims of those scholars I discuss. What I am interested in here is their positions as evidence of a historical process of modern social rationalisation. I take no position for or against their definition of sovereignty and similar concepts, but examine them as expressions of modern differentiation of politics and law, and ultimately the expansion of the state, that have come to inform the concept of sovereignty. I simply view the term as an argumentative and public resource that I believe has remained rhetorically explosive in a diverse political debate concerning invasion and defence, immigration, energy, finance, infrastructure, federalism and human rights.

I argue that the history of sovereignty can only partly be separated from the history of the *semantics* of sovereignty. Ongoing discourses become embedded into critical moments of debate, and further into constitutional history and even into the constitution itself as law. Reversibly, constitutional arguments tend to serve various ideological and dissipative motives. A hypothesis is that growing international interdependence widens the gap between fact and ideals in constitutional theory. The reasoning in terms of sovereignty, by referring to the here and now, serves as a bridge between fact and national self-description that may increasingly be questioned. The term 'sovereignty' may refer to a principle or a doctrine, but it is also pragmatically and opportunistically juggled within day-to-day politics. Its legitimacy, produced in parliamentary debate and public opinion, is sensitive as to what may pass in a political conflict.

The book largely rests on an *ex post* normativity – in confidence that the sense-making of empirical analysis will inform public debate on current issues on democracy and self-determination. The discussion rests on a general view on sovereignty that it has been, and will in the future remain, a critical concept in constitutional debate because it is interwoven with notions of the constitution, democracy and the state. This view could probably be labelled conventional or 'statist'. The norm 'sovereignty' emerges from the foundation of the state. Politically 'sovereignty' equals the people's rule and self-determination, but it implies legal and legitimated power to the government as framed in the constitution.[8] An intimate connection exists between sovereignty, the constitution and the state. According to Martin Loughlin, sovereignty is the expression of what public law formulates, about the indivisible public power to regulate governing.[9] At the centre stands the constitutional regime of a state, and not simply the constitution as a symbolic and normative order. The constitution and its language of sovereignty confirms, and is being confirmed by, the state. So far goes my normative position. I see sovereignty as rooted in equal citizenship and the state. What is called simply 'the political', a term I will address in the book, is society seen politically; the ensemble of social activity from which popular sovereignty emerges. This view I think corresponds well with a sociological perspective on conflicts on sovereignty as indicative of struggles concerning state power. Normatively this view on the close relationship between sovereignty and the state has implications for European integration. In the final chapter I comment on the implication of the EU project for sovereignty.

What is the point of stressing *sociology* in this kind of study? No clear-cut disciplinary distinction exists here between the conceptual and the political. On the contrary, there is plenty of common ground.

First, conceptual history goes beyond meaning to analyse concepts and their conventional use in political contexts, and to demonstrate how concept and context inform one another over time. In this there is no methodological difference between conceptual history and sociology. Conceptual history has, on the contrary, emphasised the importance of interpreting concepts *in concreto* to distance itself from the history of ideas, German *Geistesgeschichte* and semantic studies of meaning. In the versions of both the Bielefeld and Cambridge 'schools', social and political history became indispensable. There is methodological consensus on the necessity of diachronic and synchronic analyses, and that the two supplement one another. Studies of concepts and their interrelationships in concrete political settings over time produce history that throws light on their significance.

Secondly, there is no dispute on how to view social context. Concepts and argumentation tend to serve as ammunition in political conflict and contestation. The history of social and political concepts tends simultaneously to narrate a history of 'semantic struggle'. Research needs to be sensitive to this relationship between concepts and politics. A society of objective conflict of interests is capable, in successful cases, to resolve or handle its controversies agonistically, that is, peacefully, if with merciless rhetoric. This methodological point of agonistic treatment of antagonism is more prevalent in sociology and the political theory of Chantal Mouffe, than in conceptual history, and yet by no means absent in the central writings of Carl Schmitt and Reinhart Koselleck. Famously Carl Schmitt noted the polemical character of concepts and the construction of friend–enemy polarity in specific situations. Words like 'sovereignty', he noted, are incomprehensible if one overlooks exactly who is to be negated and refuted with the term.[10] Koselleck in *Kritik und Krise* and in the preface to the impressive lexicon on *Geschichtliche Grundbegriffe*, noted the conflictual nature of concepts.[11] Koselleck speaks of *Gegenbegriffe* – concepts as weapons in political struggle that is never solved, only replaced by other conflicts. In this book we will meet the counter-concepts in the shape of human rights and transnational integration.

Thirdly, realist sociology tends to make a note on the distinct nature of politics, that is, as a domain historically detached from general morality, into a specific *raison d'état*. This is a theme from Machiavelli and Hobbes to current political realism: after the early modern demarcation from the divine, the king turned to decision-making based on advice, and to which the people had to show unconditional respect. As the German sociologist Niklas Luhmann noted, morality was differentiated as a secondary communication code in the power-mediated function system of politics. Max Weber distinguished between two forms of political ethics, which can be interpreted as distinct forms of political communication. Conceptual history as well as sociology points out the importance of knowing the limitations and boundaries of domains to identify the reference of concepts.

In my opinion the main difference between conceptual history and historically informed political sociology is methodological in a more profound but also simpler sense. Conceptual history and sociology 'use' one another instrumentally: to conceptual history, sociology is a necessary means to understand the wider social resonance of concepts in their synchronic and diachronic changes. To sociology, conceptual history is an invaluable methodological approach to understand institutional and political change.

In particular, the mobilisation of constitutional concepts in political contestation over time in public debate ought to be considered a main entrance to understand political crisis and change.

The object of study is not so much conceptual origins and change as conceptual influence on political conflict and change. This is a matter of emphasis; the mutual constitutive relationship between concept and politics is obvious. Conceptual language narrates political conflict that provides backgrounds for rearrangements in conceptual use. Noble if contested concepts like freedom, equality or popular will are protected by institutions in society to which they conform. In this sense fictions reshape society's self-image.[12] Map and terrain vary together, but here I stress the semantic redrawing of maps. To retrace the history of political concepts is to demonstrate their swings and turns as political resources; how they have, over the years, acquired different political and moral reference in political conflict.

To see the relationship between conceptual history and sociology, one may distinguish between a) the *representational* sense: the meaning between words and concepts, how words are (and have been) customarily employed as concepts; b) the *referential* meaning between concepts and what they stand for, and the circumstances in which they can be used to refer to distinct matters; and, finally, c) the *contextual* meaning of key evaluative concepts in argument and controversy that allows them to be used in a particular way to convey distinct values and attitudes in speech-acts that disclose them as critical and contested concepts. Despite differences, this is broadly how Koselleck and Skinner view concept and history.[13] Sociology extends the contextual meaning to institutional and social structures, and to a wider social history. The sociological question here is how conceptual argument enhanced by such social structure assists in challenging or legitimating the political order, for example how 'sovereignty' is alternatively imagined as a vision, a myth, as outdated or dangerous.

A purpose underlying the following chapters is to explore a sociological approach without ignoring the connection to political theory and conceptual history. Political and institutional change takes place in and through political concepts in battle, and political and historical sociology cannot avoid the conceptual route to the heart of the conflicts. This implies that the boundary one tends to draw between concept and conflict, or between the semantic and the social, exists only to allow us to demonstrate how it is constantly transgressed. The duality of concept and context comes through in all theories of language in use, not least in major contributions in political sociology and in the research field that is now called 'political communication'. In the latter, a view is that social conditions would look for words and transform them into concepts by filling them with social, often conflictual, references. Concepts, Koselleck notes, are words where meaning and experience condense into them from their context, and thus are concentrations of substantial meaning. Concepts like freedom and sovereignty (and their reconceptualisations) are filled with significance from the concrete contexts of their public use. The question of referentiality connects conceptual history to sociology and history. Generally, Koselleck argues the history of *Grundbegriffe* from the mid-nineteenth century indicate that they undergo processes of 'politicisation', and they become filled with future expectations and 'secularised' by being implemented into ideologies and historic-political frames of reference.[14]

The context comes in with a transforming power to shape the meaning of concepts that in turn rearrange context. The historical career of the concept of sovereignty, from its reference to the king, then to the (in England) Parliament and (in America and France) the people, and then to the democratic nation and the state, has challenged various political arrangements such as the nobility and the king. In the late twentieth century, its turn came to be outmanoeuvred by concepts like human rights, international integration and constitutionalism. Recently the concept has (in Europe) been used in Britain's dragged-out divorce from the EU, and by the French president Macron to preserve French–German hegemony in the union under the banner of 'European sovereignty'. It has been used to signal greater control in specific policy areas: the incoming president for the EU Commission in 2020, Ursula von der Leyen said that 'it is not too late to achieve technological sovereignty in some critical technology areas'.[15] In a far more desperate tone, it was used by the Ukrainians during the war against Russia, and the Russian warlords relied heavily on it in their version of Russian history. Sovereignty continues to be a topic of controversy in a series of nations and states, such as Poland, Hungary, Catalonia and Scotland. The term has also entered cyberspace.

As I have hinted already, I see sovereignty as a historical thread of meaning shaped in public action. Rather than seeing sovereignty as a given, it is conceived here as an argumentative resource in processes and episodes of political controversy that provide it with meaning. My concern is *what is being done with* 'sovereignty' in political and constitutional conflict, and with what effects. Analytical weight is on its declaratory, rhetorical, confrontational, solidarity-forming and foremost *legitimating* public semantics.[16] In open democracies, public debate marks the limit of legitimacy – and *legitimacy is the limit of politics*. How legitimacy is produced depends on the given discursive and political circumstances. The wider public opinion is broadly confined to the political environment of the parliament and the government, with the news media and social media as its main carriers. Public opinion is the unpredictable and in principle open terrain where political power seeks legitimacy. In a non-ideal and non-normative context, public opinion can be characterised as episodic, unstable, contestable and contingent, without any *a priori* foundation in reason. It belongs to a vocabulary occasionally mobilised to achieve or preserve a particular constellation of power, and against economic, expert and governance-based advice.

The following chapter is concerned with some particularly relevant sociological contributions concerning the legitimacy of the modern state and the social and political role of the constitution. I will address ideas developed by Max Weber and Niklas Luhmann. The ideas of these two eminent sociologists are of particular interest for three main reasons. First, they belong to what can be called a realist perspective in political sociology, and serve as a timely alternative view, compared with, for instance, the ideas of John Rawls and Jürgen Habermas. Secondly, their sociologies can be well combined with ideas on 'sovereignty' as belonging to a contested constitutional semantics. And thirdly, they place the ideals of sovereignty into more general social theories on rationalisation and functional differentiation.

Chapter two addresses textual (rhetorical, conceptual) methodologies to be applied in empirical studies of constitutional crisis and conflicts concerning popular and national sovereignty. These include insights stemming from terms like 'clustered and essential contested concepts' and 'constitutional moments', and the methodological strategy of constructing constitutional ideal types.

Chapters three and four trace the concept of sovereignty from its early modern formulations to the beginning of the twentieth century. The purpose is not to present a conceptual history as such but to demonstrate that political and legal philosophy on sovereignty can be read as an ongoing analytical handling with paradoxes that follow political rationalisation, and that its shapes are increasingly connected to the conditions of a 'sociological' society, particularly the dramatic expansion of the modern apparatus of order, the state.

Chapter five returns to a philosophically informed sociology on sovereignty; I address insights from Schmitt, Lefort and Rosanvallon, concerning the political, to encircle popular sovereignty as a legitimating conception today. In this regard I discuss contemporary political references to 'the people', and I substantiate my point that a sociological approach to sovereignty would benefit from 'realism' in recent political theory, with, however, a greater focus on the impact of social institutions and the state.

In chapter six, I discuss the cultural and symbolic dimension of constitutions and in particular their connection to popular and national sovereignty. I attempt to demonstrate that fundamental political and legal matters are closely integrated with cultural processes related to affective responses and identification. I argue that sovereignty as symbolism and story, despite its newly reflexive character, is inherently connected to the territorial state.

During the first half of the nineteenth century, one could perhaps think that the story of sovereignty began and ended with Hobbes and the state. With Weber, the successful legitimate monopoly of violence of the state had been acknowledged (if detested) by all. The state operated with its own reasons – and this fact had become general knowledge. But history never ends, and post-war Europe opened to two fundamental turns that challenged the state: human rights emerged as a powerful language of individual protection against state dominance, and international organisations assumed power over the state. Chapters seven and eight address the most important and complex challenges with which the idea of sovereignty has been confronted: the human rights revolution after the second world war, and regional integration. In chapter eight my aim is not to question human rights as a global and successful normative discourse, but to address the debate on the tension between transnational human rights regimes, and national and popular sovereignty. Human rights as a key issue area have no doubt energised a pluralisation (differentiation) of the sovereignty concept, and I examine some propositions as to how we are to consider the relationship of the latter to the human rights discourse.

The final chapter makes the case for the concept of popular sovereignty within the framework of the contemporary democratic nation-state, and it questions the legitimacy of the federal ambitions of central EU institutions.

This introduction continues to briefly sketch out how I see history, political theory and conceptual analysis as contributions to a historical sociology of the political.

Ways of observing concepts

Sovereignty as a description of the state has gone through triumph and demise, and one could argue that both trends appear side by side in contemporary Europe. The concept of sovereignty is celebrated and challenged by autocrats who do not respect the rule of law, and by what is called constitutionalism at an international level. In very different ways, the trends involve a disjunction between the state and politics that involves a weakening of constitutions. No small matter, in as much as the invention of the constitution was a massive success legally, politically and culturally. The achievement of the constitution was grounded in its contribution to allow change under the condition of stability. An essential part of the success of constitutions lies in the combination of liberal and 'republic' values to define the limits of government and the rule of law within a framework of popular legitimacy. This tends to blur their instrumental (legal-rational) and symbolic (traditional) dimensions. Along with the emerging system of state politics, the idea of sovereignty emerged historically as a manifestation of a political ethos. It makes sense to distinguish between 1), its *heroic* phase as a project from the early 1800s towards the first world war, and 2), its *expansionist* phase in the first half of the twentieth century, and then 3), a post-war *bipolar* phase of growing ambivalence and dispute concerning the state. The latter phase is characterised by an expansive and omnipotent state that simultaneously seems to weaken its connection to democratic politics.

In the spirit of Weber's *Verstehen*, the use of 'sovereignty' and its narratives up through the decades ought to be identified as they were made sense of and actively mobilised. What I seek to present is neither a political or socio-logical 'pure' theory, nor a conceptual history, but rather a perspective on *a political-legal idea in action*. The approach involves doing historical and political sociology by turning conceptual history into a resource for analysis of political self-understanding and conflict. Although my approach is broadly termed 'sociological', it is closely tied to history, political theory, law, political history of concepts, rhetoric and media studies.[17] In the book I thus approach constitutional change by stepping outside of the legal-normative circle. Legal and moral norms will not serve as a framework from which to address constitutional transformations but rather constitute research objects in their own right. The question is what political agents do when they struggle for their interpretation of sovereignty. In this light I see debates on constitutional change as political contestation involving rival moral norms on what is legitimate and constitutionally valid.[18]

To grasp the complex, I try to avoid both timeless philosophical reading and social determinism. With Skinner, I appreciate the autonomy of the past, but unlike him, I think the analysis ought to include discourses of political non-intellectual practices and reflection. More specifically, the locus needs to be on political leadership; the key players of the parliament, political parties and social movements as they appear and perform in public opinion. Furthermore, such an approach will concentrate on points in history (critical or constitutional moments, Machiavellian moments) around which political and social forces organise themselves publicly by arming themselves with powerful, legitimating and identity-shaping language such as sovereignty.[19] Skinner argues for the possibility of clarifying the public meanings of texts, possibly also of the intentions of their authors in making a statement or issuing a text. 'Meaning' refers to why such action was undertaken there and then, in response to what. To understand a statement, we must try to make sense of it as an intervention into a specific debate with identifiable co-discussants or adversaries that follows certain rules of genres, styles and conventions. From the debate that the statement intervenes into we may infer certain meanings and intentions.

The meaning of the text refers to its conventional and situational significance. Intention has little to do with the true meaning of texts, nor about the private minds (or sub-consciousness) of the speaker or author. Rather, intention refers to opportune attempts to make a change in a political setting of importance, that led him or her to argue or 'perform' in a particular way. The 'intention' in question is in no-one's mind, but occurs in, and belongs to, a specific public, political context. Skinner argues that 'When we claim ... to have recovered the intentions embodied in texts, we are engaged in nothing more mysterious than this process of placing them within whatever argumentative contexts make sense of them.'[20] In this way I think Skinner not only handles his relativist critics well, but also demonstrates how this approach (and Koselleck's) is compatible with non-intentionalist ideas in sociology and political theory, and may play a vital methodological role in sociological analysis. In addition, when the object of study is more political than intellectual, the meaning of authorship may be less central than if the examination is on Hobbes or Locke. The intention of the authorship in analysis of parliamentary debates is institutionalised through leadership, party politics and parliamentary convention.

There are affinities from Koselleck and Skinner to Pierre Rosanvallon in that they all draw on the history of political concepts. Rosanvallon illustrates conceptual transformation as stories narrating the French post-revolutionary drama. His imaginative and transdisciplinary ways to mobilise the history of concepts are among the most ambitious for several decades. Rosanvallon addresses the very familiar democratic paradox of self-government in conceptual and political ways, that, as in the work of Luhmann, yield indetermination, contingency and conflict. He demonstrates how reflection generates ceaseless ritualism and forms of imaginary meaning that contextualise society both in its totality and in its compartmentalisation. This relates to how the concept of popular sovereignty is capable of providing legitimacy to politics as an increasingly autonomous domain and how politics has transformed popular sovereignty into a more appropriate legitimation base.

In the mid-1980s and 1990s, Rosanvallon spoke about '*histoire conceptuelle du politique*'. He has since programmatically preferred to call his approach a philosophical history of the political.[21] He continues to pay tribute to Claude Lefort's understanding of the political, as 'a set of principles generating the relations that people entertain between one another and with the world'. Lefort understands the political as a set of procedures that derive from the social order. It is not a matter of making a distinction between the social and the political. To Rosanvallon the political is 'the sphere of activities characterised by irreducible conflicts'. It stems from the need to establish a rule outside of the ordinary, and which cannot in any way be derived from something natural. The political can therefore be defined as a collective orientation that allows the constitution of an order to be shared through deliberation of norms of participation and distribution.

What I think is underplayed in Rosanvallon's understanding is the *distinction* between the political and politics. Within the concept of the state, a modern distinction should be upheld between the state as political society and the state as a centralised system of legislative, executive and administrative functions. To political sociology and constitutional sociology, it is essential that a limited sphere of politics differentiated itself with its own codes, rules and moralities. The distinction is central in the sociologies of Weber, Luhmann and Bourdieu because the distinctiveness of the political conflict between position and opposition depends on it. I will address this more closely in the chapter on the political.

The reasons Rosanvallon calls his approach a philosophical history resemble my reasons for speaking of a *sociological* history of the political. Rosanvallon's aim is to demonstrate how representative systems evolve and change, and to identify what he calls historical clusters around which new political and social rationalities organise themselves. With rationalities he thinks of representations which govern the way in which an epoch, a nation or a social group envisages its presence and future. These are self-constructed narratives, what sociology calls self-descriptions and ideologies. In focus stand key, contested concepts. Rosanvallon argues that his approach 'is a philosophical history because it is around concepts embodying society's self-representation, such as equality, sovereignty, democracy etc. that one can organise and verify the intelligibility of events and their underlying principles'. This is as much a sociological as a philosophical programme. Rosanvallon speaks of a philosophical history because he would like to do away with the distinction between political history and political philosophy of the present, and to provide a common ground for research and debate, where past experiences can provide *resonance* for present debates.[22] Like Pierre Bourdieu, who would have liked to see sociology as a social history of the present, Rosanvallon stresses the internal connection back to past controversies. Quentin Skinner, to whom Rosanvallon acknowledges great debt, has in his opinion kept his historical writings too separate from philosophical attempts to identify connections between past and present issues.

Rosanvallon stands closer to political theory than did Foucault, and I think closer to political sociology. Similarly to the approach presented here, he places concepts of ideas and ideals in a historical context beyond the chronological and the narrowly political. He brings in social and economic conditions to identify incoherent changes of conceptual meaning as it appears in the press and ministerial papers. As Skinner, Rosanvallon presents ideas as if they were speech-acts to their present past. In retrospect we see the patterns of changing theorising and contested concepts such as sovereignty as long-term expressions of intentions and contexts. Less philological than

Koselleck, who addresses conceptual changes outside of their political contexts, and less oriented than Skinner towards motives of the great minds of intellectual history, Rosanvallon comes closer to political sociology in identifying a history of conflict over issues of life and death for a nation.

The point here is to revisit ideas in history, and to examine how the reoccurring democratic paradox and indeterminacy have been sorted and transmuted to other conflicts. A narrative reconstruction will tend to look for controversies that threaten to make cracks in or blow concepts apart, or provide them with new meaning, which we then can link together (chronologically and thematically) in longer chains and bigger pictures of conceptual change. Functionally speaking, a working hypothesis is that political society constantly seeks to arrange itself to achieve a legitimate and stable form. Again, we see the historical-functional approach that I believe is evident in much of Rosanvallon's work. It moves far from general ambitions *à la* Parsons or Luhmann. Closer to history, it wants to explain political, and especially constitutional, discontinuities against the background of general social change.

A sociological approach

I propose a sociological and political approach that does not place demands and direct appeals towards political ideals or base its reasoning on moral theory and seemingly timeless conceptual frameworks. Rather, the outgoing theses here are that a) history provides political and judicial norms, and the analytical form for our understanding of long-term political debate; b) that politics is constitutive of conflict; and c) that central political concepts are moulded not in philosophical contributions but in political debate and conflict over specific issues and themes. Concepts and the wider 'stories' that apply them as frameworks, are essential as available and legitimating resources for political positions.

The approach takes inspiration from several disciplinary traditions, among them *political realism* that has appeared in Weberian sociology and recent political theory. Realist thinkers reject the idea that political decisions can be reconstructed from, and legitimated by, principles. In the spirit of thinkers such as Machiavelli, Max Weber, Niklas Luhmann, Bernard Williams and Raymond Geuss, political realism shies away from idealist, utopian and moral-doctrinal reasoning.[23] It distances itself from universal principles and Kantian ideals, such as cosmopolitanism. Such fictions, realism contends, only play an ideological role in associating politics with ideals that can never be reached. There is no modern political 'project' in sight, and to the extent one can identify political 'progress', it is a contingent result of competence and luck. Realism observes the 'truth in actual political experience' and searches political history for descriptions of inherent dynamic features of politics and how it works. The essence of politics is conflict that never dissolves in the face of any moral principle. A realist methodological starting point is that power and conflict are main features of political relations involving leadership, control, strategy, dirty hands, rhetoric and ideology, duplicity, compromise, modus vivendi, and so on. Any resolution of a political conflict is the beginning of another.

Although based in political and constitutional sociology, the approach presented here is informed by the history of political debate and legal studies of constitutional change. It reflects an attempt to reformulate the theoretical and methodological grounding for an interdisciplinary approach on trans-formations of the normative core of the nation-state. Such an approach takes aim to examine the correlations between social forces and disputes concerning basic nation-state norms. It is intended to contribute to the broader understanding of constitutionalism as a concern for historical-sociological analysis.[24]

The term 'sovereignty' has no essence beyond what it has come to be seen as historically and discursively. This is common knowledge among political agents and it motivates their struggle. Nevertheless, whereas the circumstances to which the concept refers are historically diverse, the elasticity of the concept is clearly within limits. I examine not so much its intellectual value as highlight its role as political asset in parliamentary and public dispute. The arguments, visions and imaginations it sparks refer to language, politics and social circumstances. I propose to clarify the horizon of expecta-tion concerning sovereignty and to envision the latitude and delimitations for it. The suggested tasks respond to questions concerning states' actual production and use of opportunities that can be imagined within the coordinates of a world of increasing interdependence.

Historical investigations of sovereignty feed into, and I hope will inform, current controversies by demonstrating the tensions and ambiguity of the concept. I believe the approach sketched out here sheds light on the concept of sovereignty's status. Constitutional controversy over some decades in Europe signals a revival of constitutional thinking in general, and of sov-ereignty in particular – in part as a response to liberal transnational con-stitutionalism. I do not consider it likely that national sovereignty inevitably withers away under the weight of European federalism. And yet sovereign state power is without doubt confronted by external power. This triggers popular protesting against a 'post-national' Europe that builds federalism or 'super-sovereignty'.[25]

In the modern state *the sovereign* tends to be latent. It circulates as a concept; as an attribution or fiction, to use the terms of Luhmann and

Grimm. It lives on in a historically constructed discourse but is far from emptied of power: at some significant (if unintended) moments, it demonstrates its facticity, as in the Catalonian separatist debate, Brexit or the Ukraine war. Since the events of 1989–1991, limits have been put on the functional and territorial self-determination of European states including the Scandinavian countries. 'The people' that is acknowledged constitutionally as the ultimate sovereign power, occasionally demonstrates its (de)-legitimising power during stages of disagreement and conflict. The question is how constitutional power has been defended and contested.

An ambition for a sociology of sovereignty is to throw light on differences and similarities in European state-based (anti-cosmopolitan) undercurrents, which doubt the universality of moral norms and transnational doctrines and are occasionally drawn towards questionable 'populist' articulations. With historical reconstructions of 'sovereignty' in parliament, in the media, in white papers, and so on, there is a chance that present contestations can construct antidotes to extreme identity-based struggles. Such research may present arguments for a wider appreciation of political authority. Elsewhere in Europe, feelings of resentment and longing for past arrangements seem sometimes to be immune to argument. Popular will opposes what is seen as the '*stahlhartes Gehäuse*' (Weber) of increasing power of international law and neoliberalism. The concept of sovereignty as seen from the political centre may constitute more of a problem than a celebrated credo. The concept also suggests that politics can be much more than about political representation and conflicts over distribution.

The question of sovereignty is likely to be asked with increasing volume in our world society confronted with very real and immense threats. The concept figures in political debate because it possesses rhetorical power. Transnationalisation, the 'state of exception' concerning immigration, pandemics, the climate crisis, war, energy crisis and inflation, raise concern with respect to the self-determination of states. Defenders as well as opponents of this transformation will have their political horizon changed, and sovereignty as a discursive practice and ordering principle altered. The nation-state needs to know where it stands, and a currency for making sense of this is the history of sovereignty. Searching parliamentary and public opinion history may bring to the fore potentialities and opportunities of the concept. Not least, it will be clearer whether the concept simply has fallen out of fashion and exchanged with other terms like 'welfare state', 'the cosmopolitan society' or 'Europe'.

It would be pointless here to flag an *ex ante* normative route to follow, since norms and their expressions are what are to be observed. On the other hand, one needs to adhere to some broad guiding lines. As indicated, my approach to constitutional debate can be called realist, or weberian: it distances itself from normative, such as contractarian, accounts that tend to ignore the *tension* between constituent and constituted power. Politics is about *conflict* because of inequalities and finite resources; one group's victory is another group's defeat. In a society of institutionalised interests, a focus on norms is insufficient. The question of how the problem of sovereignty is dealt with is a political and substantive problem framed by historical circumstances. The operatively autonomous political domain is a contingent and indeterminate battlefield of power, from which constitutional concepts like 'sovereignty' have emerged. In political contestation, the norms of the constitution feed into and become translated into political rhetoric and tactics.

Discourses concerning popular sovereignty and sovereign power, of constituent and constituted power, are media for reflection on the paradox of sovereignty, that the sovereign people cannot rule itself. The way out has been to operate with a concept that is unified *and* dual, fictitious *and* real, that constructs a sovereign people within a territory and its operative delegated institutionalised power. I propose to study the historical unfolding of these discourses, deriving from the impossibility of the unity of a people. This involves observing constitutional discourse – the cycles of public argumentation and polemic among institutionalised interests and their frontrunners. This, I think, provides a better understanding of what a state does when it claims its sovereignty.

Notes

1 Reinhart Koselleck, 'Introduction and prefaces to the Geschichtliche Grundbegriffe.' *Contributions to the History of Concepts*, 6:1 (2011), 1–37.

2 See for instance Richard Bellamy, *A Republican Europe of States: Cosmopolitanism, Intergovernmentalism and Democracy in the EU* (Cambridge: Cambridge University Press, 2019).

3 Wouter G. Werner and Jaap H. De Wilde, 'The endurance of sovereignty.' *European Journal of International Relations*, 7:3 (2011), 283–313, at 28.

4 Hent Kalmo and Quentin Skinner, *Sovereignty in Fragments: The Past, Present and Future of a Contested Concept* (Cambridge: Cambridge University Press, 2010), p. 7.

5 Denis Baranger, 'The apparition of sovereignty.' In ibid., pp. 47–63.

6 For a critique of political idealism, see Terje Rasmussen, *Political Legitimacy: Realism in Political Theory and Sociology* (London: Routledge, 2022).

7 Pierre Rosanvallon, *Democracy Past and Future* (Samuel Moyn, ed.) (New York: Columbia University Press, 2006), p. 45.

8 Martin Loughlin, 'Constitutional pluralism: an oxymoron?' *Global Constitutionalism*, 3:1 (2014), 9–30, at 12.

  9 Ibid.
 10 See Carl Schmitt, *Political Theology: Four Chapters on the Concept of Sovereignty* (Chicago: University of Chicago Press, 1922/2005).
 11 Koselleck, 'Introduction and prefaces'; Reinhart Koselleck, *Critique and Crisis: Enlightenment and the Pathogenesis of Modern Society* (Cambridge, MA: The MIT Press, 1988).
 12 See Edmund S. Morgan, *Inventing the People: The Rise of Popular Sovereignty in England and America* (New York: Norton, 1988).
 13 See Koselleck, 'Introduction and prefaces', 1–37; Quentin Skinner, 'The state.' In Terrence Ball, James Farr and Russell L. Hanson (eds) *Political Innovation and Conceptual Change* (Cambridge: Cambridge University Press, 1995), pp. 9–11; Quentin Skinner, *From Humanism to Hobbes: Studies in Rhetoric and Politics* (Cambridge: Cambridge University Press, 2018), ch. 12.
 14 Koselleck, 'Introduction and prefaces'; Otto Brunner, Werner Conze and Reinhart Koselleck, 'Staat und Souveränität.' *Geschichtliche Grundbegriffe*, Vol. 6, St–Vert (Stuttgart: Klett-Cotta, 1997), p. 3.
 15 Ursula von der Leyen, *Politico* (14 December 2020).
 16 John Austin, *How To Do Things with Words* (Oxford: Clarendon Press, 1962).
 17 Needless to say perhaps, a sociological project need not be conducted by sociologists.
 18 Paul Blokker, *New Democracies in Crisis? A Comparative Constitutional Study of the Czech Republic, Hungary, Poland, Romania and Slovakia* (Abingdon: Routledge, 2013); Paul Blokker, 'Politics and the political in sociological constitutionalism.' In Paul Blokker and Chris Thornhill (eds) *Sociological Constitutionalism* (Cambridge: Cambridge University Press, 2017).
 19 Terje Rasmussen, *Offentlig parlamentarisme: Politisk strid og offentlig mening: 1945–2000 [Public Parliamentarianism: Political Conflict and Public Opinion 1945–2000]* (Oslo: Universitetsforlaget 2021).
 20 Quentin Skinner, 'The rise of challenge to and prospects for a Collingwoodian approach to the history of political thought.' In Dario Castiglione and Iain Hampsher-Monk (eds) *The History of Political Thought in National Context* (Cambridge: Cambridge University Press, 2001), p. 186.
 21 Pierre Rosanvallon, 'Towards a philosophical history of the political.' In ibid., p. 189.
 22 Ibid., p. 198.
 23 See Rasmussen, *Political Legitimacy*, ch. 2.
 24 Constitutions tend to point out lines of research on themselves. The vast majority of the contributions to analysis of the Norwegian constitution leading up to the bicentennial addressed the nineteenth century, and were informed by the history of law. For the last decade a turn towards research on constitutional law in contemporary political and legal sociology has been noticeable.
 25 French president Emmanuel Macron used the term 'European sovereignty' on several occasions in 2019 and 2020 concerning the development of the EU and NATO. Given that there can be only one sovereign, one ought to expect some debate on the matter.

1

A sociology of constitutions

Early political sociology from Marx, Durkheim and Weber on, implemented legal positivist and historicist ideas into a conception of democracy that focused on the formation of the state. It rejected the radical legal positivist idea that the state was merely legally legitimated. Enlightenment ideas of sovereignty and citizenship were followed into their practical implementation in society. Democracy was seen as an idea with material and practical origin and loaded with new paradoxes, since the role of free citizen cannot be separated from the collective forces of society.[1] Weber argued that the modern legal idea of the citizen had evolved as an effect of the domination of state bureaucracy and viewed modern representative democracy as an effective instrument for social and administrative order. Parliaments were another impersonal element within the formal-legal rationalisation of society with insecure legitimate grounding, to which the individual had to be subjected. According to Weber, the German parliament suffered from both efficiency and legitimacy problems. Essentially Weber saw democracy as an unavoidable inconsistency between on the one hand the ideal of sovereign citizens and their institutions, and on the other hand state power with its political system that strategically extracts legitimacy.[2] More than any other sociological theorist, Niklas Luhmann has laid out the specifically legal and political, and the constitution as their connection. Methodologically he has provided sociology with the theory of the paradox as a mode of questioning and observing.

Unlike normative theories on legal and political constitutionalism, sociology examines the *de facto* social agreement or acceptability of political arrangements, the tensions and controversies regarding legitimacy that constitutional debates are embedded in, and the historical trajectories leading to actual circumstances of dissent and conflict. It addresses processes that in part involve *self-legitimation*, where constitutional norms are referred to as rational, prescriptive guidance for 'necessary' change. Blokker calls this 'sociological legitimacy', as opposed to the idealist appeals to legitimacy in much normative theory. The approach suggested here regards norms in society as influential on constitutionalism, but also that, as a rule, there would be competing and conflicting normative views in play, in combination with non-normative powers of interest.

Versions of constitutionalism

To the constitutional term *par excellence*, sovereignty, the constitution itself lends legal and political authority. After a decline of interest in constitutions after the second world war, formalist-normative approaches appeared within the fields of normative philosophy, legal theory and history of law (Rawls, Dworkin, Habermas). However, with the early writings of Luhmann on law and constitutions, a more dispassionate and historically informed sociology of constitutions emerged. Together with important work on the state by Norbert Elias, Charles Tilly, Theda Skocpol, Michael Mann and Pierre Bourdieu, Luhmann's sociology of the political and legal function systems provided important context for the re-establishing of an empirical sociology that questions normative theories as theory, and rather views them as objects of study.[3]

Constitutions are here ideal-typically considered as the essential link, what Luhmann calls structural coupling, between law and politics. Precisely in this position inside and outside of law and politics it equips political agents with legal authority. It bridges the gap between political-legal normativity and institutional facts. Norms and facts are sewn together into the same argumentative resource that then places itself as the locus of the most fundamental conflicts of the state.

The legal-political innovation of constitutions can be preliminarily understood as a document at the core of the political system that signifies the legal regulation of political power and subject for parliamentary and public discourse. They were a product of political struggles in the nineteenth century, particularly in its second half. Constitutions are documents of legitimation of the state with some distinct legal, productive and symbolic features.[4] From the nineteenth century they were seen by public law as the external organisation of the people, to use the words of Johann Caspar Bluntschli.[5] The Norwegian *Grunnloven*, for instance, came into being during dramatic circumstances as early as 1814, after Napoleon and the Kiel Treaty, and just before the Vienna conference and the backlash of the Restauration. It was heavily inspired by the French and North American revolutions a few decades earlier. In the nineteenth century a series of constitutional conflicts with the monarchs followed that basically confirmed the idea of constitutionalism, understood as a historically generated political theory about legal control. After the revolutions in America and France, constitutionalism acquired a sharper normative profile under the flag of sovereignty, division of powers and rights of citizens. It addressed expectations to political society at safe distance from political power.[6] It appeared after liberal and radical political forces had conquered political power from absolutist rule in the eighteenth and nineteenth centuries, and a modern state had been established under republican or moderate royal power, and then became the legal norm. The sovereign nation understood as the people (Rousseau) and as the legitimate state monopoly on the use of force (Weber) developed.

After the revolutions, the idea of popular sovereignty coincided with the idea of the autonomous nation-state – sovereignty referred to the people within a territory, the nation. The first French declaration after the revolution stated: 'The principle of all sovereignty resides essentially in the nation. No body or individual may exercise any authority which does not proceed directly from the nation.' The innovation of *the social contract* had already been created and modified by philosophy as a metaphor for legitimate rule in the paradox of a political society of equals *and* non-equals. In the late nineteenth century, 'democracy' came to be associated with the idea of a national and political constitution for a sovereign nation-state. The turn to positive law meant that the state could bind itself legally and become its own primacy: the procedures of legislation were legally decided.

After the revolutions, the state described itself in terms of popular representation, and Emmanuel Joseph Sieyès's concepts of *pouvoir constituant* and *pouvoir constitué* were instrumental in operating with representation as a function of popular power. Constitutional power was seen as creating and regulating legitimate rule that is bound by the constitutional framework. A question is how the interplay between the two powers is given shape in constitutional controversies. We may distinguish between three ways to observe constitutionalism.

Legal constitutionalism, the predominant approach, tends to emphasise the constitution as a self-limiting device, and thus a paramount example of legal-political rationality. It views constitutionalism as a special and particularly ambitious form of legalisation. Grimm describes it in five frequently cited points, of which the most essential is that constitutional norms emanate from political decisions and are meant to regulate comprehensively, exclusively, with primacy and full validity, the exercise of political power, in the name of, and legitimated by, the people.[7] Legitimacy, the democratic element, is a precondition for the rule of law. Legitimacy is a condition for efficiency. It cannot tolerate private, or external, competitors; the borders between the public and the private, and between the internal and the external, are constitutive for the constitution. As Grimm states, 'Only a constitution that comprises both elements is capable of fulfilling the expectations of constitutions fully.'[8]

In this approach, the constitution offers procedure for its own reforms. It cannot solve disagreements on constitutional change but may settle them peacefully if temporarily. The classical 'legalist' view is that constitutional law is a written set of norms that stem from agreed principles of reason and is teleologically directed towards a public good. The central legitimating function of constitutions lies in their capacity to present their power as under independent legal control and so contribute to the acceptability of political decisions. Constitutions allow politics and law to operate independently of each other and of the environment, yet to register eventual necessity for internal modification according to external (national and international) change. Legal constitutionalism tends to define the constitution as a document that is superior to ordinary legislation and justifiable and constitutive for the legal and political system.[9] It draws on an idealised version of legal procedure, where basic questions are decided by judicial review. According to critics, it tends to assume the non-political and individualised character of issues that are fundamentally political and collective. As is illustrated by the bitter constitutional conflicts in the US, hardcore constitutionalism seems to ignore the vital point of political legitimacy. Its legal rationality overlooks how central values may be articulated and embodied in the constitution, for example on the limits of human rights.[10]

Political constitutionalism emphasises the role of political contestation and controversy in such questions, and notes that in constitutional matters, little or no room for compromise exists.[11] Questions concerning rights and popular sovereignty are seen as political constructs rather than moral principles. The constitution locates itself at the centre of collective conflicts and decisions. The political process towards constitutional change *is* the constitution, argues Richard Bellamy.[12] For instance, political constitutionalism argues that human rights are contestable and subject to debate and justification beyond judicial deliberation.[13] They do not constitute a moral demarcation of politics, but exist as claims and demands on behalf of competing interests and ideologies. Only formal and legitimate decision-making can resolve disputes on rights. Consequently, the object of study ought to be the political circumstances *that favour selected arguments and disfavour others*. Political constitutionalism and recent political realism are important contributions to a political sociology of constitutions, particularly since they stress contestation as a political logic, and politics as a distinct field of power struggle. However, political constitutionalism as a political theory, Bellamy's contributions among them, presents itself as a normative theory that locates itself close to its object. In addition, political constitutionalism ignores vital differences and couplings between law and politics. These points are given more attention in sociological constitutionalism.

Sociological constitutionalism enters here on the level of theory in that we view the constitution and its interpretations as a *social structure that provides normative stability by producing self-descriptions for society*. And yet for reasons of legitimacy, this point often also places constitutions at the centre of political controversy. A sociological approach will tend to study constitutions as interfaces between politics and law, and as vital for the legitimacy of political power. As Blokker argues, 'Constitutions are continuously put to test, also in terms of being both evaluated from an internal, juridical view, and from extra-juridical, political, normative and societal points of view.'[14] Sociological constitutionalism addresses critical concepts (like 'sovereignty') in their formative and conflicting context and points out that societal differentiation and inclusion of groups in the political realm in the nineteenth and twentieth centuries had severe consequences for the concept that referred to a unified people. In general, functional differentiation leads to revised or reinterpreted structural couplings between law and politics.

Sociological constitutionalism tends to situate constitutional conflicts wider in time and space than the two other modes. If constitutional texts themselves appear to lack drama and conflict, their concepts and meanings have often appeared central in conflicts over basic questions for the nation-state and its citizens. As text and condensed normativity given an authentic and 'timeless' present tense, and with an apparent undisputable and self-created authority, the constitution places itself at the centre of political struggle as a political instrument for performative acts in and outside of the parliament. To provide arguments and positions with legitimacy, constitutional backing is vital. Sociological constitutionalism agrees that rights are *claims* – but focuses more broadly than legislative decision-making, to include social movements and associations, outside the formal political institutions, that influence such political processes. Political activity in the civil society and the public sphere are central in the formation of legitimate rights.[15] Only by a broadening of the perspective of constitutionalism can practices like squatting, civil disobedience, political strikes and other expressive or non-conventional modes of political expression be considered in accounts of constitutional interpretation. This is evident for example in environmental struggles as well as in conflicts over ethnic rights and the right to abortion.[16]

Some examinations make clear that constitutions are best seen as a programmatic shaping of law in ways that provide the community a legal foundation in a concrete historical situation. Grimm argues that 'The constitution traces back to a political decision by the political forces that determine the instituting of the constitution.'[17] Grimm emphasises its historical dimension and indicates that it must transcend politics and law to encompass a legitimate base. Ultimately, as Wahl writes, individual and collective recognition give the constitution its normative force.[18] Its legal and political effectiveness can only be explained by its shared normativity – from the energy it receives from political and social sources, and its origin in a critical or revolutionary moment. Its norms have achieved primacy in society. Its explicit relationship between the state and the people is simply recognised as a set of principles of value. Wahl states that 'Constitutions were and are parts of political-social movements and real political forces stood and stand behind them.'[19] Constitutions in the state, about the state, are the locus of political power and general legitimacy. Wahl speaks of a 'complex constitutional-state constellation' to stress the law in context; 'the constitutional question does not only concern the legal quality of the norms of constitutional law; the field is much broader.'[20] It is important, as Wahl notes, not to underestimate the political process that plays up the acceptance of the constitution. To this we should add the centrality of the circulation of social-political norms in civil society and public opinion that reproduce the validity and legitimacy of the constitution. The nerve of the constitution concerns the political being and its relation to the state in a wide sense.

This is what is meant by 'sociological constitutionalism', a term that must not be confused with 'societal constitutionalism'. It goes beyond the formal text and places the constitution in the crossfire of controversy under the condition of stability. Two sociologists stand in the foreground: Max Weber and Niklas Luhmann have contributed extraordinarily to the sociology of politics and law, as well as to a sociological understanding of the constitution as a legitimating social structure. Their works form radical critiques of political idealism and liberal notions of reason, as inherited from the Enlightenment – Weber as the great observer of political and legal authority, and Luhmann as the observer of paradoxes. Both scholars formulate historically informed theories on political rationality and political legitimacy of democratic nation-states of Europe in the twentieth century.

Weber on the state

Weber's political writings address the interrelationship between state and society, between state power and nation, and, as a running theme, the need for legitimacy. One can easily argue that Weber put too much emphasis on the need for a strong state, and that the normative question of the good society was completely overshadowed by his realism. That is, as Kelly notes, part of the appeal of writers like Weber and Carl Schmitt.[21] Weber's aim was different and more modest than the political theory of the Enlightenment: it was to ensure stable conditions for democratic governments and state

formations, by pointing out the constitutional arrangements for their legitimacy and integrity. Weber's main thesis was the rationalisation of society,
and his political question was how politics, formally and substantially, could
be secured under these conditions. The age of Chancellor Bismarck was
history, and modern politics had irrevocably differentiated to bureaucracy,
the parliament and the mass, which somehow had to relate to one another
rationally. The risk that they would not, however, was acute. Educated and
effective leaders was the key.

A beginning point is Weber's view on politics as a particular value sphere
that he calls the state. It is characterised by institutional structures, like the
formal bureaucracy, the political parties and their elites, the parliament and
the chancellor, where political power is constructed and deployed. Weber
sees the state as a set of institutional structures that gives shape and form
to politics, to which action must accommodate and motivate *post facto*.
Politics, with its distinct approach to morality and power, is a product of
objective rationalisation, which is met by subjective and meaningful steps
among individuals and collectives. Rationalisation enhances an internal
political logic and distinct political values. This was also seen to be the case
in other spheres like religion, science and law, a fact that occasionally would
bring them into conflict. To Weber, this pluralisation of society set its ultimate
mark on modern society.

The institutions of democratic politics that Weber addresses are bureaucratic
administration, and legislative and executive politics. The state is characterised
by the separation of administration from politics. Weber explains this separation of powers not as a normative mechanism for neutralising power *à la*
Montesquieu, but historically and sociologically: traditional legitimacy, which
the prince expropriated from the aristocracy and later lost to his staff,
became undermined by officialdom and the first 'bureaucrats'. Legal-rational
legitimacy emerges in the process as rationalisation of the state and law.
Politics ultimately becomes an exercise of power without direct access to
the means of power, leading to an understanding of executive political power
as the business of the state. Political parties and their elites are left with the
responsibility of mass democracy.[22] Parties have no territorial power but
adapt to their role as mediators between politics and the citizen.

The modern state takes responsibility for new dimensions of human
welfare and protection, as was evident under Bismarck. It expands its sphere
of responsibility and is forced to reproduce its authority through bureaucratic,
systematically ordered and directed routines. To Weber, bureaucratic *Herrschaft* appears superior because there is no other way to carry out the tasks
of the state in a large-scale society without some form of legal routinisation
and specialisation.[23] The need for control grows in such a society, and so
does the need for *Fachwissen*; science-based knowledge.

The concept of 'popular sovereignty' had no explicit place in Weber's thought.[24] As he wrote to Simmel, concepts like the 'true will of the people' did not mean anything to him. To him they were fictions.[25] Weber presented a model of a leadership-democracy where popular participation had little analytical place. To Beetham, Weber's understanding of democracy centred on the charismatic figure and 'has very little to do with democracy at all'.[26] Curiously, Beetham wrote this in Britain during the Thatcher decade characterised by a strong-leader democracy. The point is rather that Weber, in his typology of legitimacy and in his political ethics, demonstrated how democratic politics was possible despite inherent tensions and contradictions. A leadership democracy with an elected president and parliament is a democracy all the same, and so 'leadership democracy' and 'elite democracy' were quite accurate terms to Weber. No doubt Weber had limited confidence in public participation by the public and the intellectuals. Certainly, his cool-eyed view on politics prevented him from projecting an expanded democratic model of politics that included a civil sphere and a critical debating press. His theory concentrated on politics and its ways to attract legitimacy in the 'mass'. What one largely could expect from the 'mass' was ordered response or absence of protest. Weber was critical of Michels's moralism in his writings on the oligarchical tendencies in modern party organisations: to Weber, the emotional and unorganised nature of the mass needed strong leadership. The leader recruited his mass of followers by demagogy, rather than, as normative theory of democracy would have it, the mass giving birth to its leaders. This was the nature of politics in all democratic societies.[27]

Weber's 'sociological constitutionalism' is indicative of his marrying German constitutionalism with his own ideas of social action and legitimacy. As a proponent of strong leadership and democracy, Weber advocated plebiscitary democracy in the form of direct election of the charismatic leader (as opposed to a 'leaderless democracy'), which combines routine party-dominated democratic rule and charismatic leadership, and which derives its legitimacy directly from the ruled. The stability of parliamentary politics needed to be supplemented with the extraordinary political will of the political leader. Weber acknowledged the parliament as a source of legitimacy as far as it goes, but as secondary to its educational and selective functions. The parliament does not represent the state in its totality, but rather sector- and class-related interests in perpetual struggle with one another. Voting on the chancellor is the way the masses actively subordinate themselves under the chosen leader. Weber argued that direct election of the leader was necessary to not let the future of the nation in the hands of an omnipotent parliament, whose majority could paralyse governmental rule. The power of the chancellor needed to be severely restricted in case of all eventualities, but he had to stand on his own ground directly from the will of the people.[28] At stake for Weber here is the ability of the nation to act rationally in an unstable international community. Weber was wary of the power of the masses, not least the proletariat that could be led astray by demagogical and charismatic leaders. The political maturity of the masses was simply at a level that made full democratic power to the elected parliament too risky.[29] Only plebiscitary democracy could lift politics to the level of the nation among other nations. In this way Weber wanted to combine representative politics with the grandeur of charismatic leadership.

Weber thus had limited expectations as to what representative democracy can fulfil: 'The demos in the sense of an unstructured mass never "administers" itself in large groupings, but is administered, and alters only the mode of selection of the ruling administrative head and degree of influence.'[30] This view has been interpreted as a sort of aristocratic scepticism, even a down-grading of people's political and societal engagement. I think it ought to be seen as respect for how people live their lives and what they are concerned with. It connects to a realist view on power and hierarchy as an unavoidable dimension of all organised life when the bureaucratisation machine sets its mark on it. Consequently, he too, as a believer in the *Recht-Staat*, or rule of law, viewed division of power as a key principle.

In his final years, Weber was concerned with constructing an analytically viable concept of the state, by eliminating any organicist and supra-empirical or *normative* conceptions, as he wrote in 1913.[31] The war experience made him increasingly engaged in constitutional questions. His very last lectures, in May 1920, were on 'General Theory of the State and Politics (Sociology of the State)' at the University of Munich. He died on 14 June that year. In the lecture series it appears from the students' notes and his lecture plan that he was typically not interested in constructing a normative theory to resolve the fundamental paradoxes of the state. In a familiar manner, Weber had laid out the antinomies for states in general and Germany in particular. Again, at the centre of his interest were the paradoxes concerning the production of types of legitimate rule. The influence of his colleague Georg Jellinek's work on 'The General Social Theory of the State', to which I return, appears to have been considerable.

Of overall interest here is, first, that Weber's writings on politics and the state (bureaucracy, monopoly of violence, types of rulership, types of political ethics, types of law, political rationality, and more) can all be seen as contributions to a theory of political legitimacy.[32] And, secondly, that theory of political legitimacy in a modern nation-state is a theory of sovereignty. What differs from legal writers of sovereignty is that Weber neutralised the normative question of its ontology, its foundation of obligation, will or reason, and so on. He refused any essentialism regarding the general will or the *Volksgeist*.

Given his nominalism, he probably saw sovereignty as basically a historically shaped concept, more or less suited for social analysis. He concentrated on the ideas and beliefs that were set to work in an actual society, such as nationalism. Weber concentrated on the sociological question *per se* on modern politics: how legitimate authority is constructed and reproduced. A lesson from Weber is that legitimacy is not to be fundamentally embedded in a normative outlook *ex ante*, but needs *to be observed as a social fact*.

Weber's concept of sovereignty

To Weber the legitimate monopoly of force of the state was naturally connected to state sovereignty, as a 'material attribute of today's institutional state'.[33] In *Economy and Society* he discusses the 'illegitimate power' of regimes that cannot avoid endemic conflict between *'politische Verbände'* within a territorial community, because there is no monopoly of power. To Weber 'illegitimate power' or 'non-legitimate rule' simply describes a sovereign's lack of a legitimate monopoly of power. Weber referred specifically to the ability of the state to legitimately *defend* its sovereignty through force. Quite noticeably, Weber's emphasis on the state as the legitimate monopoly of force works for him also as an understanding of sovereignty. Following Andreas Anter, the concept of sovereignty works in Weber's discussion to unite the domestic emphasis on monopoly of violence with its external dimension. Sovereignty, seen as a 'material attribute' was to Weber a dimension that is activated to a variable degree according to the international situation.

I think the nationalist Weber, when seeing his sociological and political writings together, did in fact present a sociological approach to sovereignty. This conclusion is in part based on his definition and analysis of the origin and functioning of the state. Although much of his thinking on these matters directly responded to the German situation after the collapse of the *Kaiserreich* in 1918, his ideas ought to be read as contributions to the debate about the internal and external dimension of sovereignty in general. Weber advocated a balance between a strong legislative power and the directly elected chancellor as the executive head of the state apparatus. Representative democracy had its advantages compared with plebiscitary democracy in that it encouraged institutional collective action with some clear advantages concerning recruitment and order. After all, politics governs the legitimate monopoly of use of force (*Gewalt*) within a territory, which makes it imperative to prevent abuse or misuse. The potential third corner of politics, public opinion outside the parliament, was not seriously addressed by Weber. Popular sovereignty was already institutionally accommodated by the parliament and addressed by Weber in his typology of political legitimation. Politics as an institutional activity was, according to Weber in his 1919 talk on the vocation of politics, about the leadership of political parties and associations (*Verbände*) capable of autonomous action, which makes up the state and its legitimate violence monopoly. Politics would mean the competition to control the distribution of power between and within states, as Weber stated in the address. This implies that no organisation can claim the right of using force to improve its purposes without permission of the state. The state has no overall purpose or end point, only a function: ultimately to guard and protect its territorial monopoly within a constitutional framework. To the extent that politics has a purpose, it operates in conjunction with law, to secure social order.

To Weber the state was of course a historical product, entangled in western rationalisation. In his theory of a legitimate state, Weber presents a sociological understanding of sovereignty in that he constructs historically and ideal-typically the sovereign state as a necessary and legitimate regulation of means of power by the enforcement of formalised law. Rationalisation (formalisation) towards the 'rule of law' increasingly provides the legal framework for the expanding state, which in turn must rest on legitimation, and finds it in parliamentarianism. Consequently, to Weber sovereignty emerged from western political rationalisation that establishes the legitimate *Gewalt*-monopoly of the state regulated by formalised law and parliamentarianism, *not* to accord with normative principles or Enlightenment ideals, but for 'real' reasons of stability and legitimacy.[34]

Weber distinguishes between four types of legal validity that can be ascribed to a legal order by those who must obey it. A legal order, including its constitution, is legitimate by virtue of tradition; by virtue of affective faith; by virtue of value-rational (substantively rational) faith; and by virtue of positive enactment of recognised legality.[35] Three of these correspond to the types of political legitimacy. The value-rational type was reserved by Weber to be a thing of the future, possibly from anti-formalist tendencies such as in Leninism and German nationalism. As often, Weber notes that the types tend to combine in real life: 'The forms of domination occurring in historical reality constitute combinations, mixtures, adaptations, or modifications of these pure types.'[36] Weber points out the rise of positive law in western society towards formal rational legal thought, modern contract law being the prime case. He argues that there is a growing tension between formal and substantive law, and that the increase of formal law in modern societies has consequences for human freedom. Substantive rationality of law entails the application of values (ethical, political, utilitarian, conventional) in legal decision-making, and thus is *not* informed by modern general norms.[37] Rationality also leads to irrationality emerging from law's blindness to human character, ultimate values and sincere motives for action. Formal legal rationality gives rise to bureaucracy run by technical expertise, where individual variation is filtered out by formal procedure.

Weber's sociology of law thus demonstrates how the 'order system' is loaded with inherent tensions between formal and substantive rationality (and irrationality) as a consequence of the rationalisation of modern society. Formal rationality refers to the increasing tendency of modern law to take unambiguous and general characteristics into account by explicit formulas, at the expense of the specific and unique, as in contract law. The Prussian constitution of 1794 failed, Weber argued, because it attempted reform of a substantial kind. In Weber's view, constitutional law is no exception to his general diagnosis – the tendency towards increasing formal rationality is pervasive and not to be avoided.

Luhmann and the concept of 'the state'

In a sociological view, the state changes itself by structural and semantic means. From the function of continuing its tasks the state enhances loyalty and conjoining behaviour. As a rule, a minority will tend to be unreachable or in opposition. Consensus goes in tandem with conflict. To enhance adherence to state purposes and norms and to construct topics of identity-sharing, a key function is to stabilise complexity. To make sense of themselves and the state in one and the same frame of reference, citizens need symbolic, narrative and affective simplifications. Following Niklas Luhmann's sociological theory of political semantics, the state produces meanings that are capable of lasting beyond specific events and operations of the state, and that can be retrieved at later stages. Such descriptions simplify the nature of the state for its citizens: 'Self-descriptions reconstruct the complexity of the system in such a way that they can be re-introduced into the system in a simplified form (e.g. as unclear goal-settings) and used as a guidance factor.'[38]

The state is a concept that refers to the political system and its main sub-systems that to a large extent overlap with legislative, executive and judicial powers.[39] At the level of political and conceptual history, Luhmann presents the hypothesis that the need for self-description arises with increasing differentiation of the political system. We may expect that as the state retracts its welfare functions for fiscal reasons (but expands its administrative and steering capacities), a self-description is likely to emerge that can bring new expectations together. Self-descriptions generate new (liberalist) *reflection theories* that generalise and connect descriptions to previous philosophical norms, to explain origins and consequences.[40]

As the description of the welfare state is currently stated as a fiscal *problem*, new reflection theories will revise the semantic self-reference of the state, but certainly not without struggle. After the self-description of the state as welfare-state, it seems that Europe (no doubt influenced by the US) approaches a liberty-oriented state where citizens are increasingly left to their own individual freedom and rights within the limits of law, at the same time as the state dramatically expands its control and steering functions. The liberalist metaphor of freedom of choice relieves the state from some of its responsibilities and enables it to grasp itself under conditions of immense complexity.

The concept of 'the state' signifies continuity and unity throughout modernity, with self-descriptions marking its development. In this respect the state is a stabilising formula referring to the artificial man (Hobbes), the object of the people or the general will, the legitimate monopoly of violence, and so on. In the Renaissance the political system began to refer to 'the state' as it assumed a formula that simplified and stabilised the political system and its environment. It protected the necessity of allocating societal power to legislative politics and later indirectly to the idea of 'the people'. The concept of the state began its career by legitimating the king based on tradition and the divine, and later disconnected itself from external control and encompassed the national through positive law and rights. The state prepared the ground for the invention of the constitution in the late eighteenth century. Following Luhmann, this assisted legitimation of the political system as it connected to political parties and representation. The challenge was however to construct unity and stability amidst conflict and social differentiation: 'The nineteenth and twentieth centuries experimented with institutional solutions to this problem and used "constitutions" as the instrument to settle and vary them.'[41]

The state became a reference for the collective within a national territory and connected to the symbolic and legal bearer, the king and his government. Gradually 'the state' as self-reference allowed the emerging political system to understand its purpose. Differentiation (of government, parliament, administration, courts and their internal differentiations) could proceed in a controlled manner. The state originated as a divine formula attached to the king, but gradually acquired independent status and handled the demand for the right to protest. Parliamentary opposition was institutionalised and legitimated within the description of the state and ensured a surplus of steering possibilities in the political system. It enabled the political system to improve its observation and stabilisation of its political environment, and to rearrange itself institutionally (the separation of powers, rights) and semantically via concepts like representation, sovereignty and democracy.

What Luhmann calls *political theory* refers to the conceptual and comparative orientation of political communication within the political system that contributes to the performance of the system. At a certain level of sophistication and justification, one can speak of reflection theories.[42] As a theory of the system within the system, it contributes to general self-descriptions: 'In this way it is a political theory that no longer understands itself as a political theory, but as a state theory.'[43]

Constitutional semantics

Luhmann's theory of society projects a social evolution at two levels: a structural level of communicative differentiation and a semantic 'super-structural' level of reflection. In modern societies the two levels have developed in tandem. With the turn to functional differentiation, emerging function systems have developed structural couplings or connections, such as constitutions between the political function system and law. On the other hand, stabilising, system-specific semantics have developed in the shape of system-specific contingency-formulas and self-descriptions in the form of reflection 'theories'. At the structural level I will address constitutions as inter-system couplings, and then the semantic level of politics.

Societies tend to differentiate the notion of societal rationality in alternative ways: in what is economically efficient, in what kind of research sector generates truth, how art can transcend the mundane and how to win in sports. Politically the question of rationality concerns political legitimacy.[44] Legitimacy rests in a constitutional state as guarantees for subjective rights, particularly freedom of speech, and by securing differentiation by limiting politicisation of the economic and private spheres. The legitimacy function is covered in the political environment of public opinion, and with structural couplings to other function systems, which depend on politics economically and legitimately.

To Luhmann, the constitution is not simply seen as a legal text for the control of political power. Rather, it is a mechanism for controlled differentiation of politics and law, and for production of political legitimacy. Luhmann addresses it as a structural coupling between the function systems of politics and law that allows for the systems to open themselves to one another without losing their specifically coded communication. Politically the constitution produces and legitimates political institutions oriented towards power. Legally, it provides law that validates legal norms. The political and legal systems are linked through differences from their environment – the constitution allows for their coupling despite their communication autonomies. Observed from each system, the constitution belongs to the system, but also to its environment. It is mirrored in law or politics. Law and politics observe their boundaries through the constitution-in-context and the distinction between system and environment that at any point in time lends the constitution its validity.

As indicated, sociology assumes a close connection between the differentiation of society and its constitutional development. The constitution can be read as the self-description of the modern rule-of-law state. With the development of European bourgeois society during the nineteenth century the old ethical-political unity was laid aside and a constitutional political society emerged. The distinction between state and society was a consequence of the gradual primacy of the political, and the state left the metaphor of the body to be a branch (or social system) within society.[45] The constitution formulated the tasks and functions of the political system and specified its relation to other social systems.[46] With *representation* as formula, the constitutional state developed in early modern society. Representation assumed a notion of unity in the plurality that with increasing complexity became more difficult to defend. Parliamentary politics had to rely on other categories, such as *reflection* (self-determination, self-selection, procedure (*Verfahren*)).[47] With the labour movement, the category of *participation* followed from the mid-nineteenth century. The abstract framework and boundaries for this were already set in many constitutions.

The textual facticity of the new constitutions denoted principles for the order of the state: the separation of powers and the general organisation of political-legal processes stabilise the power relationship. In a functionally differentiated society, its function is to mark the difference and compatibility of the political system with society and its sub-systems.[48] The internal differentiation between formal politics and public administration helped to designate their respective functions.[49] As self-descriptions of the political system, constitutions clarified the complementarity of state and society: the state is the force that guarantees the freedom of society.[50] By preparing the state to confront and protect society, the constitution allows for a more complex political system.[51]

Unlike the validity of law, politics must somehow draw on the public for political legitimation, which entails that the public must be brought to comply with policies and candidates. Politics produces its legitimacy by handing the public identities and values that follow every decision and statement. The public receives, understands (if often disagrees) and accepts political communication *qua* such. However, the public itself is not included in the sub-system of politics, only the political observation of it. The demos is 'present only with its absence', as Luhmann typically puts it. Politics must produce its own representations of the public as 'the people' that suitably generate legitimation from the political environment. The public is thus only indirectly implicated in legitimation. The absence of naive and unstable confidence must be filled with the fiction of a constituent demos that produces critical questions and that keeps politics and law at proper distance from one another.[52]

From such 'realist' considerations presented by Luhmann in the late 1960s and early 1970s, a sociological theory of constitutions subsequently evolved. Contributions in legal and political sociology, and in what is now called constitutional sociology, observe state power as co-originating with normative and legitimating statements on sovereignty and rights.[53] How the constitutional description of politics and law is interpreted to ensure autonomies and stabilities when being at the centre of conflict is a central topic. For example, when international interventions into state public law lead to the rethinking of constitutions, friction occurs.

The constitution is made meaningful by its inception that in many instances has been dramatic. Conversely the background (history, the political moment) is given meaning by the elevated and symbolic document. The circular reference between text and context enables a series of constitutional discourses tied to democracy and legitimacy. The constitution provides interpretive discourses and energy through various sources slowly shifting in time. This tends to enable stabilising power that protects society against legal bureaucratism and political absolutism. Thus, the document we call the constitution marks a connection between law and politics that keeps them in a regulative and mutual 'irritating' relationship where the influence of the one on the other is kept within limits.[54] By enabling law and politics to observe their boundaries and their difference from the environment, the constitution functions as a selective filter. It assists politics and law to cope with increasing differentiation and complexity such as internationalisation.

Constitutional legitimacy

According to Luhmann the constitution is a paradox that protects another deep paradox of popular sovereignty: the sovereign people cannot rule. As a functional equivalent to direct democracy constitutions as evolutionary achievements mark a particularity in the reproduction of politics and law. They are products of the reflexive invention of writing that allowed for both autonomy and societal influence of politics and law. Luhmann argues that they evolved in ways that allowed for increased technical and functional administration, based on the destruction of old hierarchies and the positive construction of abstract legal regulation. Constitutions are self-limitations on political power, and yet they increase state power by enabling the political system to handle problems that the political system observes as political. They sanction normatively the differentiation, centralisation and rule-based administration of political power; they regulate inclusion of citizenship and responsibilities; and they select power in society that can be distributed through politics. In this theory complex, law serves to stabilise expectations by providing legal identities to social arrangements over longer spans of time.[55]

The fact that law performs not only legality but legitimacy in modern societies has not been a controversial position among sociologists and philosophers since Weber. Habermas argues that legal power is legitimate through discursive opinion- and will- formation. In a realist view the condition for legitimacy of law lies rather in the historically defined ways it is applied by the system of law and the apparatus of state violence. The first constitutions helped the early modern states in their relatively stable functional differentiation by allowing for positive law and detailed legislation.[56] They served as what Luhmann calls contingency formulas. With the assistance of constitutions, politics could obtain normative and reflexive justification for its expansion and as an explanation for inclusion and exclusion of state matters. The formal ordering and stabilising effect of positive law transformed the legitimacy of legality into a non-normative fact. In Luhmann's early analysis, legal administration emerged as a self-legitimating procedure of society. Legitimacy was ensured, as he saw it, through successful legal and administrative performance. The price to pay was increased complexity that forced legal and political systems to perform more efficiently in and through their selections. This suggests that only as long as the welfare state can fiscally compensate for its dysfunctions, will it remain sufficiently legitimate.

The constitution viewed sociologically is a collection of normative statements about the power of the nation-state that as a rule is capable of constructing a sense of legitimate collective reality.[57] Legitimacy denotes the way politics expresses the necessity of social order under conditions of reflexivity and complexity. It explains the way the political system operates rationally by way of messages of inclusion, and by explaining to citizens their responsibility for the future. Legitimacy refers to the mutual adjustment of politics and the political environment. It somehow entails attributing to the political authority its entitlement to rule. The question is how and under what circumstances such an attribution is generated. We cannot assume a 'contract' or any other form of discursively based agreement between state and society, only discourse under the condition of history and contingency. The vast majority of Norwegian citizens, for example, associate the constitution *Grunnloven* with the date and place of its foundation. For some it is associated with controversies concerning admission to the country, conflicts between the parliament and the Swedish king, and with conflicts concerning EU membership and rights. More recently some of its articles have been intimately connected to a heated debate on transfer of sovereign power to the EU. As a social and political 'fact' *Grunnloven* is shared and passed on in education and culture as a thread of Ariadne that lays out and orders the nation's history of independence, democracy and national identity. It symbolises and organises popular sovereignty and the legitimate power of the parliament, *Stortinget*. At certain critical moments, however, it stands out as a text of rival expectations and interpretations. Although the unique feature of constitutions is their legal formalism, their sources and implications go beyond law into the social and political environment.[58]

Concepts and structure

Constitutional sociology benefits from seeing itself as a *political* sociology, where the historically grounded legitimacy of political power stands at the centre of interest. From its first generation of scholars, sociology has targeted the production of political legitimacy of the state as the foundation for state cohesion without assuming that legitimacy is simply generated by citizens in their spontaneous practices.[59] It shared similarities with the constitutional theory of Carl Schmitt, in the critique of legalistic, positivist and normative thinking, without, however, Schmitt's non-liberal decisionist ideas. After the second world war, sociological reflection on constitutions appeared in writings by Talcott Parsons and Niklas Luhmann in particular. Political sociology offered a range of historical studies on the origins of the modern state and its legitimacy, which provided background for further analysis of constitutions. From the 1990s, political and legal contributions within a broadly defined sociological field emerged that addressed sociological aspects of constitutions. In the last couple of decades, general efforts have appeared that explore the social origins and developments of constitutions as normative structures beyond legal and political normative theory.

Political legitimacy relates to self-descriptions of the political system from the eighteenth century.[60] Such theories, in the light of a waning societal totality, emerged in conjunction with structural change, and as a preference for (particularly with the assistance of the printing press) identity in the form of new distinctions. Such political theories of reflection took on a 'modern' semantic form as conceptually elaborated theories to ensure a favourable environment. In Luhmann's distinction between social structure and semantics, *concepts* are a key entry to system-definitions that emerges from a structural-functional differentiation. Conceptual and intellectual history is therefore a vital methodology that assists the understanding of historical and evolutionary transitions and tensions between social forms.

Luhmann's methodological approach was influenced by his colleagues at Bielefeld: Otto Brunner and Reinhart Koselleck. Luhmann's general theory, such as his last main work on modern society, can be read as a European history of concepts. The impressive work on *Geschichtliche Grundbegriffe* by Koselleck and his colleagues took the reflection on formation of concepts to a new level within the German historical tradition from the 1960s, in interaction with hermeneutics and the history of ideas.[61] I will point out two insights. First, concerning the relationship between language and reality: political events such as speeches are at once political events and narratives of these events. By examining a speech, we are *eo ipso* studying the event insofar as we can situate the speech as a response in a political discourse. The challenge is to see speech and historical context in a reciprocal relationship. Describing the world and the world itself cannot be assumed to be the same thing. Metahistorical context concerns temporal, spatial (social) and political boundaries that stand outside of language.[62] While historical reality is expressed in language, it is conditioned by a wide range of factors such as infrastructure and political organisation. This essential point, that Koselleck shares with Skinner, marks a difference from prolific versions of hermeneutics and post-structural theory, and I believe also from conventional historical research that often ignores *language* itself as a source about what happened.

Secondly, of basic importance is Koselleck's notion of *Grundbegriffe*, understood as basic, controversial and inescapable concepts like sovereignty, that political discourse circulates and performs as the core of conflict in their own right. Their status positions them into objects of new or revised understandings, that can be diachronically reconstructed. Continuous conceptual reconfiguring in political debate is an expression of political hegemony. Conceptual reinterpretation represents a core aspect of political and rhetorical conflict. There are many examples on how basic concepts attain the centre of interest (democracy, rights, globalisation) or, conversely, become marginalised (patriot, nation, empire). What does 'Europe' mean in political discourse today?

Niklas Luhmann focuses on how functional differentiation releases new paradoxes that must somehow be dealt with through meaningful semantics. This produces new possibilities for society to develop. Conceptual and semantic history thus appears as the study of the availability of meaningful (deparadoxing) ideas that are crystallised and generalised in concepts like 'state', 'freedom' and 'citizen' that provide immediate and general expectations. This approach provides insights as to how specific concepts are connected to structural transformation. Meaning is a precondition for their availability and their ability to assist expectations in communication. Semantics provides communication with condensed distinctions of meaning that inform societal communication, at the same time as specific communication over time serves to reproduce its influence – until structural change inevitably enhances new concepts. The essential point is that all disputes are unique in that they invest specific meaning into essential concepts – but they cannot avoid drawing on previous debates and literature. In debating the future, they must operate recursively. Again, this is a sociological matter of co-evolvement between structural semantics and situational speech-acts.

Political semantics

The research strategies of Koselleck and Luhmann suggest that conceptual history is well suited to serve as a sociological methodology. Conceptual history is a methodological entrance to semantic paradoxy. The key concepts of the political system that Luhmann addresses acquire their significance in distinct dimensions of meaning.[63] Luhmann frequently applies three dimensions informed by Parsons and Koselleck to frame empirical phenomena through his consistent application of distinctions. First, the *social* dimension of meaning concerns who is addressed as opposed to who is not, who is recognised as an agent, as opposed to the Other, who is included and excluded, who is provided with identity as opposed to the abstract Other. A version of this distinction was applied by Carl Schmitt in his infamous friend/enemy distinction. Secondly, the *thematic* agenda-setting dimension concerns which issues are conceptually addressed and which are not. What is, and what is not, a 'nation'? Thirdly, and possibly most importantly, the *temporal* dimension induces a distinction between past and future, or before and after, which defines the interface we call 'now'. What is traditional and outdated – and what is modern or utopian?

Semantics and their concepts mark social existence by applying the three dimensions in their production of meaning. There are aspects here of particular importance to the study of political concepts like sovereignty. First, there are tensions or conflicts between what a concept covers and everything else, for instance the concepts of nation or class. Consider the twentieth-century discussion between Marxism and liberalism: what is a democracy? Secondly, rival social interests will work to influence the definition of concepts as a part of their social struggle. As pointed out, sociologically there is no *ex ante* definition of sovereignty, since definitions are themselves part of the political struggle. That fact, I must add, does not prevent an author (such as the present) to take explicit part in that debate. Thirdly and relatedly, concepts (that always refer to something, and therefore not something) will produce counter-concepts. Inherent counter-conceptions lead to the mobilisation of oppositional concepts. In the history of sovereignty, for instance, monarchical sovereignty was replaced by a notion of balance between state powers, then the concepts of human rights and international cooperation delineated aspects of 'sovereignty'.

How the three dimensions of meaning are played out in discourse will have implications for how underlying paradoxes are handled. Meaning and conflict are closely connected, a point stressed in other forms of semantic and discourse analysis as well. This is not always emphasised by Luhmann although he is clear on the point that transitions imply tension. He is more interested in stability than disruption. His main point is nevertheless of great importance in a study of sovereignty as a phase in the evolution of political semantics: the political system enables its own reproduction by inducing new semantics of expectations that resolves its paradoxes by 're-entering' new distinctions with new paradoxes. Society handles complexity by adding complexity.

Political theory from Hobbes on, marked a tradition of not only political and moral philosophy, but the beginning of a theory of the state.[64] The principle of *representation* as authorisation that appeared with Hobbes became a reformulated element in conceptions of popular sovereignty and was adopted in the late eighteenth century. The paradox, in that *all* have the ultimate power and *some* are in power, yielded representation as a principle. Authority rested no longer solely in the body politic of the monarch, but on the loyalty and unity of the subordinate, which then required legitimacy that from now on had to be *earned*. Similarly, theories of the system inside society were developed in science, economics, education and art. Descriptions influenced the system, which called for new descriptions – that is, public reflections on new demands and future directions.

The demand for legitimacy is presented by Luhmann as a strategy for dealing with the paradox of sovereignty that followed the era of the divine monarch and the coming principle of the division of powers. The emerging political system could no longer rely on general notions like confidence, trust and loyalty, but needed to develop its distinct foundation for power based on the possibility of negative sanctions.[65] From this, the medium of power differentiated itself as a specifically political form. Ascribed and politically specialised justifications were developed to ensure the good of the nation. The codification and turn-taking of government, and opposition in particular, could more flexibly resolve potential legitimacy problems.[66]

With the introduction of printing and diversity of genres an audience was invented that reached beyond the control of the author. Books and pamphlets became objects for reflection. Text constituted documents for a growing public with increasing freedom to read and interpret. Society developed new efficient ways to handle modern paradoxes. Sovereignty, after Jean Bodin's writings in the late sixteenth century, referred to the power of the king as the state. Later, 'the state' referred to a collective, although the king remained the sovereign.[67] Questions of legitimacy rose with reference not only to God and king but also to 'the supreme power' and 'the people' as sources of sovereignty, with the contract as a productive metaphor. The secularisation of the concept after the French revolution did not, however, equalise it with democracy or rule of the people. As in Locke's *Two Treatises of Government*, popular sovereignty implied that the supreme power (the king) was to remove or change the legislative assembly during an interregnum. As Ihalainen demonstrates, even after the American and French revolutions 'popular sovereignty' was related to the people as an abstract reference, and barely in any 'democratic' sense.[68]

The semantics of the welfare state

Luhmann accounts for the historical semantics of the concept of *the state* in modern society, from representation, sovereignty and democracy to the welfare state. Self-descriptions and their concepts of society were produced by politics and its public opinion. Descriptions and semantics change as conditions of social acceptability (legitimacy) follow the total transformation of society.[69] In the eighteenth century, the liberal understanding of the state relieved itself by referring to public opinion as the medium of popular sovereignty. It greatly improved the ability of the state to interpret its environment and provided an answer to growing expectations. The state reached a higher level of ability to observe society politically and acquired increased capacity to react to movements and demands in society.[70] 'The people' emerged as an abstract reference in the political system.

Values of the Enlightenment, such as what Montesquieu called the principle of 'honour', served to motivate and maintain normative stability, and contributed to legitimacy as reflexivity.[71] The nature of public disagreement and pluralism began with the printing press when books of divergent views appeared side by side in the library and could be compared, introducing inconsistency as a topic.[72] Tolerance was to be granted to others by those who did not seek trouble but wished to achieve something. Purposive rationality proved itself more productive than value rationality. With the concept of the public, voicing one's opinion played a more central political role because it marked a distance from given privileges. The public increasingly referred to individual rights and interests.

In Luhmann's perspective, *democracy* marks another phase of the out-differentiation of the political system.[73] It secures its coming decisions through a self-image that is generally accepted in society. Democracy means openness, or *the known ignorance* of what will happen beyond the next election. The short-range openness or ignorance of the future creates a focus on decisions as operations. In systems-theoretical terms the difference between system and environment is produced in the system through operations. When politics speaks of 'democracy', it functions adequately for society.

After the second world war the concepts of sovereignty, democracy and the *Rechtstaat* prevailed but another understanding of the state developed alongside it; the concept of *welfare state*. In the Nordic countries it was dominant even before the war. Welfare became another wish-formula for social inclusion. The state was to have responsibility not only for those unable to survive without assistance, but for all disfavoured groups in society under the parole of universal welfare. The welfare formula emerged from the need for reconstruction of European states after the war and provided guidance for politics by providing markets with social responsibility. Welfare is, as Luhmann puts it, another formula to ensure consensus for an unknown future.[74] Today the concept is another historical concretisation of old ideas of equality and individual freedom that not even European conservatives can go against. It is widely accepted as a mode to handle the need for projections about the future. For ruling social-democratic parties in the 1950s it meant a way of handling the expectation of socialism in a non-socialist way. It involved general political responsibility for the welfare of the population and served as an economic label beside 'democracy'. Up to a certain point this provided legitimacy, but when pressed further after the 1960s it produced growing disappointment.[75] Important here is that the welfare state was explicitly understood as a nation-state.

To Luhmann and Weber, political legitimacy is a product of ways to handle rationalisation of society and politics. Along with the structural dimension of differentiation, an emerging dimension of theoretic and semantic reflection co-evolves that sorts out what politics can and cannot do, and how it is to operate *vis-à-vis* other function systems like the economy and education. Constitutions represent the axial point between the structural and theoretical (semantic) dimensions of the state. They are evolutionary effects of structural and reflexive transformations leading to the self-referential circularity of legitimate politics. Constitutions are issues of power because they cannot be ignored. They were once handed legally and legitimately to the political system. The constitutionalised state and the monopolisation of the means of violence signified a tremendous mobilisation and centralisation of power, which required a constitutional legitimating base. Another word for this is 'constitutionalism' – in the development of which administrative and legal institutions formally deal with issues of power. In the cold war period, politics itself became increasingly 'de-politicised' and constitutionalised in the sense that issues were exported to autonomous administrative organisations, linked to national and international law.

From Max Weber we learn that modern politics emerges through rationalisation and that legal-rational legitimacy in particular is a fundamental and normative aspect of this structural transformation. What is described in heroic terms in normative political theory is in many respects mundane effects of the emerging modern state. Following Luhmann as well as current political realism, applied political theory is integral to legitimation as articulation and naturalisation of concentrated political power. Chris Thornhill argues that:

> The modern idea of legitimacy, and the theories of *human rights* attached to this idea, emerged as concepts that traced the distinctions between the political system from what is not political, forced the state to preserve an autonomously political description of itself and its preconditions, and so ultimately clarified the positive grounds of the state's statehood.[76]

Ideas of rights and constitutions as responses to the emerging question of legitimacy were fed into the development of the state and served its self-descriptions, which again led to stabilisation of its operations in an increasingly complex environment. Particularly after the second world war, European states were in control not only of monopolies of legitimate means of violence, but also of steering devices by which they could bind and test their own operations against a self-constructed environment of norms. The idea of individual universal rights became particularly influential.

In his historical analysis, Thornhill demonstrates in a luhmannian sense how theories of legitimacy in Europe developed integrally with factual political functions in defining society as a political community, within, however, a societal setting that furthered similar trends in function systems like science and art. Thornhill argues that functional differentiation took place in an extended space where the adaptation and accumulation of political power required legitimacy in concordance with its political character, as norms.[77] Of particular interest here is how modern societies continue to validate their political functions in normative ways. A critical sociological approach therefore cannot take these normative political theories for granted but views them as semantically constructed in interchange with structural transformations. By considering political theory as second-order communication in the political system, the projected contradiction between reality and norms, or between democratic development and liberalist ideas, evaporates. Liberal norms are communicated in and by the political system, as inherent in political power. Consequently, the norm 'sovereignty' needs to be examined as a 'super-structural' self-description, which stabilises political power in its environment.

In Luhmann's theory, notions like the 'sovereign' and the 'state' emerged as self-descriptions or 'fictions' with which politics could stabilise itself as a distinct and autonomous political set of meanings. A task for sociology in this perspective is to inquire critically into the historical conditions that paved the way for sovereignty as a legitimating norm, and how it developed further. For Luhmann it is a precise observation that politics leans on the legitimacy of *legality*.[78] Politics and law are structurally coupled function systems that operate and legitimate themselves according to different codes. Only by realising their mutual autonomy can sociology examine how politics is second-coded by the constitution for the production of stability and narratives of plausibility.

A historical appreciation

From Luhmann, contemporary sociology of constitutions developed in two (interacting) directions.

First, a radical, autopoeitic direction with central terms like 'societal constitutionalism' and 'constitutional pluralism'.[79] In Gunther Teubner's work, constitutional politics develops side by side with, and allows for, the differentiation of the political system. Teubner modified the term 'constitution' to denote general production of self-descriptions and contingency-formulas in function systems, and observes a gradual self-constitutionalisation of global self-referential function systems. Quite radically, Teubner describes a development of political-legal self-constitutionalisation of *all* function systems, particularly in light of globalisation. The legal pluralism of Teubner emphasises that transnational institutional arrangements in political as well as non-political areas tend to constitutionalise themselves, outside state structures. Constitutional pluralism entails constitutionalism without states in global society that produces self-reference and replaces the former need for integration and identity. Without leaning on unreal appeals to a cosmopolitan constitutional order (Habermas), Teubner has presented a series of works that argue in favour of a societal constitutionalism for a world society.

This view has met decisive criticism. Verschraegen argues rightly that Teubner's theory underplays the role of the state.[80] Social rights developed by the territorial welfare state, for example, can be seen as ways to affirm its significance. Also, territorial internal differentiation of politics and the state can be seen as a stabilising element in globalisation. There might be no contradiction between strong nation-states and global functional differentiation.[81] Clearly, the state as a constitutional framework can, when the balance between constituent and constituted power is tilted, cause serious harm in the direction of totalitarianism or liberalistic atomism. Yet nation-state differentiation is without a credible alternative related to identity-formation and self-description. In contrast to arguments about universal political arrangements, individuals and institutions alike depend heavily on nation-state protection, stability, security and solidarity.

Secondly, a historic and comparative sociological direction has developed, mainly through the work of Chris Thornhill, that emphasises the stabilising function of the constitution in the contingent development of nation-states in Europe.[82] In a series of publications, particularly in the opus *A Sociology of Constitutions*, Thornhill reopened a classic, non-normative historical sociological path of analysis of constitutions, and paved the way for a Luhmann-informed perspective on constitutional change, particularly linking it to the question of political (self)-legitimation.[83] Unlike normative theory, under scrutiny were the self-reflections and self-descriptions of politics and surrounding constitutional change, which may serve (or undermine) legitimating purposes. Constitutions were seen as normative political structures concerning the elimination of private political power and regulation of state power.[84]

This sociology is not settled with stressing the ceremonial and integrating role of constitutions. A historically informed political sociology of this kind explains how constitutions as documents, conventions and debates locate themselves at the centre of parliamentary and public debate, how they attract social and political interest, how they (fail to) legitimate politics and how they themselves acquire legitimacy. To study the constitutional structure of society is understood here as to analyse descriptively a concentrated set of norms concerning the relationship between the individual and the nation through the vocabulary of rights, citizenship, representation and sovereignty. In Thornhill's approach, constitutions play a central role in the political stabilisation of society. Seen by Luhmann and Thornhill as the structural coupling between politics and law, constitutions express a legal framework for political power that cannot be overruled without serious consequences. They restrict the application of public power and private force and instruct politics to operate in accord with principles of the state by formulating boundaries of political, public administrative and legal powers (the state–society boundary) and formalise the selective inclusion of citizens through constitutional rights.[85]

Conclusion

Constitutions are seen here as outcomes of an evolution of societal differentiation, and as effects of a contingent development, that established 'real constructions'. Constitutional change, including its interpretations, takes place in distinct constitutional and discursive moments of unrest concerning fundamental questions of sovereignty and rights. Reformed constitutional expressions are seen as a route to enable social change via a higher consolidated level of stabilised normative structure for society. In other cases, constitutional change is initiated from political elites, and seen as a threat to established values and interests by broader sentiments of society. Even beyond revolutionary moments that clearly establish a new constitutional order, constitutionalism ought to be supplemented with a wider view on social and political engagement in constitutional affairs. Actual social and political circumstances should be seen in explicit connection with parliamentary deliberation and wider public debate, while keeping distance from the normative ideals and grand declarations of the constitutions. The purpose would then be to address paradoxes of political society where constitutions play a formulaic role – paradoxes like liberty and force, equality and inequality, democracy and capitalism, national sovereignty and globalisation.

Constitutions are evolutionary and historical products. They are socially generated and essential principles, they are condensed 'moral facts' (Durkheim) produced politically and socially. In a non-idealist view, constitutions are the link between politics and law. Constitutions are products of political deliberation and social conflict. This view does not dismiss the idea that the constitution reflects widely shared social norms but leaves open for analysis whether they reflect social consensus. Because constitutional norms are outcomes of social processes that cannot entirely be described as rational, they may be described as, for example, ideology, symbolic power (Bourdieu), social imaginaries (Castoriadis, C. Taylor) or, as here, political self-descriptions (Luhmann). Their stabilising function derives from their constraining and cohesive character, which regulates the use of political power and formally defines popular sovereignty.

Politics is the political sub-system characterised by conflict between position and opposition about the power to make binding decisions on behalf of citizens. Politics legitimises itself in its political environment, for instance as in the Machiavellian term *virtù* to counter the arbitrary *fortuna*. It has differentiated its morality, reasoning and rhetoric. Politics is defined semantically as the domain where political self-descriptions unfold historically. Politics mirrors society in that it involves inequality and pluralism. It is endemic of controversy. Its symbolism is a resource for unity *and* ammunition in the struggle for political influence. It cannot produce its own legitimacy out of thin air, and I will return to the legitimating role of society seen as political.

The concept of popular sovereignty is ambiguous, as it is conventionally (substantively) understood. To understand its nature, we cannot stick solely to political theory and public law theory, since they are less historically designed to understand institutions of social order. Sociology casts the net wider, to include symbolic, aesthetic and moral communication as effects of structural transformation. To be sure, sociological constitutionalism is a form of political observation and reasoning. However, with its rejection of explicit normativity and its criticism of idealism and moralism, sociological constitutionalism observes from a second-order position, more firmly placed in the sciences. Unlike liberal political theory, sociological constitutionalism has limited confidence in unifying processes of justification, and it remains at a descriptive-analytical level. From Montesquieu on, sociological constitutionalism *observes* political normativity; liberal political theory is seen as self-descriptions and formulas with the function to handle contingency and paradoxes.

Sociological constitutionalism in the version presented here can be seen as 'realist' but more importantly it is *historical* and draws upon *its own normativity* in the history of the state and its theories. For instance, rather than working its way from a given definition of a concept, it traces the meaning of concepts like sovereignty (Bodin), representation (Hobbes), the constitutional monarchy with its honour (Montesquieu), the general will (Rousseau), and constituent and constituted power (Sieyès). Sociological constitutionalism rejects any attempt at constructing an ideal model of democracy by which society is to navigate. Sociological constitutionalism organises a historical set of social rules, ideal types, typologies, generalisations, and observations of the differentiated and specialised power related to political governing. It intervenes with its hypothesis and explanations on a structural and a semantic level. On a structural level is politics seen as distinct communication about the power of the state as a legitimate monopoly apparatus of violence. Semantically, sociological constitutionalism examines the self-reflexivity of the political system. At this level sociology has the capacity to exercise second-order critique against idealisations of politics.

Notes

1 Chris Thornhill addresses the history of sociology in relation to the state and politics in *The Sociology of Law and the Global Transformation of Democracy* (Cambridge: Cambridge University Press, 2018).
2 With a formulation of Chris Thornhill about Weber that resembles Luhmann even more: 'Democracy could not be legitimated by the people – only by its construction of the people.' Thornhill, ibid., p. 103.
3 For a history of constitutional sociology from Hegel to Luhmann, see Chris Thornhill, 'The sociology of constitutions.' *Annual Review of Law and Social Science*, 13 (2017), 493–513.
4 Definitions presented in this text are tentative and preliminary. Note that many constitutional conflicts may not affect the constitutional text directly but concern

constitutional matters of rights and sovereignty nonetheless, and may be included in an analysis. The British constitution does not appear as one unified text.

5 Johann Kaspar Bluntschli, *The Theory of the State* (Ontario: Batoche Books, 1875/2000), p. 508.

6 For a brief history of the concept of constitutionalism, see Dieter Grimm, 'The constitution in the process of denationalization.' *Constellations*, 12:4 (2005), 445–584.

7 Dieter Grimm, *The Constitution of European Democracy* (Oxford: Oxford University Press, 2017); Petra Dobner and Martin Loughlin (eds), *The Twilight of Constitutionalism?* (Oxford: Oxford University Press, 2010).

8 Grimm, *The Constitution*, p. 364.

9 Richard Bellamy, *Political Constitutionalism – A Republican Defense of the Constitutionality of Democracy* (Cambridge: Cambridge University Press, 2007), pp. 1–12; Martin Loughlin, *Against Constitutionalism* (Cambridge, MA: Harvard University Press, 2022).

10 John Gray, *Enlightenment's Wake* (London: Routledge, 1995); Matt Sleat, *Liberal Realism: A Realist Theory of Liberal Politics* (Manchester: Manchester University Press, 2013), p. 169.

11 Gray, *Enlightenment's Wake*.

12 Bellamy, *Political Constitutionalism*, p. 5.

13 Ibid. Jeremy Waldron, *Law and Disagreement* (Oxford: Oxford University Press, 1999); Guy Aitchison, 'Rights, citizenship and political struggle.' *European Journal of Political Theory*, 17:1 (2018), 23–43.

14 Blokker, 'Politics and the political', p. 195.

15 Aitchison, 'Rights, citizenship and political struggle'.

16 For instance, considerable media debate circulated around the Norwegian High Court case concerning petrol exploration plans in the Barents Sea. Civil society organisations, among them Greenpeace, sued the state on the grounds that the plans, if realised, would signify a breach of *Grunnloven* and international treaties. More conflicts of this kind are likely to come.

17 Peter Badura, quoted by Rainer Wahl, 'In defence of "constitution".' In Dobner and Loughlin (eds) *The Twilight of Constitutionalism?*, p. 221.

18 Ibid., p. 221.

19 Ibid., p. 234.

20 Ibid., pp. 235–236.

21 Duncan Kelly, 'Revisiting the Rights of Man: Georg Jellinek on the rights and the state.' *Law and History Review*, 22:3 (2004), 493–529, at 499.

22 Peter Breiner, *Max Weber and Democratic Politics* (Ithaca, NY: Cornell University Press, 1996), p. 148.

23 Ibid., p. 137.

24 Duncan Kelly, *The State of the Political: Conceptions of Politics and the State in the Thought of Max Weber, Carl Schmitt and Franz Neumann* (Oxford: Oxford University Press, 2003), p. 118.

25 From Andreas Anter, *Max Weber's Theory of the Modern State: Origins, Structure and Significance* (Houndmills: Palgrave Macmillan, 2014), p. 72.

26 David Beetham, *Max Weber and the Theory of Modern Politics* (Cambridge: Polity, 1985), p. 266.
27 Max Weber, *Political Writings* (Peter Lassman and Ronald Speirs, eds) (Cambridge: Cambridge University Press, 2010), p. 28.
28 Ibid., p. 307.
29 Ibid., pp. 25–27.
30 Max Weber, *Economy and Society: An Outline of Interpretive Sociology*. Vols I–II (Berkeley, CA: University of California Press, 2013), p. 568.
31 Gangolf Hübinger, 'Max Weber's "Sociology of the State" and the science of politics in Germany.' *Max Weber Studies*, 9:1–2 (2009), 17–32, at 20.
32 Rasmussen, *Political Legitimacy*, ch. 4 and 5.
33 Anter, *Max Weber's Theory of the Modern State*, p. 26.
34 Gregor Fitzi, 'Sovereignty, legality and democracy: politics in the work of Max Weber.' *Max Weber Studies*, 9:1–2 (2009), 33–49, at 37.
35 Weber, *Economy and Society*, Vol. II, ch. 8.
36 Ibid., p. 110.
37 See Stephen M. Feldman, 'An interpretation of Max Weber's theory of law: metaphysics, economics, and the iron cage of constitutional law.' *Law and Social Inquiry*, 16:2 (1991), 205–248; Martin Albrow, 'Legal positivism and bourgeois materialism: Max Weber's view of the sociology of law.' *British Journal of Law and Society*, 14:2 (1975), 14–31. Weber also addresses subtypes and irrational types of his two main legal rationality types that need not concern us here.
38 Niklas Luhmann, *Political Theory in the Welfare State* (Berlin: de Gruyter, 1990), p. 121.
39 For an overview of Luhmann's theory of the political system, see Rasmussen, *Political Legitimacy*, ch. 7.
40 Luhmann, *Political Theory*, p. 127.
41 Ibid., p. 131.
42 Ibid., p. 142.
43 Ibid., p. 143.
44 See Chris Thornhill, 'Niklas Luhmann: A sociological transformation of political legitimacy?' *Distinction*, 13 (2006), 33–53, at 49.
45 Niklas Luhmann, 'Politische Verfassungen im Kontext des Gesellshaftssystems.' Parts 1 and 2. *Der Staat*, 12:1 (1973), 1–22, 165–182, at 5.
46 Ibid., 6.
47 Niklas Luhmann, *Legitimation durch Verfahren* (Neuwied: Suhrkamp, 1969).
48 Luhmann, 'Politische Verfassungen'.
49 Ibid., 9.
50 Ibid., 165.
51 Ibid, 168.
52 Luhmann, *Legitimation durch Verfahren*.
53 Chris Thornhill, 'State building, constitutional rights and the social construction of norms: outline for a sociology of constitutions.' In Mikael Rask Madsen and Gert Verschraegen (eds) *Making Human Rights Intelligible: Towards a Sociology of Human Rights* (Oxford: Hart Publishing, 2013), p. 27.

54 Niklas Luhmann, *Law as a Social System* (Oxford: Oxford University Press, 2004), pp. 404–409.

55 Ibid., p. 143.

56 Chris Thornhill and Samantha Ashenden (eds), *Legality and Legitimacy: Normative and Sociological Approaches* (Baden-Baden: Nomos, 2010).

57 Kim Lane Scheppele, 'The social lives of constitutions.' In Blokker and Thornhill (eds) *Sociological Constitutionalism*, p. 3.

58 Blokker, 'Politics and the political', p. 178.

59 Chris Thornhill, *A Sociology of Constitutions: Constitutions and State Legitimacy in Historical-Sociological Perspective* (Cambridge: Cambridge University Press, 2011), p. 2.

60 Niklas Luhmann, *Die Politik der Gesellschaft* (Frankfurt am Main: Suhrkamp, 2002), p. 33.

61 For their treatment on sovereignty and the state, see: Brunner, Conze and Koselleck, 'Staat und Souveränität'.

62 Melvin Richter, 'A German version of the "linguistic turn": Reinhart Koselleck and the history of political and social concepts (*Begriffgesichte*).' In Castiglione and Hampsher-Monk (eds) *The History of Political Thought*.

63 Luhmann, *Political Theory*, p. 21; and Niklas Luhmann, *Introduction to Systems Theory* (Cambridge: Polity, 2013), p. 18.

64 Luhmann, *Introduction to Systems Theory*, p. 232.

65 Luhmann, *Die Politik der Gesellschaft*, p. 72.

66 Ibid., p. 100.

67 Pasi Ihalainen, *Agents of the People: Democracy and Popular Sovereignty in British and Swedish Parliamentary and Public Debates, 1734–1800* (Leiden: Brill, 2010), p. 9.

68 Ibid.

69 Niklas Luhmann, 'The third question: the creative use of paradoxes in law and legal history.' *Journal of Law and Society*, 15:2 (1988), 153–165, at 154.

70 Luhmann, *Die Politik der Gesellschaft*, p. 355.

71 Charles Montesquieu, *The Political Theory of Montesquieu* (Melvin Richter, ed.) (Cambridge: Cambridge University Press, 1977), p. 189.

72 Luhmann, *Introduction to Systems Theory*, p. 132.

73 Luhmann, *Die Politik der Gesellschaft*, p. 105.

74 Ibid., p. 365.

75 Ibid., p. 364.

76 Chris Thornhill, 'Towards a historical sociology of constitutional legitimacy.' *Theoretical Sociology*, 37:2 (2008), 161–197, at 188.

77 Thornhill, *A Sociology of Constitutions*, p. 143.

78 Chris Thornhill, 'Legal revolutions and the sociology of law.' *Social and Legal Studies*, 23:4 (2014), 491–516, at 503.

79 Gunter Teubner, *Constitutional Fragments: Societal Constitutionalism and Globalization* (Oxford: Oxford University Press, 2012).

80 Gert Verschraegen, 'Hybrid constitutionalism, fundamental rights and the state.' *Rechtsfilosofie & Rechtstheorie*, 40:3 (2011), 216–229.

81 Ibid., 226.
82 Thornhill, *A Sociology of Constitutions*.
83 See Přibáň's comparison of Teubner and Thornhill in Jiří Přibáň, 'Constitutionalism as fear of the political? A comparative analysis of Teubner's *Constitutional Fragments* and Thornhill's *A Sociology of Constitutions*.' *Journal of Law and Society*, 39:3 (2012), 441–471.
84 Thornhill, *A Sociology of Constitutions*, p. 11.
85 Thornhill, in *A Sociology of Constitutions*, makes the point that in the formation of nation-states the emergence of rights that accompanied the French and American revolutions played a central role for the semantics of nationhood in the mid-nineteenth century. Rights allowed for inclusion but also limited the extension of state power to society.

2

Political uses of 'sovereignty': sociological methodologies

The methodological path of a political and constitutional sociology presented here can serve to examine ideas and arguments in political practice as they come together over time. The raw material is political statements as they occur as impact points in public debate. In this, words are deeds: arguments must be seen as practices in larger discursive networks. In addition, there are other contextual and structural elements to account for – such as the nature of genres and media, and the larger political and cultural situation.

This chapter addresses research strategies concerning constitutional debate. For a theme so wedded to centuries of philosophy and law, it is central to highlight not only its sociological non-normativity and thematic delimitations, but also its grounding in empirical analysis. Pertinent here is that to understand political society, it is necessary to account for concepts like sovereignty, representation and rights that in their instantiation legitimise and provide meaning to society over time. It is a well-known insight, from Tocqueville to Lefort, Skinner and Luhmann, that such terms and the generative principles they mediate, assist the political self-understanding in society. This symbolic and formative dimension informs 'the political' in political and legal philosophy as a precondition for politics. The concepts and the shifting debates that contextualise them, demonstrate how paradoxes about politics and power are tackled. Since power in democratic societies cannot function without its inherent legitimation, debates, as political acts, are not simply mirroring power – they *are* power and the means for challenging it.[1] In what follows, I address some key insights that I consider to be particularly helpful in historical-sociological studies of constitutional conflict.

Parliamentary deliberations

I have emphasised that it is essential to not (only) study the ideas of great texts, but also to take the effort to study how they are used in public debate by political actors. That implies studying parliamentary debates, newspaper chronicles, pamphlets, petitions, celebrations and the like, that not only express ideas but also intervene in specific conflicts in crucial moments of change. Sovereignty discusses itself in and through the public sphere, including the parliament. The contextual aspect is critical: the challenge is to understand these expressions in their context of time and place. History is read as successive conflicts, often reflecting large contradictions between classes and groups and long-lasting ideological positions. Let me first make a note about the study of parliamentary debates.

The tradition of parliamentary sovereignty in Britain and Scandinavian countries has come to imply that the parliament has the right to change laws that no government can set aside. Sovereignty as a functional relationship between the parliament and the constituent power had, in the second half of the twentieth century, been understood as a communicative relationship regulated by elections, public opinion, public hearings, corporate and post-corporate pluralism, and referendums. The sovereignty of the national assembly was historically opposed to the powers of the king, nobility and courts. The current parliamentary concern, I might add, is compatibility with super-parliamentary powers and the power to regulate multinational capital. Analysis of the public use of 'sovereignty' renders visible the topical transformation itself, and highlights aspects of the dynamics of parliamentary history, as well as the diversity of views on the status of the nation-state and the parliament. Rhetoric and substance can be considered analytically distinct only up to a point, since they tend to become fundamentally inter-woven in the political debate that they essentially constitute.

The rhetoric of parliamentary debate displays ideological visions and party agendas of the interests they represent.[2] By debating proposals and opinions, representatives are potentially constructing and reshaping general positions of government. Parliamentary deliberation means to approach a problem from different positions, which often coalesce to two contrary sides. The aim is simply exhaustive consideration leading to a decision.[3] Parliamentary politics is about reconstructing disagreement within an agreed formal structure on how to conduct affairs. Parliamentary rhetoric displays, following Ilie, a duality on confrontation and compromise. Its development has followed two discursive genres; it has adopted internal and specialised conventions, and more open and audience-friendly styles. Parliamentarians are constrained by such conventional and institutional genres, as they rely on certain recurrent *topoi* or communication codes that contextualise (generalise and specialise) debates to enable coherent communication.[4] Sovereignty as meta-discursive representation calls internally to parliamentary communicative rationality and externally to how the concept is subject to contestation in actual controversies. Internally, the analysis sheds light on the debating powers of the parliament (and its alleged decline), and externally on the development of the democratic nation-state. Importantly, these are sides of the same coin of the autonomy and legitimacy of deliberating and legislating politics. When a parliament gathers to debate national sovereignty, it addresses *eo ipso* its *own* capacities and limitations.

Politics and law are produced in and through their generalised and functionally coded communication. To use Luhmann's terms, politics communicates about power while legal communication revolves around legality. In the study of constitutional moments, to which I return below, the object is discourse taking place in politics and law, as well as in their respective environments. Political and legal vocabularies can be analysed to see how politics and law have reproduced and delimited themselves from other function systems over time. More specifically, the development of constitutional discourse producing constitutional conflicts can be analysed in parliament and the public debate.[5] Significantly, the history of political concepts like representation, democracy and sovereignty has been studied by Koselleck and Skinner in their respective Bielefeld and Cambridge schools, rightly seen as critical for constitutional law and the role of parliament. However, sociological analysis of constitutional debate wants 'more' out of this than a history of concepts. The sociological interest lies with how concepts and their transformations appear as comments to paradoxes between the state and the people and between the state and the world. It indicates how the nation-state steers itself by recontextualising and redefining key concepts in conflict and crises.

As political philosophers can be read as politicians, one may read parliamentarian debates as signals of the constitutional spirit of the time. Arguably, a sociology of constitutions would benefit from reconstruction of a methodology based on the history of concepts and more generally the history of parliamentary deliberation and public debate. Kari Palonen and Pasi Ihalainen have therefore developed their insights into studies of parliamentary vocabularies more generally.[6] With the digitalisation of parliamentary proceedings and newspaper debates, frequency measures can assist research in mapping constitutional moments in a broad sense. Contextual analysis of parliamentary concepts in debates on parliamentarianism and constitutional affairs discloses in what ways their self-description and self-understanding change over decades and centuries.

Rhetoric is a central dimension of political and legal communication, and serves as a sociological method for examining such communication. Skinner notes that concepts reveal what distinctions the speaker makes, what questions the speaker tries to answer, and how the speaker makes sense of the world.[7] Values and beliefs are played out in argumentation as the sincere and rhetorical 'truth' of the speaker. Nominalism rules: validity beyond the words is inaccessible and of no concern to the historian or sociologist. The point is not the concepts themselves, but their public implications, their 'uses in argument' or (with Austin's terms) perlocutionary speech-acts. Parliamentary politics is 'to do public things with words', and parliamentarians' words are public 'deeds'.

I share Palonen's view that studies of parliamentary debate benefit from being informed by insights of Koselleck and Skinner, and indirectly by Weber's methodological construction of the ideal type.[8] Weber scholar Palonen distinguishes between three ideal types of parliamentary communication: *representation*, *legislation* and *deliberation*, each with their own vocabularies, time-orientations, key events, type of politician and momentum. Representation refers to elections, majorities and connection to the people. Legislation refers to votes, laws and the role of legislator, while deliberation refers to the typical plenary *pro et contra* debates. Compared with the dominating legal studies of constitutional history, sociology of constitutions implies strategic reinterpretation through recontextualisation of constitutional change.[9] Until recently, sociologists rarely turned to rhetoric and speech-act theory in designing methodologies, and still political rhetoric is generally addressed as *parole* rather than *langue* – as speech-acts in their immediate context rather than as discourses over time. Now, rather than putting the emphasis on solely legal reasoning in a first-order fashion, sociology observes deliberation and debate as rhetoric involved in contestation and conflict. Parliamentary debates are seen as a particular arena of political contestation on behalf of social groups and classes over economic and ideological interests. It can hardly be different in a society of political equality in an environment of growing social and economic inequality. There has been a misunderstanding since around 1980 to project the aim of politics as 'consensus', whether through an inner linguistic drive towards mutual understanding or through a pragmatic interest in deliberation to gain support. The emphasis on consensus as a political norm through communicative or contractarian formulas in political theory enhances a de-politicised view of politics. Sociology and political realism can provide critical responses to this view. In my 'Weberian' view, dissensus and deliberation for the purpose of advancing a given position is an ideal-typical feature of parliamentary debate. Parliamentary politics can be understood as a never-ending (Weber: 'slow drilling through hard-boards') deliberation and contestation on how to reform and discipline individual and collective self-interest, so that it does not destroy one's own and others' freedom from dependence. Such a tentative definition is informed by republican and realist views, from Machiavelli on. Constitutional adjustments and amendments can be seen as legal specifications and generalisations of such political contestation.

Weber's views on political conflict have influenced Skinner's and Koselleck's priorities towards the study of specific cases, periods and types as contingent outcomes of modernisation. Koselleck was more interested in long-term macro-changes of concept formation than Skinner.[10] Skinner addresses changes in intellectual texts and in situations of dispute and argumentation and is more interested in the question of legitimacy as predominantly a rhetorical problem. Skinner in particular shares Weber's interest in the modern (democratic) kind of political legitimacy as an inherent political achievement involving the image of the people. Following Weber, the belief (*Glaube*) in legitimacy differs according to types of sources (custom, legal-rational, charismatic). In the history of modern political politics all three sources of legitimacy are in play.

As noted, sovereign power can be taken to mean the absolute control over a politically defined territory. Different forms of sovereign statehood exist, and they have changed profoundly over time. Competing descriptions of sovereignty take various examples as their empirical referent to universalise it and to stabilise the meaning of the concept. It no doubt marks a site of political contestation. A purpose here is to present some ideas on how to examine sociologically how the concept of sovereignty became fixed historically in nation-states, and how particular norms about sovereign identity became justified during decisive moments. This refers to the transference of judicial, political and symbolic representation from constituent to constituted powers, to apply Sieyès's terms, that are woven together in political struggle.

Parliamentary public debates, their speech-acts and rhetorical practices, are considered as material for analysis of parliamentarian practice and the meanings of constitutionalism. The contesting modes of debate are recognised here as their way of demonstrating political freedom. Kari Palonen argues that the parliament

> is the site of dissensus par excellence, based on the rhetorical epistemology that an item cannot be properly understood unless it is considered from opposing perspectives and subjected to the debates between them. The parliament offers us an institutional procedure in which the dissensus between agents is not only legitimate, but also a condition for the understanding of the singularity of the parliamentary style of politics.[11]

Palonen suggests that one may 'judge parliamentary procedure as an institutionalization of dissensus that refers to a rhetorical theory of knowledge, for which items on the agenda can be properly understood only when they are discussed by confronting opposed points of view.'[12] Parliamentary deliberations (explications, justifications, etc.) are then observed more broadly than in the conceptual histories of Skinner and Koselleck. Considerable insight is also to be gained from Ihalainen's study of British and Swedish early modern parliamentary debate and the changing meaning of terms like 'sovereignty', 'democracy' and 'the people'. Ihalainen presents a conceptual and contextual history of the reception of the concepts of sovereignty of the people and democracy in the late eighteenth century based on close analysis of politicians' concepts and arguments in speeches and debates.[13] Based on comparisons between England and Sweden, he demonstrates the significance of national context and influence of English debate on the Swedish.

One may concentrate on political *pro et contra* deliberation and disputes in speeches, addresses, debates and writings in parliaments on constitutional topics that highlight controversies, positions and dealing with paradoxes. An example of relevant source material where political vocabulary comes to the fore is the records of the official openings of parliament with the subsequent debate, where contested and controversial concepts, expressions and opinions concerning constitutional affairs are challenged. Political speech-acts ought to be observed in the context of their occurrence. A challenge is to stick to the wider contemporary use of the terms in the past, to avoid implicitly current meanings of the terms. Not only does the word or language mediate between the observer and reality, but the *context* also indicates how 'sovereignty of the people' and 'democracy' were historically understood. Key phrases cannot be deemed to have any value or meaning independent of their occurrence in history and their 'uses in argument'.

Public opinion rhetoric

It makes sense to distinguish between *parliamentary* and *public* debate due to their modes and rhetoric. A distinction between parliamentary deliberation on the one hand, and a wider public engagement in the press and on the streets, is essential in the identification of constitutional moments.[14] During the late nineteenth century, parliamentary debates in Britain and France connected increasingly to the emerging press and civic associations. Politicians took their disputes further into the public arena in publications and meetings as covered in the press. It must be remembered that until the 1970s, the national political agenda of public debate in Europe was probably set more by the parliament than by the press. Following Charles Tilly, it is more appropriate to say that the press took part in the 'parliamentarisation' of popular politics.[15] Representatives of parliament as well as politics itself had a higher political standing in the formation of public meaning than today. Naturally, this connection varies among political and press cultures and over time, and its influence should not be exaggerated.[16]

A central task in explorations of constitutional contestation would also be to identify the role and tactics of non-state, non-legal actors, like *ad hoc* manifestations and social movements as they turn to the press and the streets. Of relevance in the study of press coverage is discourse and frame analysis that have been widely applied in media studies, along with conceptual analysis to systematise and crystallise the complexity of meaning in media texts.[17] In constitutional struggle, such mobilising of collective and critical actors has played a decisive role. In at least the Scandinavian countries, it is not satisfactorily assessed how political interests have mobilised the law to exercise political change. The question of legitimacy in most western nation-states is closely connected to such nation-state collective actors, although this fact is rarely recognized as such by formal law and politics, since the sovereign subject remains the citizen represented by the parliament.[18]

Ideal types

In the second half of the nineteenth century, Wilhelm Dilthey was concerned with the scientific achievement of comprehending human activity in a world in which the observer was also a member. To Dilthey, categories must have their origin in the time and experience of human life and cannot be reserved to the faculty of human reason. On the contrary, *because* of our full involvement in social life we may also be capable of understanding it analytically. The epistemological dualism between everyday life activity and the scientific interpretation of it (reality and concept) must be overcome by reflection. Theoretical studies of history and culture must be approached through grounded and well-connected concepts. What helps the hermeneutically inclined researcher is that human behaviour is generally coherent and purposively oriented and can be interpreted from its historical and cultural context. Just as the natural scientist exercises the controlled experiment as the prime method to establish truth, the human sciences lean on hermeneutics as the art of interpretation. Meaningful behaviour and texts provide data for the human sciences, that, unlike in the natural sciences, can be studied 'from within', by way of exegesis. Interpretation gives rise to more general rules of human conduct that seeks justification against other interpretations to produce a methodology of interpretation of human records.[19] In contrast, Kantians like Rickert worked with prescriptive, formal and logical categories rather than with rules of interpretation.

These were not routes that Weber followed, although they helped him in formulating a neo-Kantian, nominalist critique of Dilthey on the irrefutable gap between the categories of the scientist and the actual world. This led to Weber's perspective of *Verstehen* and to his idea of the ideal type. Between Dilthey's vitalism and Rickert's transcendentalism, Weber presented his view on sociological methodology. In his essay on the 'objectivity' of knowledge in the social sciences published in 1904, Weber clarified the notion of objectivity and the ideal type as a prime methodological tool for the social scientist.[20] It becomes quite clear that Weber had no faith in the Kantian search for the complete meaning of human events that can provide prescriptions to society about its preferred development. Scientific analysis can inform political debate but never make any fundamental legitimate change outside its own domain.[21] Value judgements from scientists should not be conflated with scientific analysis. Worldviews are shaped and exist in perpetual struggle with other views and ideals at a distance from scientific truth. Science, Weber argues, has a conceptual relationship to reality; reality can only be identified or supposed as existing through our conceptual thinking.

The bridge Weber provides is the ideal type:

> The concept of the ideal type can direct judgement in matters of imputation; it is not a 'hypothesis'. Nor is it a representation of the real. Rather it seeks to guide the formation of hypotheses by providing representation with unambiguous means of expression. One does not construct the concept of for example 'town economy' as an average of the economic principles that are observable in all towns, but as an 'ideal' only in that they accentuate and elucidate relevant meaning.[22]

Weber writes that these thought constructs are ideal only in a 'logical' sense. They highlight what is to be seen as significant, and they sharpen the historical profile of social phenomena like the capitalist spirit or the charismatic leader.

More than hermeneutics the ideal type serves as a 'modelling device'. As in modelling, empirical complexity is simplified in a meaningful way. Meaningful to Weber means that its historical background is brought into the light. The aim is to interpret singular events as cases with historical causes. Purification of messy realities may indicate historical and contemporary underpinnings and values. Whether the type will provide useful depends most of all on the creativity and knowledge of the researcher. Ultimately the ideal type is a product of scientific imagination guided by reality.[23] 'We are concerned with the construction of relationships, which seem to our imagination sufficiently motivated and "objectively possible", hence appearing adequate from the standpoint of our nomological knowledge.'[24] The notion of the 'ideal' can be understood in light of Weber's view on social facts as historical facts. Social facts are products of historically produced ideas. The ideal type captures analytically this relationship between idea and fact. As Whimster states, 'Ideas are historically effective, existing as a psychological reality in the minds of men and causing them to act in certain ways.'[25]

Weber makes clear that there is only one standard here: that of success in developing knowledge of concrete cultural phenomena in their context, their causal determination and their significance. The construction of types is not an aim, but a means:

> All careful observation of the conceptual elements of historical representation shows that as soon as the historian seeks to go beyond the mere registration of material relationships and 'characterize' the cultural significance of even a very simple process, he is forced to work with concepts that can only be defined sharply and unambiguously in ideal types.[26]

Weber states that the ideal type

> is a thought construct: not historical reality, and most certainly not 'genuine' reality. It is not for employment in the service of a method for which reality is reduced to an exemplary instance, but which functions instead as a purely ideal limiting concept (*Grenzbegriff*), against which reality is compared, so that particular significant component parts of its empirical content can for the sake of clarification be measured. ... The ideal-type is in this function an attempt to comprehend historical individuals or individual components through genetic concepts.[27]

Clustered and essential contested concepts

Political discourse is constituted by key concepts with common, as well as rival, understandings that give debate coherence. Participants must largely share these concepts to interact meaningfully. Contests over the proper or legitimate interpretation of concepts are themselves intrinsic to politics.[28] Understanding this conceptual system is necessary to make sense of key discourses involved in constitutional disputes. 'Sovereignty' has been viewed as an 'essential contested concept'. The phrase was coined by Gallie, and later elaborated by William Connolly and John Dunn.[29] According to Gallie, the applicability of such terms in political discourse are multiple, complex and normative. A concept is essentially contested if its rival uses express competing moral and political perspectives.[30] Concepts involve standards and norms for their correct application, indicating larger disputes and broader frameworks of concepts. They are inherently attracted to controversy because of their reference to critical interests and norms. Their meanings are relatively open and invite interpretation of even shared norms differently in conceptual and substantive terms. Universal criteria of reason do not suffice to settle such controversies. Nevertheless, their definition and some root judgements are shared and make communication possible.[31]

The formulation 'essential contested concepts' helps to explain the role of sovereignty as fixed and at the same time how it is given meaning in networks of other terms and in wider social and conflictual frameworks. Such terms also tend to have a distinct philosophical character.[32] They tend to occur in pluralist and democratic societies where disputability is allowed to develop, and where the appropriate applicability of the concept never ends. Their open-textured character implies that they can constantly be recontextualised and challenged. They appeal to a common core of meaning developed historically through controversies on its proper application. Such conflicts also tend to involve related concepts. The use of a concept systematically presupposes or endorses whole networks or constellations of concepts in a way that indicates rival views. These conceptual divides cannot easily be resolved by empirical evidence, since to describe is to characterise from the vantage point of distinct interests and purposes.[33] The relationship between the criteria of a concept and its purpose is what makes concepts such as 'sovereignty' the subject of conflict.

Political opponents (and theorists) tend to structure their arguments around rival conceptions of the same concept that enable it to be understood in terms of different relevant conceptions.[34] The different conceptions tend to be anchored in rival theories, with different practical and evaluative consequences. Following Connolly and Dunn, investigations of contested and disputed terms of political discourse should involve examination of common vocabularies involved in conflict, how their meanings establish frameworks of political reflection, and what they represent in actual political conflict. The descriptive-normative content of conceptual clusters indicates what such applicability of essentially contested concepts helps to constitute. Analysis is then a matter of conceptual as well as political clarification of conceptual 'clusters' that represent and endorse particular positions. The term 'sovereignty' is thus embedded in semantic families of related concepts given meaning by rival positions. 'Sovereignty' is a clustered and essentially contested concept in that it refers to different aspects of power and is grounded in different value-systems. Most evidently it mobilises different and rival political camps. This allows for meaningful and peaceful contestation.

Constitutional moments

Conceptions of 'sovereignty' concern a supreme power and the ascription of that power to political and legal authorities in particular events. Analysis of constitutional semantics needs to be re-asserted in its proper historical-sociological light. There is no need to analyse the creation of, or change of, law, or to rewrite the history of the constitution in its entirety. Rather, a purpose in constitutional sociology is to address the influence of social structure and semantics on decisive episodes, critical moments or *constitutional moments*.[35] Such moments are points in history around which political and social forces organise themselves publicly to institute and prevent change by arming themselves with powerful, legitimating concepts such as sovereignty. In the spirit of Weber's *Verstehen*, the task is to grasp the use of 'sovereignty' and related narratives as they were made sense of and actively mobilised in particular circumstances of the past.

I have noted the sociological relevance of the distinction between structure and semantics with reference to Luhmann. Structure refers to media of longer-time change in the economy, politics, culture, demography, and so on. Semantics refers to documents, debates, speech-acts (including judicial white papers, etc.). Constitutional conflict is considered here as an effect of structure and semantics in combination: as a result of historical processes, and as *momentary*, often dramatic, circumstances of political conflict. Bruce Ackerman's concept of 'constitutional moments' is methodologically useful to identify disruptive episodes of constitutional innovation.[36] The term can be understood as a decisive constitutional phase or stage, or the discontinuity or rupture between events preceding and following constitutional change, or simply the moment at which the difference between the constitution and its social context becomes visible and contestable.

The term might suggest that structural preconditions such as economic growth and demography yield rising expectations, a self-produced sensation of crisis and a momentum of constitutional change. Such moments are fractures in time where the constitution imposes itself on events and becomes a visible and critical object between politics and law. It may be a moment in time publicly understood as a constitutional crisis, where the past as well as possible futures are highly contestable. It then appears as compressed political time where politics and law stand against each other, and legitimacy is drifting. The civil rights movement in the mid-1960s leading up to changes of law is one of Ackerman's examples of a constitutional moment, but there can be briefer moments as well, and quite a few failed such, as Ackerman demonstrates. Their significance can generally be seen in retrospect.

Ackerman's theory of American constitutional development indicates that transitions between constitutional regimes have taken place through processes of what he calls 'higher law-making', consisting of heavy involvement from outside the legal-political system by social movements and organisations among 'the people'. The considerable changes that the American constitution has undergone since the federalist constitution have often been the outcome of civil engagement outside the normal constitutional process, but still perceived to be legal and legitimate at the time. Constitutional moments consist of situations of extra-legal constitutional change, where formal rules that are designed to regulate constitutional change fail and mass mobilisation, along with strong voices and organisations of 'the people', take the lead. Conventional 'legalist' explanations of constitutional change, Ackerman argues, cannot account for 'unconstitutional' transitions between constitutional regimes in American history. Ackerman's claims may also elucidate the contemporary constitutional divisions in the US.[37] To Ackerman the term 'constitutional moment' was initially referring to moments of hope, such as for the civil rights movement in the 1960s. Notion of 'hope' or 'progress' probably needs to be replaced by a view that is more sensitive to power, such as in J. Pocock's work *The Machiavellian Moment*. After all, the 6 January 2021 attack on Capitol Hill was a constitutional moment.

A 'moment' of this constitutional kind is filled with contingency – a momentum that causes an extraordinary rupture and unexpectedly opens space for manoeuvres for political actors that may reorder the current power constellation. Such momentum may escalate into a revolutionary moment, as with the conquering of the Bastille. The Norwegian constitution was born in a brief revolutionary momentum in the spring of 1814. The duration of a moment may vary from days to months although political and moral erosion is inescapable.[38] As a moment of opportunity, connected to a constitutional topic of importance, it brings new players and their views into the chain of events. It is a rhetorical turning point, a *kairos*, where able politicians apply time and communication in their tactics. The skill of timing is vital, but then also unexpected opportunities allow for just as unexpected outcomes.[39] Palonen describes such moments with Weber's concept *Chancen*, translated as realisability or probability. The concept links Weber's political, methodological and historical analyses: 'The point is that even unrealised possibilities (whether they have simply yet to be realised or never will be) play a crucial role in the understanding of politics as a contingent activity, as they too represent the chances (whether taken, missed or unrecognised) in a given situation.'[40]

Constitutional change reflects changes outside and inside of formal procedures for such change. Those transitions suddenly become no longer illegal but celebrated as highly legitimate milestones towards greater freedom and sovereignty. Actual constitutional interpretation interacts in an immediate sense with social groups without any mandate. Constitutional moments occur when legal-political processes interact intensively with circumstances of non-legal populist, moral and counter-legitimate mobilisation. Such dramatic constitutional moments of 'higher law-making' illustrate the influences of social and political forces in the environment of politics and law.

Conclusion

I have argued that insights from studies of essential concepts in their contexts are useful methodological ingredients in 'thicker' analysis that includes controversies over political and constitutional matters that might apply the same key concepts, although in conflictual rhetorical contexts. Also, conceptual use is seen as intervention in debates that run over longer spans of time about essential matters such as freedom, justice and democracy. The sociological element comes in with the recovering of problems and their 'agonistic' parts in a wider social and political story of social and political change. The concept of sovereignty and related concepts often forms the centrepiece of a constitutional dispute where different definitions collide in the debate, while in other cases the concept is ignored precisely for the connotations it carries. For political sociology, I suggest, key contested concepts are traces to follow from moment to moment (case to case) through history, to make sense of the relationship between political communication and political change.

Notes

1 Claude Lefort, *The Political Forms of Modern Society: Bureaucracy, Democracy, Totalitarianism* (John B. Thompson, ed.) (Cambridge: Polity, 1986); James D. Ingram, 'The politics of Claude Lefort's political: between liberalism and radical democracy.' *Thesis Eleven*, 87:1 (2006), 33–50, at 43; Wim Weymans, 'Freedom through political representation: Lefort, Gauchet and Rosanvallon on the relationship between state and society.' *European Journal of Political Theory*, 4:3 (2005), 263–282, at 263.
2 Cornelia Ilie, in Paso Ihalainen, Cornelia Ilie, Kari Palonen (eds) *Parliament and Parliamentarism: A Comparative History of a European Concept* (New York: Berghahn, 2016), p. 133.
3 Kari Palonen, in ibid., p. 239.
4 Ilie, in ibid., p. 137.
5 Parliamentary records are increasingly digitally available in full-text searchable databases. The same is the case for extensive collections of public debates in the press, where debates can be traced according to their constitutional topics, and subsequently interpreted as rhetorical interaction.
6 Kari Palonen, 'Towards a history of parliamentary concepts.' *Parliaments, Estates and Representation*, 32:2 (2012), 123–138; Ihalainen, *Agents of the People*.
7 Quentin Skinner, 'A reply to my critics.' In James Tully (ed.) *Meaning and Context: Quentin Skinner and his Critics* (Cambridge: Polity, 1988).
8 See Kari Palonen, *Politics and Conceptual Histories: Rhetorical and Temporal Perspectives* (Baden-Baden: Nomos Bloomsbury, 2014), p. 79.
9 Kari Palonen, 'Quentin Skinner's rhetoric of conceptual change.' *History of the Human Sciences*, 10:2 (1997), 61–80, at 61.
10 Ibid., 73.
11 Palonen, *Politics and Conceptual Histories*, p. 13.

12 Ibid., p. 300.
13 Ihalainen, *Agents of the People.*
14 Hauke Brunkhorst, 'Globalising democracy without a state: weak public, strong public, global constitutionalism.' *Millennium: Journal of International Studies,* 31:3 (2002), 675–690, at 677 revises Nancy Fraser's distinction between weak and strong publics, also applied by Habermas in *Factizität und Geldung.* The strong public has moral and political power and decisions are made and linked to legal procedures framed by the constitution. The parliaments would be a typical strong public in this sense. Unlike Fraser and Habermas, Brunkhorst includes networks of public debates, publications, advertising, television, talk-shows, teach-ins, protest movements and more. What is left in Brunkhorst's weak public type would be, in the spirit of Dewey, the more or less uncoordinated action of the people such as in Paris 1789 and in East Berlin in 1989. Brunkhorst argues for a possible global order based on rights. His analysis ends, however, not in a critical analysis of sovereignty, but in a diagnosis of its dated status, and an idealist speculation of what the global weak public might achieve.
15 Charles Tilly, 'Parliamentarization of popular contention in Great Britain, 1758-1834.' *Theory and Society,* 26:2/3 (1997), 245–273.
16 Palonen, *Politics and Conceptual Histories,* p. 127.
17 One may for instance benefit from the methodologies in critical discourse analyses of national identity: Ruth Wodac, Rudolf de Cillia, Martin Reisigl and Karin Liebhart, *The Discursive Construction of National Identity* (Edinburgh: Edinburgh University Press, 2009).
18 One may focus on four groups of actors in constitutional conflicts: a) parliamentarians and governmental figures as they operate in plenary debates, commissions and so on; b) constitutional experts (for instance through judicial review, white papers); c) central figures in public debate (editors, commenters, intellectuals); and d) leading figures in social movements in civil society initiatives for or against constitutional reform. Each institutionalised group of actors will tend to be informed by certain modes of justifications and claims (interpretations of justice) and rhetorical ways to enter the debate. It can be argued that 'hegemonies' or prerogatives may shift among groups that make alliances, formulate common claims, and influence formal political debate and legal procedure.
19 On Dilthey, see Sam Whimster, *Understanding Weber* (London: Routledge, 2007), p. 85.
20 Max Weber, *The Essential Weber: A Reader* (Sam Whimster, ed.) (London: Routledge, 2004), p. 360.
21 Whimster, *Understanding Weber,* p. 103.
22 Weber, *The Essential Weber,* p. 387.
23 Ibid., p. 39.
24 Ibid., p. 387.
25 Whimster, *Understanding Weber,* p. 112.
26 Ibid., p. 389.
27 Ibid., p. 390.

28 William E. Connolly, *The Terms of Political Discourse* (Oxford: Martin Robertson, 1974/1983), p. 39.
29 Walter B. Gallie, 'Essentially contested concepts.' *Proceedings of the Aristotelian Society*, 56 (1956), 167–198; John Gray, 'On the contestability of social and political concepts.' *Political Theory*, 5:3 (1977), 332–348.
30 Connolly, *The Terms of Political Discourse*, p. 36; John Gray, 'On liberty, liberalism and essential contestability.' *British Journal of Political Science*, 8:4 (1978), 385–402, at 392.
31 Connolly, *The Terms of Political Discourse*, p. 3.
32 Gray, 'Contestability of social and political concepts', 332.
33 Connolly, *The Terms of Political Discourse*, p. 22; Gray, 'Liberty, liberalism and essential contestability', 344.
34 Neil MacCormick, 'Sovereignty and after.' In Kalmo and Skinner, (eds) *Sovereignty in Fragments*, p. 152.
35 Bruce Ackerman, 'Why dialogue?' *Journal of Philosophy*, 86:1 (1989), 5–22.
36 A similar term is 'critical moments' in Luc Boltanski and Laurent Thévenot, *On Justification: Economies of Worth* (Princeton, NJ: Princeton University Press, 1999).
37 Sujit Choudhry, 'Ackerman's higher lawmaking in comparative constitutional perspective: constitutional moments as constitutional failures.' *International Journal of Constitutional Law*, 6:2 (2008), 193–230, at 198.
38 Palonen, *Politics and Conceptual Histories*, p. 189.
39 Ibid., p. 218.
40 Ibid., p. 246.

3

Paradox: early modern formulations
of sovereignty

Among my intentions with this book is to clarify the contested and political adaptability of the concept of sovereignty.[1] I see this as a contribution to political and legal history, and as a resource for the assessment of multiple nation-state challenges today. As a discursive attribution a question is how the concept performs today, when no state is sovereign in a pre- 1945 sense. The term has been adapted to national transformation as well as globalisation, and no 'proper' concept of sovereignty can be found. The suitability of the term remains a political question. Precisely because of this fact it is essential to present at least elements of 'sovereignty's' journey through history. As a backdrop to current debates, I hope to provide some sobering historical insights to its political dimension. In the words of Dieter Grimm, Georg Jellinek argued that it is essential 'to take into account the circumstances, ideas and interests to which the various interpretations of sovereignty owe their origins and ascertaining the functions that the various concepts of sovereignty fulfil in their shifting constellations'.[2] Only then can one examine 'whether they will be able to endure even under current conditions or are so connected to the conditions of their emergence that they are no longer suited to the present'.[3] More than his fellow jurists within the positivist tradition, Jellinek stressed history as the legitimating and explanatory factor concerning the status of constellations of the state. I address Jellinek's perspective on the democratic state in the chapter that follows this.

I propose to focus on the concept as a key to handling paradoxes of power. In this chapter I argue that debates on sovereignty move along two dimensions, or tracks, that benefit from being observed sociologically: *externally*, debates are influenced by social inequality and the abilities to articulate it in paradoxical ways. The social medium here is the institutionalisation of interest (in movements and parties) and the institutionalisation of conflict in parliament. *Internally*, political and philosophical debates are driven by the motivation to sort the unsolvable paradox of the sovereign people that cannot govern itself. Of the many rhetorical and discursive methods to make legitimate space for the state, I highlight one: the differentiation (the introduction of distinctions) of the concept of sovereignty and related concepts. Historically, the two tracks lead to the out-differentiation of a political system dedicated to making and executing legitimate decisions for all to abide by. The background for the internal paradox that constantly interacts with social and political conditions is the fact that the sovereignty concept refers to philosophical, ontological, even metaphysical speculation, and at the same time to distinct issues of policy. In the constitution the two discourses connect.

The following discussion includes some of the contributions to the idea of sovereignty that came to influence political sociology as well as politics. French theorists will dominate here because they influenced and were influenced by a political revolution that changed Europe, and therefore caught the interest of early sociology. The purpose is to demonstrate that the early modern political philosophy and sociology of sovereignty can be read as a series of interventions in search for ways to situate *the people* as idea and fact; and how this search reopens paradoxes that can be examined sociologically. Theoretically the understanding of sovereignty moves on a bumpy path away from absolutism. It oscillates between voluntarism and rationalism, both giving way to public, centralised institutional responsibilities. The debate increasingly considered Hobbes's early absolutist ideas of the sovereign *state*, and then, in the nineteenth century, as a legal-political fact within a liberal constitutional order.

The brief narration in the chapter illustrates the tendency in modern political theory to move towards differentiation and complexity, with which the state is brought into theory as an ordering device. What sociology tends to ask is how sovereignty legitimates ruling power. Another, more sober way of formulating this is how politics organises *and describes itself* to handle new expectations of democracy. To some French post-revolutionaries, British utilitarians and many nineteenth-century legal scholars, such demands lead to rationalism, which views the state as a cohesive legal-administrative apparatus, with only an abstract view of the state as a 'person' enabled by the people. Liberal rationalists and legal positivists tended to bracket popular sovereignty from political discourse. Populists of many shades, however, kept the door open for civil self-government and socialism.

The sovereign state

The state has of course been subject to rival definitions throughout the centuries. In the seventeenth century the term began to refer to the body of the people as the owners or authors of the true sovereignty.[4] This came from the writings of Bodin, Grotius and Hobbes onwards. It came to be the name of the nation and the people and the actual sovereign power of the king. It was a concept in service of presenting the sovereign in a collective unity of power *and* submission. From the late nineteenth century, it referred to nation-states and empires. Then, at the beginning of the twentieth century, it tended to be instrumentalised in the sense that it referred to the government and its organisational resources. After the second world war in particular, international treaties and regional integration reached beyond the state.

International law emerged in the 1500s, and the Westphalia Treaty followed in 1648, in the common interest of nation-states to prevent external pressure and control from other sovereign states. It referred to sovereign states, never to their citizens.[5] Machiavelli, already in *Discursi*, probably completed in 1519, asked the question of why certain ancient cities (particularly Rome) had become free from political servitude whether imposed internally or externally from an imperial power. The *libertà* of the cities he addressed is understood as independence from any authority except the authority of the city itself.[6] A 'free state' was a state that governed itself, a state in which the rulers were the people. He attached much importance to the founding fathers of the cities and their *virtù* because they are law-givers.[7] The post-Westphalian order and the legitimate monopoly of force laid the foundation for the depersonalised state, which subsequently became the holder of sovereignty to avoid fragmentation. Only the constitutional state could fully recognise popular sovereignty and the demographic necessity of representation and constitution-making as well as separation of state powers. Changes to this arrangement came with the Hague Peace Conference and its multilateral conventions and treaties from 1899 on.

Jean Bodin was probably the first to account more substantially for the early modern state. He referred to the term 'sovereignty' in his main work, *Les six livres de la Republique* published in 1576, and it became *topos* for the construction of the nation as absolute monarchy. The king was conferred complete sovereignty by God. The French revolution fundamentally changed the meaning of the principle that had been discussed by Montesquieu, who combined the principle of the separation of powers with the British system of parliamentary monarchy. During the revolutionary years, Emmanuel Joseph Sieyès first formulated a principle of national sovereignty to arrange for the *de facto* jurisdiction of the representative National Constituent Assembly.[8] Article 3 of the Declaration of August 1789 (that Sieyès drafted) defined the national sovereignty as the sole possessor of the indivisible sovereignty of the *nation*. The members of the assembly were 'representatives of the nation'. The principle of sovereignty appeared as paradox: a national assembly ruling over a sovereign people.

Under the conditions of stronger royal power in France and during the wars of religion from 1562, Jean Bodin connected the concept to the superior authority of the state to enforce peace and create laws within a territory.[9] Bodin made the concept of sovereignty into a public and legal principle based on a territory, no longer by necessity connected to the divine king. It rather referred to an absolute and singular, but still more abstract power. It included legislative and executive powers, but he made a notable distinction between legal and non-legal ways of executing power.

The influence of Bodin's ideas was considerable, but shifting political conditions led to variation of the term, for instance the divisibility in English parliamentarism ('the king in Parliament') that did not fit his concept. With Hobbes, a stronger conception of the sovereign was imagined: only the artificial legal person of the omnipotent state could prevent civil war. With the natural law theory version of social contract theory, ideas of rights as superordinate to the state began to emerge.[10] The idea of the contract led to a stronger emphasis on the role of the people and the necessity of distinguishing between possessing and exercising sovereignty.[11] Hobbes introduced the concept of *authorisation* in *Leviathan* to explain how the king may stand in for the people. The king's conduct is authorised by each member of the people.[12] The people remain the authors and responsible agents of the actions of the king. Thus, authorisation handles the paradox that the king rules over the people as authors.

After the Reformation and the civil wars, the time came for concentration of powers in the hands of a single ruler, and, increasingly, the absolute and sovereign *state* as the legal and (to a variable degree) legitimate monopoly of force. In Europe, the end of this period began with the French revolution. The meaning of sovereignty as the highest and indivisible authority remained intact, argues Grimm, but in practice new laws took on the form of an agreement between the ruler and the privileged estates within the territory.[13] The state, from which citizens demanded to be protected, was a precondition for constitutions. The ruler's right to rule was not questioned, but the ruler was nevertheless encircled by natural and positive legal bonds. The ruler's legitimacy was grounded in the consent of the popular, rather than in divine or secular monarchical will. Its task was to protect the state and the rights of the citizen. Positive law was acknowledged as political, with the purpose of delimiting politics, in a process of never-ending reflexivity involving the circulation of power between individuals composing the nation as *l'assemblage des individus* and the Assembly. Sieyés's dual conceptualisation of constituent and constituted power is an expression of this distinction.

Sixty years after Machiavelli's *The Prince*, Bodin based his understanding of sovereignty on public law, and he targeted the state. Bodin was the first to offer reflections on the modern sovereign state and its legitimacy. His heritage marks the first serious attempts at a clarification of the question of sovereignty. He made distinctions between the state (*l'etat*) and the government (*la police*), and between the state and the study of the state within a legal framework (*politique*).[14] In the first book of *La République* he examines the concept of sovereignty, before in the second book examining three forms of government: monarchy, aristocracy and popular rule. (The 'republic' in the title refers to states in general.) He initiated a tradition of sociology and political philosophy that reflects on the modern state, its powers and legitimacy, and in constantly novel ways unravels handlings of the paradox of rule. Bodin lived in a time of emerging 'democratisation' of law and politics, but also in a time of war. The printing press in the sixteenth century played a vital role in the dissemination of legal documents and political pamphlets; concepts referred to a wider, more complex religious and secular world, concerning not only the state but also the good, the just, the natural, of monarchy, aristocracy, even democracy. The apparatus of royal power had to put more effort into retaining hegemonic understandings of law and political power. Sovereignty was accounted for through the legitimacy of the state as a legally regulated organisation for the nation.

Bodin was obliged to balance the consistent image of royal sovereignty as indivisible, eternal and unmixable with the protection of the commonwealth against tyranny. Bodin, we must bear in mind, looked for political order at a time of religious conflict and massacre, and viewed the monarch as a stabilising force. He thought monarchy was superior to democracy and aristocracy because it could limit conflict. He had to make the unsatisfactory assumption that the monarch would, due to his conscience and greatness, act rationally and according to law. The sovereign capability to change laws without consent was a logical result of the concept of sovereignty, but so was the king's self-made choice to act according to law.

Jean Bodin opens the first book by declaring that sovereignty is the absolute and perpetual power of a *republique*; in Latin *majestas* and what the Italians call *segnoria*. He explains at length why sovereignty cannot be temporary and divisible, and concludes that 'sovereignty then, is not limited either in power or in function, or in length of time'.[15] For logical reasons the king cannot be subject to his own laws, nor can a sovereign obligate himself to the estates.[16] The sovereign cannot be divided among separate agencies, which Bodin inferred from the fact of the nature of absolute power. It must be one way or the other, he writes – either the king is bound by his laws and the advice of the general assembly, or he is sovereign.[17] The *summum imperium* was to be supreme, absolute, indivisible and perpetual. And yet Bodin modified his strong words about undivided sovereignty by indicating that the monarch needs *consent* to tax the citizens. He tended to follow central ideas from the Roman Republic and Athens, where sovereignty was shared in different ways. Thus, already in Bodin, one can trace the never-ending paradoxical questions concerning transfer of sovereignty and the self-binding of a sovereign, where logic collides with life. Political and legal concepts step in to bridge the two.

Later in Book I he added attributes to these traits, above all the right to make laws, including the privilege to make, and end, war.[18] One the one hand, the sovereign monarch could not subject himself to nothing or no-one without cancelling his sovereignty, but on the other hand, sovereignty was not tyranny. The sovereign was morally bound by laws given by God. In Bodin, a beginning differentiation emerged between sovereignty and the personal agent that embodied sovereignty and acted temporarily in its name.[19]

In his discussion of the 'Republic', he famously makes a distinction between a principate and sovereignty. The problem of perpetual sovereignty unlocked discussion of legitimacy as an *institutional* requirement. Magistrates, Bodin concludes, could exercise minor tasks on behalf of the king. This distinction, and in fact the beginning of a notion of the state, could be traced in Machiavelli's *Principes*, as well as in *Leviathan* from 1651, forty-five years after Bodin's work appeared in English.[20] In the latter Thomas Hobbes emphasises in chapters 16 and 17 that the sovereign person is an artificial person, and he explains how the sovereign with his non-essential persona can represent the authors as a 'mortal God', as an institution. That the sovereign person is artificial means that he represents others and not himself. He is a legally accepted 'person'.

In *Leviathan* Hobbes comments on proposals regarding representative government, and he focuses on the act of responsible actors as authors who can grant someone the authority to act in their name. Authorisation is granted by a multitude of 'particular men', each with their desires and interests in the natural condition of war of every man against man. From this situation, with no body of people in need of representation, Hobbes begins with the difficult claim that representation means using persona, someone's mask, and acting in someone else's (a person's) name, and speaking the lines of those one is representing as an 'artificial person'. The sovereign is this person, also called the Representor or Representative person. The problem of how to represent a multitude then seems solved. Hobbes makes clear that the Representer carries the Person, and only one Person, because that is the only way to understand the Unity in the Multitude. It is the *authorising* from each person in the Multitude to the artificial Person, that makes him a sovereign, and by that authorisation he 'becomes' a sovereign, and by this the representer of the people as a whole:

A multitude of men, are made *One person*, when they are by one man, or one Person, Represented; so that it be done with the consent of every one of that Multitude in particular. For it is the *Unity* of the Representer, not the *Unity* of the Represented, that maketh the Person *One*.[21]

The authorisation converts the multitude into one person, and this true subject of the sovereignty, over which the sovereign Representer (the king) simply holds the right to exercise, is the persona civitatis, a Common-Wealth, or a civitas. 'This is the Generation of that great Leviathan or rather (to speak more reverently) of that *Mortal God*, to which wee owe under the *Immortal God*, our peace and defence.'[22] Transforming the multitude into one fictitious person who can serve as the sovereign representative of the multitude was an astonishing contribution. The actions of the state are attributed as the bearer of sovereignty, so that the person commanding it is the person of the state. All must agree to put all power upon one individual man or assembly. That agreement reduces the plurality of wills into one will. The essence of the commonwealth, Hobbes writes, is One Person: 'And he that carryeth this Person is called Soveraigne, and said to have *Soveraigne Power*; and every one besides, his Subject.'[23]

Hobbes's argument no doubt became highly influential in Europe because of its sophisticated meddling between extreme positions. *Leviathan*, Skinner points out, was not simply a timeless philosophical reflection but an intervention against both conservative catholicism and 'democratic gentlemen', his liberal adversaries. With the term *authorisation* Hobbes tried to solve the problem of authority (the right to action) without succumbing to the notion of popular sovereignty.

Sovereignty differentiated

The ambitious work of Montesquieu, based on journeys and readings over several decades, represents an early modern attempt to identify types of relationships between a political society, its political regime and law. Montesquieu presents three *principes*, his three central types of government, and the society and fundamental attitudes produced for their stability. The typology appears as pre-sociological ideal types of political culture. It is rightly observed that Montesquieu, in his *Spirit of the Laws* from 1748, casts the net wider than the particular political regimes and he addresses a wide range of features of societies. Although it would be mistaken to argue that he describes types of societies in general, he addresses political societies; precisely *the political* is what captures the society in its totality.[24] When he uses the term 'society', it often means what we call a state, and in other places seems to include what we today call a political culture, a vibrant social spirit or national character partly independent of the state. What he calls *L'esprit general* refers to a political atmosphere, or a set of norms that have their origin in phenomena like religion, law, even climate. The norms express what is praised and condemned, and signal to each individual what conduct is expected. Laws are norms and therefore a product of the political society which they shape.

Montesquieu addresses relationships between types of political society and law. His ideas on law appeared during the heyday of the idea of natural law where law was seen as universally given through a social contract or by nature or God. Montesquieu breaks with this tradition by viewing law in a secular natural sense as a social phenomenon, if ultimately emerging from the nature of things. Law depends on a multitude of social and physical conditions, and for that reason it takes different forms. This was a major step forward at the time and it formed the beginning of a sociology of law and constitutions. Montesquieu studied law between countries and cultures, and Emile Durkheim argues that he 'instituted a new field of study, which we now call comparative law'.[25]

As products of society, laws are different in different states. They derive indirectly from society via the law-giver; while customs spring directly from social life and as such are beyond the power of the legislator. But laws too have to be largely in accord with customs and manners; they represent nothing that does not already exist in custom and would wither away if they did not serve certain functions. By studying laws, we learn about the society of their origin, and which they in turn regulate. And clearly, by their definite form and their inevitability, they mediate a social force of their own.

Types of government and *principes*

In Book II of the *Spirit of the Laws*, Montesquieu famously describes three types of government: republican, monarchic and despotic, and he accounts for the political institutions typical of each. In Book III he goes on to describe the individual *principes*, the principal attitudes and passions that drive each type. *Principes* are both causes and effects of a type of government, and we may say that they reproduce themselves functionally, just as the regime is fairly well adapted to its social and physical environment. Montesquieu stated indirectly that none of these *principes* would operate in pure form, implying their status as types. In Book VIII he provides examples of political societies that do not fit well with his model, implying again that this is a purified typology, but also that societies are not static. There are republican features in the British monarchy, and despotic features in the Polish republic, and so on. Montesquieu never speaks of types or models, nor of regimes. That kind of sociological (and in part functional) language was not yet invented. There are nevertheless clear parallels to Weber's famous discussion on ideal types and his analysis of the relationship between the protestant ethic and the economic spirit of the emerging industrial capitalism in Europe.

Montesquieu attempts a typology of political cultures based on the cases he had observed on his travels in Europe and readings about the empires in the east and south. He describes three types of political society dominated by honour, virtue or fear, as an exhaustive typology from his knowledge of the world at the time. He makes clear in the conclusion of Book III that people are not all honourable, virtuous or fearful within each type of government, but that they ought to be – the types exist because the political culture produces expectations that people tend to meet. If they don't, instability might cause the regime to fall and the society to move towards another type. Expectations would likely be met because people prefer stability. They generally also wish for the preservation of their political institutions because they would tend to be in accord with the spirit of society.

In *monarchy* a code of *honour* or self-esteem drives central political action and regulates society. Honour refers to action that is prized and highly valued; it is a particular code for political institutions, that does not derive from nature or God but from political roles and tradition. Honour also refers to the quality of character of the individual and its public recognition.[26] Honour exists between self-interest and self-effacing civic virtue; it comes forward as character or integrity. Honour provides, we could even say, a sense of personal authority that is legitimated socially and politically. Again, we may see a thread forward in time to Weber and his *Gesinnungsetik*, a political ethics (or political leadership type) that Weber illustrates with Martin Luther's famous words: 'Here I stand and can do no other.'

The monarch does not have all powers, and honour accommodates the separation and distribution of power. Honour serves the institutions that link the people with the monarch: the assemblies, clergy, nobility, government, the courts. Honour emerges from this division of power among institutions and is oriented towards their tasks and boundaries according to law. Its partiality is attached to membership in classes and estates and connected to particular institutions. There is no total vision of society enforced from the monarch – that would have been, or approached, tyranny.

To Montesquieu honour is a 'prejudice': for the individual it highlights and assumes a particular set of values and distinctions that is attached to their roles in institutions and segments. Nevertheless, central to the sense of honour is an ambition to do great things that would serve the individual and the country. Krause notes that it has certain similarities with Machiavelli's *virtù*, in that the holder of honour seeks public acknowledgement, even glory. It provides courage and moderation.[27]

In the *republic* central agents are motivated by a distinctive principle of a civic political *virtue*, a selfless love for the country. Here the sovereignty lies with the people. The republic may exist in aristocratic or democratic form. Ancient Rome is an example of a republic with a certain distribution of power according to virtue. Without virtue society would fall apart because there is no monarch or despot to hold it together. All citizens must sacrifice themselves for the common good by obeying the laws and defending the state. The public interest is all, individuality means little.

In a *despotic* society political statements and actions are regulated by the passion of *fear*. All powers are concentrated in the hands of one ruler; there is no security or safety, no shelter from the arbitrary rule of the despot. Fear undermines everyone's courage and feelings of personal ambition.

About the blessings of the separation of powers in a monarchy Montesquieu had learnt much from his long stay in England and from his discussions with the leader of the opposition, Bolingbroke. In his famous chapter in Book XI on England he acknowledges a constitution that serves as a 'mirror' to liberty. Its separation of legislative, administrative and the judicial kept state powers in an internal balance, that inhibited arbitrary abuse of power. It brought forward the significance of parliamentary control. That Montesquieu's image of England was not entirely accurate was of minor importance. Nor was Montesquieu the first to point out this practical but essential liberal measure. Yet Montesquieu formulated the principle in a way that made it into a key liberal constitutional doctrine, and, as we know, it found its way into several constitutions.

It is however important that the principle of distinction between state powers did not alone define the nature of government and the liberty of citizens. Rather, it was one element in a wider discussion of monarchy, particularly the English variant.[28] Nor did Montesquieu simply distinguish between three types of political societies, but between three types of sovereign power with their types of legitimacy. In Book VIII he makes clear what happens if a regime undermines its principles. Then, its basic political nature deteriorates, and the laws begin to work against the state.[29] As a typology of political cultures it is a theory of legitimacy and sovereignty in early modern societies. As Durkheim notes, we ought to see Montesquieu as a pioneer in political sociology. He presents a prelude to, for instance, Weber's theory of modern political legitimacy. He also pioneered constitutionalism in seeing the constitution as not only a normative instrument for political values like equality and liberty, but also in pointing out how it reflects its political environment. This is most clearly seen in his famous attempts to make explicit the norms in the English constitution. His normative and empirical statements about constitutions were entangled in his discussion, but nevertheless one could see him as beginning, if not with sufficient clarity, a sociology of constitutions. As Richter and Neumann argue, it was not the constitutions alone that were his prime interest, but their social substructure, that is, their proclamations of certain values in society; how they reflect and may influence such values, similar to the working of *meures* and *manières* in other parts of society.[30] The *Esprit* in the title of Montesquieu's central work refers to the essential and underlying meaning of laws and constitutions *and* to the distinguishing character of a nation.

Montesquieu was sceptical of popular sovereignty for the reasons basic to European liberalism. However, he also acknowledged its existence. To later readers of Montesquieu, and particularly after Rousseau, believers in the will and the power of the people had little problem in seeing how the principle of division of power could be unified with the basic premise of *volonté générale*. Montesquieu had in fact advocated ways to prevent popular sovereignty from turning against itself. One can easily see how Montesquieu's rationalist points complemented weaknesses in the later voluntarism and republicanism of Rousseau. Modern constitutions in Europe in the late eighteenth and nineteenth centuries therefore implemented insights from both thinkers.

Popular sovereignty celebrated

'Democracy' was a disputed term that overcame great obstacles before its current celebrated status. One could boldly argue that the terms 'democracy' and 'popular sovereignty' have exchanged places since the days of the first revolutions. Their semantic content overlaps considerably, but while 'democracy' in France came into use after the revolution and was in common use in political discourse after 1848, the term 'popular sovereignty' was formulated and recognised earlier.[31] In the 1700s, 'democracy' referred to the ancient Greek and Roman republics. To many it designated a direct form of legitimation and one in opposition to political representation. In Jean-Jacques Rousseau's writings, the notion of popular sovereignty has priority over the notion of democracy. In *Emile*, Rousseau states that democracy means that the sovereign can entrust government to the people, or a great part of the people. In *The Social Contract*, democracy as such is not a central theme. Pierre Rosanvallon writes that 'For Rousseau, democracy is a form of government and a method of decision-making, but it does not constitute the essential thing: the very foundation of the social bond and the political order.' To Rousseau the central problem is how to build central institutions within a modern order: 'Hence the centrality to his writings of the concept of the sovereignty of the people breaks with the previous scholastic and monarchical resonances (the exercise of power in the service of the people).' In this view 'the question of democracy takes second place to that of sovereignty of the people, amounting to nothing more than a subtheme'.[32]

Rousseau famously begins *The Social Contract* by stating a paradox: 'Man is born free and everywhere he is in chains. One who believes himself the master of others is nonetheless a greater slave than they. How did this change occur? I do not know. What can make it legitimate? I believe I can answer this question.' It is a reformulation of the Hobbesian question about legitimate power, but without Hobbes's answer. The individual is free from nature, and it increasingly sees through traditions and custom; it recognises itself and its freedom, and therefore is better placed to see the contrast between human freedom and religious dogmas that hold humans down. What was once seen as natural, appears constructed, and therefore changeable. Conventions and commands are experienced as more intense and only accentuate the sense that the individual is chained.[33] Claims to authority need to explain themselves; the issue of legitimacy becomes more explicit.

Rousseau believed he had the answer to the question of legitimacy. No longer can divinity do the job, and self-interest only corrupts social order. The answer could not be *la volonté de tous*, the opinions of all particular wills. It can only be the collective and congruous spirit of the people that reflects on what the common good entails. *La volonté générale* posits the problem of reconciling rationality and popular sovereignty. With the replacement of the king with popular sovereignty, the true sovereign benefits from freedom and autonomy in spite of the necessity to obey political power. *La volonté générale* expresses – in principle – the unity of the common will, the will of the people created from the singular will of free and autonomous individuals. Rousseau points out in his discussion in Book II of *The Social Contract* that sovereignty is the power and exercise of the general will. It is the collective character of (the political) society, on the basis of the dynamics of customs, habits and trends. The sovereign is the king as the keeper of sovereignty. As Durkheim interprets Rousseau: 'The sovereign is the people in action; the people is the sovereign in a state of passivity.'[34] Sovereignty lives in each individual and is at the same time the foundation for the actual sovereign power.

In his discussion of Rousseau, Durkheim distinguishes between three features. First, sovereignty is unique and inalienable. It cannot be exercised by any other than the people, not even through representation, because that would mean that the general will would be exercised by an individual or institution. Secondly and relatedly, it is indivisible in that one part of society cannot speak for the whole since that would not be a general will. The sovereign consists of individuals and groups, but its power derives from the unity of the general will. The legislative and executive power might stand for or represent parts of the sovereignty of the people, but assemblies and governments are not parts of sovereignty, only manifestations of it. Sovereign acts spring from the general will, which emanates from the entire people. Durkheim is critical to this vitalist view because it neglects what came to be Durkheim's key point concerning a modern division of labour:

Rousseau demonstrates a mechanical view of society; as a homogeneous society with few political institutions, based on individuals sharing the same soul.[35] Rousseau thinks, argues Durkheim, that cohesion is necessary and the only possibility. What are we to make of this today, Durkheim asks, as if modern society had not developed from being a dense, homogeneous community with few individualistic particularities. It seems however that Durkheim ignores that this is a treatise on the *political* dimension of society; it primarily concerns the principle of *political equality* as a basis for law and government.

Durkheim's third feature is that, in Rousseau, no external force exists to check or control sovereignty. Law is the language of sovereignty, the way it commands over itself, internally. What he calls political law, including constitutional law, addresses the political organisation of society, and emerges directly from sovereignty. To formal law, Rousseau added customs, manners and public opinion, as collective practices that influence individuals in much the same ways as laws.[36] To Hobbes, law was only possible as long as individuals submitted freely to the law of the sovereign to avoid war of all against all. The individual trades security with his obedience. To Montesquieu, proper law derives from social and political conditions manifested in distinctions of state power. Rousseau, however, introduces the subjective and collective dimension of these conditions as the acting subject of sovereign action on itself. For this to work, each individual mind must work together towards the same general aims.

Rousseau states that sovereignty is never corrupted, although it *can* occasionally be linked to particular interests. Sovereignty cannot legitimately single out individuals and groups and treat them as non-sovereign. Then it would no longer speak for the whole. The social contract is a social bond between equals, not between master and subordinate. Sovereign rule goes beyond majority rule. From this, a standard criticism of Rousseau from rationalist liberals after the revolution – and as a lesson from it – was that the general will is unable to reconcile individual rights with the collective will. As an extension of this concern comes another serious criticism: Rousseau's *La volonté générale* may become precisely what the charismatic and manipulating leader needs to proclaim himself as its voice. Since Rousseau, therefore, a key question has been how the general will can be expressed, if at all, within a liberal framework. The answer, as we know, was the principle of public opinion and then a reformed view on representation.

Constituent power

With the American and French revolutions and several new constitutions, sovereignty became a fundamental constitutional issue, guided by natural law theories. In France the conception of national sovereignty appeared in the Declaration of 1789 and the constitution of 1791, while the constitution of 1793 further specified and granted assemblies with legislative powers on behalf of the sovereign people. At the time of the first revolutions, the concept referred to the indivisible people and entire nation. Those emphasising the nation and a more ordered political rule were criticised by adherents of popular sovereignty for preventing the people from exercising their political power.[37] The concept of sovereignty itself was from early on inherently loaded with the conflict between the people and the institutions of the nation. Intense debates over constitutional revision took place. To the central revolutionary figure Emmanuel Joseph Sieyès the best government was representative government. On the other side, radical voices of the *Club des Cordeliers* defended the term 'popular sovereignty'. The point was to denounce the oppression of deputies and administrators that in this way usurped the power of the people. The point was not so much self-rule as the popular power to monitor government and ratify their law proposals.[38] In 1790 and 1791, the central theme was sovereignty – such as how to make laws and keep representatives connected to their constituents. To the abbé Fauchet, democracy referred to governmental affairs, while sovereignty designated the much more important problem of keeping politics in touch with the people. Some few years later (1793–1794), the potentially conflicting terms 'democracy' and 'representative government' rested upon a principle of people's sovereignty. The two terms emphasised different forms of power and legitimacy but met in their reference to the people. What they grappled with was the paradox that Joseph de Maistre formulated eloquently after the revolution: 'the people are the sovereign which cannot exercise their sovereignty'.[39]

Emmanuel Joseph Sieyès's conception of constituent power is seen by some as a variant of popular sovereignty and by others as an alternative approach. Rubinelli argues that many scholars since have misinterpreted constituent power as a theory of sovereignty.[40] She holds that, from the point of view of Sieyès, there is little evidence that popular sovereignty and the concept of constituent power were having the same meaning.[41] Rather, she argues that the latter was presented as an alternative to the former, and she traces the concept of constituent power from the French revolution to post-war debates. She argues that Sieyès put forward an understanding of popular power as authorisation of the constitution that accommodated theories of individual liberty. Rubinelli argues that Sieyès offered a way to handle operative political power without being absorbed by the problematic aspects of popular sovereignty. As soon as the constitution was sanctioned, constituted power took over within constitutional limits imposed by the people. The opposition between the two concepts was fundamental as it underlined the role of the people in the new French state. The tension clearly lingers on: history has shown how the revolution both liberates and terrorises its disciples.

In fact, Sieyès said very little about this conceptual duality. Only in the fifth chapter of his famous pamphlet about the Third Estate does he declare that fundamental laws (*lois fundamentale*) for the legislative and executive bodies are absolutely inviolable, and emphasise the essential point that both bodies in the first instance were constituted by the nation, the constituent power. From this he concludes that *no body with delegated power can in any way change the conditions of its delegation.*[42]

Sieyès provided the revolution with a rhetorically masterful differentiation between the people as nation and its constitutionally delegated bodies that enabled him and the assembly to take proper distance from Rousseau's paradoxical view on popular power governing itself. He did not distance himself from Rousseau's contract, and in the pamphlet on the Third Estate he is very clear that without the common will, individuals would be powerless: 'Power exists only in the aggregate. The community needs a common will; without singleness of will, it could not succeed in being a willing and acting body.'[43] This point was then supplemented with a constitutional view on what he called 'the representative common wills'. He understood the necessity of combining legitimacy with efficiency. The latter had probably never been in Rousseau's mind. In the introduction to his constitutional observations, Sieyès notes that democracy is a direct and impossible mode of governing, while representation could contribute to the development of society. Democracy was the root of the representative system.[44] As he argued in one of his other pamphlets:

> In a democracy, the citizens themselves make the laws and appoint their public officials directly. In our conception, citizens elect – more or less directly – their delegates to the constitutional convention. The legislature is thus no longer democratic but rather representative. The people exert a lasting influence on the [selection of their] representatives – no-one can become a representative of the people who does not have the trust of his constituents … yet the people can in no case pass laws, let alone take the implementation of those laws into their own hands.[45]

Sieyès's conceptual innovation transformed the representative national assembly into a legitimate medium of sovereign power. The innovation was a success; the concepts were later elaborated in various directions by Carré de Malberg, Carl Schmitt and Hannah Arendt, who contributed to a more specific debate on what representative democracy entails and located the ontological tension inherent in representation. Sieyès cunningly addressed a conceptual problem that lingered with the principle of representation. The dual concept marked a step further into a more modern and specific conception of the people's power.[46] The people as the sovereign was protected from its own revolutionary excesses. Constituent power of the people as an articulation of popular sovereignty could not be transferred to sovereign powers, but it nevertheless placed constitution and law-making in the hands of representatives as the constituted power within constitutional limits, most evidently articulated through the separation of state powers and fundamental rights.[47] Sieyès offered a way to handle the paradox of a people that cannot govern itself. The constitution, as a vehicle to resolve paradoxes, was interpreted as a legal instrument for constituent power and ultimately sovereignty.[48]

In a philosophical context, the concept of popular sovereignty is still often addressed as 'constituent power'. The term combines individual and collective power within one frame of reference, as mutually constitutive entities in a political order. It is always addressed in relation to a settlement within a particular historical setting, and wider sources of meaning and legitimation.[49] Sieyès stated that 'the constituent power can do everything in relation to constitution making. … The nation that exercises the greatest, the most important of its powers, whilst carrying this function must be free from all constraints … except the one that it deems better to adopt.'[50] A collective subject (the nation) stands over another arrangement (a representative assembly) to which it delegates power. The constituent power recognises the internal dynamic of the citizen and the nation as subject. Insofar as it addresses a collective subject, it recognises the political, from which it derives. Constituent power is a legal-political construction where two subjects institute and confirm one another in a settlement of an assembly, the constituted power.[51] Constituent power mediates constitutional change through the recognition that such change, under normal circumstances, may best be initiated by formal procedure.

Sieyès's terms originated in the Calvinist reinterpretation of Bodin's concept of sovereignty, which resolved the paradox of operating with a binary concept of personal (the ruler) and real sovereignty (vesting in the people or 'nation' that authorises personal rule). According to the French jurist Raymond Carré de Malberg, Sieyès's great achievement was that he attributed sovereignty to the 'nation', in order to restrict its influence to political institutions of the territorial and indivisible state.[52] Historians have generally emphasised Sieyès's thinking as a way to moderate and resolve Rousseau's abstract account of a general will, whereas Carré de Malberg considered Sieyès's political conception as fundamental to the political structuring of the modern *state*. According to Carré de Malberg, Rousseau did not himself see the danger of a *volonté majorité* that demanded the submission of the minority.[53] Sieyès's contribution to the conceptual enigma of power and freedom was to underline that while the people is the ultimate and original holder of sovereign power, it exercises it indirectly through the principle of political representation, as this arrangement is authorised in the constitution. The dual concept was for Sieyès a way to conceptualise the paradox of political power without relying on either the radical concept of popular sovereignty or the moderate concept of national sovereignty. He considered both to be inconsistent with the new situation characterised by the political separation of powers.[54]

It is of course highly relevant for a sociological emphasis on political and social circumstances (rather than normative principles) that Sieyès's thinking was intervening in a heated revolutionary period, where order could be restored only if the notion of sovereignty were adequately adapted to the structure of the new constitutional state. The notion of popular sovereignty was at the time associated with the Jacobin terror. The constituted power of the government is delegated authority, a delegation that the nation has the right to withdraw. Democracy, as it was then understood, was to Sieyès out of the question, but he argued indirectly in favour of representative democracy. In 1789 he argued that

> The people or the nation can only have one voice, that of the national legislature. ... The expression of an appeal to the people is therefore mistaken. ... The people, I repeat, in a country, which is not a democracy (and France would not be one), the people may only speak and may only act through its representatives.[55]

A key term here is 'political representation'. As delegated authority, the government cannot change the premises for its own power – that is a matter for the nation through the constitution as its instrument.[56] The constitution was recognised by Sieyès as the key medium for resolving the impossible imperative of self-determination.

Constant and the *parlement*

We need to consider briefly how French liberalism after Napoleon got around the revolutionary demand for popular rule without falling back on the values of *L'ancien régime*. We have seen that Rousseau's concept of sovereignty rested on a general will of a unified people that could act without reservations on behalf of that will. This demanding concept of sovereignty could not meet the social and political reality in any other specific way than legitimating utopianism and absolutism. Emmanuel Sieyès moderated the concept by making it the *source* of authority; he could then make it more practicable. The constituted power became the decisional body, and the portal whereby proposals to amendments to the constitution could enter.[57]

Constituent power represented the will of the people that cannot be ignored. After the revolution and the Napoleon years, Rousseau's manifest and unconstrained concept of sovereignty was seen as dangerous by liberals like Guizot, Germaine de Staël and Benjamin Constant. Rousseau's republicanism came under attack from rationalist and pragmatic liberals stating freedom of expression and state non-interference as ideals. A revolution, terror and Napoleon were between Rousseau and the modern liberals as three walls between two worlds. As Vincent reminds us, what was essential to Constant and fellow liberals was to avoid a return to the absolutism of the Old Regime by reconciling individual liberty with monarchy.[58] The emphasis had shifted from public solidarity and positive liberty to the protection of individuals' private rights. More weight was put on reason (particularly in Guizot) as opposed to Rousseau's *amour propre*, his emphasis on hearts and souls. Liberals like Constant, Germaine de Staël and Tocqueville were concerned with the risk that the people could be seduced by demagogues. Local agencies emerged as a response to the problem of how popular sovereignty could be realised in the widespread French territory.[59] For the sake of popular rule without instability, ideas of social institutions were preferred to the amorphous and unpredictable power of the people. Popular will needed to be delegated to a corporate body or person to achieve political authority. To Constant, this was essential to minimise and withhold the distance between people and government.

Constant did value the notion of sovereignty as the expression of an ultimate or supreme power. But he had no faith in a notion of a single voice of the people from which a constituted power could exercise unlimited rule. On the contrary, this was the kind of theory that was

> responsible for most of the difficulties the establishment of freedom has encountered among various nations, for most of the abuses which worm their way into all governments of whatever type. ... It was just this theory which inspired our Revolution and those horrors for which liberty for all was at once the pretext and the victim.[60]

There were two stages of revolutions: when the old regime is overthrown, and then 'when by means of an artificial prolongation of a movement no longer nationwide, there is an attempt to destroy everything contrary to the viewpoint of a few'.[61] As Geenens and Sottiaux argue, 'Constant wanted to maintain – within the constitutional order – a symbolic reference to the people as the source of sovereignty, without succumbing to an illusion of a genuinely existing "people" that would precede its own constitution, that is, that would precede the establishment of a constituted order.'[62]

Constant's main target in his criticism of Rousseau from 1806 and 1815 was the idea that sovereignty was absolute and could not make mistakes, as Durkheim later described it. Constant wrote in his *Principes de Politiques* that

> No authority upon earth is unlimited, neither that of the people, nor that of the men who declare themselves their representatives, nor that of the kings, by whatever title they reign, nor, finally, that of the law, which, being merely the expression of the will of the people or the prince, according to the form of government, must be circumscribed within the same limits as the authority from which it emanates.[63]

Ultimate sovereignty, to Constant and other liberals, could justify terror and despotism. The general will and its sovereignty contained the seeds of tyranny if not kept divided. The general will could be the base from which powerful interests, groups or individuals could concentrate power. Napoleon was the example for all Europe, a man Constant detested but also served.[64] To counteract concentration of power, Constant advocated freedom of expression and proper political procedure protected by the constitution.[65] A division of state powers could work as a controlling mechanism if institutionalised in the way he recommended.

Constant held the law as a manifest expression of the people's will but not of a unified, general will in Rousseau's sense. To Constant, a division of power was essential to check all forms of state power, and, as he wrote on the legislative power after the revolution: 'Now, when legislative power is quite limitless, when the nation's representatives think themselves invested with boundless sovereignty, when no counterweight exists to their decrees either in executive or judiciary power, the tyranny of those elected by the people is as disastrous as any other, whatever name it bears.'[66] Similarly, his close collaborator Germaine de Staël wrote in 1798 that the principle of the sovereignty of the people was applied falsely by the representatives of the Directory. Popular sovereignty was acceptable as a principle but turned into fatal power when not divided.[67] To de Staël, the principle of popular sovereignty could only be applied within a constitutional order that would divide political sovereignty. With Constant she advanced individual rights as a protection against unlimited sovereignty and political power. The rights of the citizens, Constant stated, 'are individual freedom, religious freedom, freedom of opinion, which includes the freedom to express oneself openly, the enjoyment of property, a guarantee against all arbitrary power'.[68]

Liberalism and democracy

In the aftermath of the revolution demands were articulated in the language of individual and collective rights. As in Montesquieu, a connection was identified between structural change and values. A general orientation towards freedom as something achievable, the contingency of power and powerlessness, the moral significance of injustice – all point towards *an expansion of the political* which the new political elites and intellectuals could accommodate. To Constant and his fellow liberals, personal freedom and protection from arbitrary power were a fundamental concern. Therefore, in addition to the separation of powers, public involvement in political affairs through openness, debate and the freedom of the press were basic requirements that Constant probably considered unstoppable. In the political theory of the new bourgeoisie, public, elevated debate was the fundamental medium of sovereignty.

Constant's conception of sovereignty was given a novel interpretation by French scholars in the group working close to Claude Lefort in the 1980s. In particular, the philosopher Marcel Gauchet held that a more nuanced and complex reading would identify democratic elements in Constant's ideas. Gauchet reads Constant in a way that allows for seeing popular sovereignty as a collective subject within the political sphere. For individual power to fulfil itself, it is necessary to recognise the political society as a self-reflecting and constitutive producer of power that protects the individual from 'omni-politics'.[69] Stephen Holmes as well argues that Constant was able to combine liberal and democratic ideas involving freedom and self-rule, or individual liberty and popular sovereignty within a liberal constitution. In its historical and intellectual context, Constant's work can be located within a larger liberal-democratic tendency in European thinking. Then the emphasis is on Constant's discussion on how to preserve liberal autonomy by limiting, but never sacrificing, popular sovereignty. To Constant, limitation of popular sovereignty was not a problem.[70] This balance of popular sovereignty with a safeguarding of individual freedom through sovereignty of the king was a common bourgeois idea at the time. In contrast to the holistic tendencies in Rousseau and republican thinking, Constant was not willing to compromise on individual and independent existence. When he argued that sovereignty only exists in a limited and relative manner, and that its jurisdiction ends where individual existence begins, he intended it as an argument for combination, not replacement.[71] Constant helped to show how differentiation between state and society, or state sovereignty and individual liberty, could co-exist and benefit from their respective authority. For instance, the new emphasis on rights in the nineteenth century assisted the state in observing the boundaries of its power.

Sovereignty of reason

The revolution followed Rousseau in resolving the implausibility of the divine right of the monarch that had been hidden with the dogma of the king's two bodies.[72] Irrevocably, 'the people' was now the name of the true indivisible sovereign, a view, however, that re-actualised Rousseau's paradox and made it into a practical problem. Rousseau had rejected the existence of an individual sovereign, and advocated an 'absolute' general will, without developing any theory of representative government. The Doctrinaire circle in Paris with the historian and statesman François Guizot as its most prominent member, proposed an enlightened sovereignty through the capacity of an elite from the bourgeoisie. That was their attempt to find a way between the traps of aristocracy and democracy. Deliberations among notabilities would be capable, as was the ideal in England, of distinguishing between private interests and the public good. Sieyès had done the groundwork by differentiating the concept of sovereignty, but scepticism towards representative assemblies and what was later called 'politicians' during the Restoration was widespread.

The doctrinaire school of conservative liberals made a conceptual space for themselves between aristocracy and radical republicanism. In his uncompleted work on sovereignty, François Guizot simply rejected Rousseau's idea of the general will. It was absurd, if not blasphemy he thought, to argue that 'man' (the individual) should be in absolute power over himself, and that only his will could have power over him.[73] The protestant Guizot pointed at another version of the unresolved rousseauian paradox. As liberals elsewhere in Europe, Guizot addressed the liberation from dogmatic religion, towards public reason, truth and justice, mediated by men of capacity in assemblies, the government, the university and the press. In this view, universal suffrage was based on a misplaced belief in democracy as primitive majority rule.

Several elements are juxtaposed in Francois Guizot's liberal model: parliamentary debates, separation of powers, public opinion, scientific reflection, freedom of the press and limited voting rights. The separation of powers between parliament and government was a *de jure* element in a more comprehensive *de facto* social model for negatively limiting abuses against the minority, and positive for producing legitimate policies. To Guizot, reason became effective when individuals were able to transcend themselves through conflict of opinion, an ability given by God. No man can claim to be perfectly reasonable in his judgements. Nevertheless, social inequality meant that some had more capacity than others and had to be given precedence in the representative system. The right to vote had to be reserved for those with education and an independent position. Like the invisible hand of the market, this capacity-motivated reason to Guizot was seen as irresistible, legitimate and sovereign. The invisible hand of politics was impersonal, social and separate from the self-serving character of economic liberalism.

Power cannot *belong to* anyone, Guizot declared:

> I do not believe in the sacred right or in popular sovereignty. ... In these, I
> see nothing but violence. I believe in the sovereignty of reason, law, and justice:
> it is the legitimate dominion the world seeks, which it will always seek – for
> reason, truth, and justice there is nothing comprehensive and flawless. No
> man, no group of men possess them and cannot possess them without defects
> and limitations.[74]

Tyranny in the form of one individual or the mass had to be defeated from
a sense of right. 'The consciousness of law and reason, which God has given
man, this right beyond the will of man, is strong and inscrutable and will
win at last.'[75]

Guizot's 'ontological liberalism' was based on the norms of truth, reason
and justice. He highlighted three conditions for a representative system:
separation of powers, elections and publicity. *Separation of powers* prevents
a single person or power from claiming all legitimate power.[76] The separation
of powers is the natural consequence of sovereignty not being 'owned'. It
allows their interdependence to prevent them from considering themselves
as without responsibility. Collectively, they can legitimise laws, and through
elections they can also be changed. *Elections* must build on the recognition
of the principles of morality and judgement that society celebrates and that
prevent power from becoming entrenched. Representation also ensures
pluralism within a unified framework. The overriding purpose of representative
rule is to combat all forms of absolute power.[77] *Publicity* is the main com-
ponent of the representative system. In the public anyone with the right to
do so can seek reason and justice. Publicity is the link between society and
government. These elements ensure that the minority is not wiped out, for
the majority is not always right and not right forever.[78]

François Guizot rejected the revolutionary 'pure reason' informed by
Rousseau's idealism, and equally the Old Regime. The Doctrinaire generation
of academics and political actors respected some of the principles of the
revolution but worked in the restoration years for a modernised nation
based on a proto-liberal view on how politics could achieve legitimacy.
Politics was to continue the unstoppable evolution of social change and
progress by changing institutions like schools and universities, but under
the condition of political stability. Political institutions needed to be reformed
to the extent that they dealt with the challenges of a new age. The programme
of Guizot proclaimed political stability (restricted) representative government,
political freedom and other restrained liberties.

The concept of 'sovereignty of reason' was made into rhetorical credo
by conservative intellectuals like Guizot, Royer-Collard and de Maistre as
a reply to demands of democracy.[79] The reformed sovereignty concept came

to refer to the qualities of knowledge, truth and justice – to function and reason rather than will. To produce the necessary legitimacy, institutional arrangements would have to do the job: the assembly of two chambers, division of powers, the informed public opinion deliberating on behalf of the abstract notion of 'the people' and veto of the king.

The concern of the liberals was that if they rejected both the king's divine right to arbitrary domination and popular sovereignty, they had to come up with an alternative foundation for legitimacy. Their theoretical task was to elaborate a position on where to situate sovereignty to prevent the practical sovereign power from being undermined. Political life during the Bourbon restoration, writes Craiutu, was characterised by creative disputes between rival theories of sovereignty and political obligation.[80] Constant and later Guizot advocated limitations on the general will by basing their defence for a limited government on reason. Guizot went further than Constant in pointing out the necessity to prevent majoritarian power (*souveraineté du nombre*) from becoming *de jure* sovereignty. To avoid the majority's oppression of the minority, a 'sovereignty of reason' could be secured beyond the immediate will of singular individuals and the people. Constant's theory of sovereignty and Guizot's sovereignty of reason advocate the institutionalisation of bourgeois power. The suspension of popular sovereignty could be justified by insisting that its *functions* were situated in a concrete set of political institutions. The representative government was obliged to constantly justify its actions and accept critical commenting in public opinion, and the elected assembly had to play by the rules of the constitution.

As I have noted, in the nineteenth century *public opinion* became a decisive input to the idea of democracy. The value of disagreement and pluralism began to be acknowledged in the sixteenth century, when books of divergent views appeared side by side in the library and could be compared.[81] Inconsistency of texts became a topic and uncertainty more of a normal state. With the expansion of the state apparatus, purposive rationality proved itself more productive than value rationality. With the concept of *the public*, voicing one's opinion played a more prominent role because it marked a distance from given privileges. It referred to individual rights and interests, but appeared social, and was given political weight. The distinction between public and secret was replaced by the distinction between public and private, and a public opinion domain emerged in the eighteenth century. In liberal theory it included the millions of individuals located in the nation as a unity. The press justified its business as a mission – as a medium of the people that tied contexts and groups of opinion together in larger issue networks. In the late 1700s this phenomenon was given spiritual qualities, as the invisible hand or a secret sovereign of the political system.[82] The *esprit public* raised its ambitions as the voice of the true sovereign. It was seen as the equivalent to truth in the sciences, and the closest one could get to a yardstick for rightness in political questions.[83] It consisted of individual voices and at the same time expressed the *volonté générale*, from which it condensed meaning.

A notable exception to the liberal rule of public opinion as the voice of popular sovereignty is famously examined by Alexis de Tocqueville. The overall point in the proto-sociological work *Democracy in America* from the 1830s is that popular sovereignty was not an abstract principle in the New World as it was in Europe. At the beginning of the first volume, Tocqueville makes the point that in America popular sovereignty 'is reduced to practice in the most direct, the most unlimited, and the most absolute manner'.[84] In chapter four he specifies the principle of popular sovereignty to be integrated in customs and laws at all levels of society. Unlike in other nations, it is openly recognised and spreads freely: if there is a nation where the doctrine of the sovereignty of the people and therefore its dangers and advantages can be judged, he writes, it is assuredly America. It has acquired 'all the practical development which the imagination can conceive. It is unencumbered by those fictions which are thrown over it in other countries and it appears in every possible form.'[85] Towards the end of Volume I he concludes with the 'great maxim on which civil and political life in the United States is based. Extended to the whole nation, it becomes the dogma of popular sovereignty. Thus, in the United States, the generative principle [*principe générateur*] of the republic is the same principle that governs most human action.'[86] With the concept of popular sovereignty Tocqueville connects sociological and political sentiment to underlying economic, and technological, change, and foremost to America's brief history as a colony, while democracy referred to the system of government. Due to the shape of popular sovereignty, American democracy had no real enemy, only dilemmas resting in the inherent paradox of federal rule. Three decades later slavery actualised that paradox and resulted in the immensely destructive civil war.

Despite the abstract texture of the *volonté générale* in France, the revolution and the semantics of the nation in its wake made evident that a self-organised political system was in the making.[87] The first half of the 1800s were golden years for political semantic innovation and import. In the absence of the divine body politic of the monarch, the secular principles and semantic conditions of the political had to be addressed. Ideas of human rights, the freedom of the individual and the reason of public opinion emerged from Rousseau. His social contract was not, as in Hobbes's covenant, the exchange of liberty for law (of the sovereign), but a reconciliation of liberty, equality and self-prescribed law. Natural inequality was replaced by political equality that could only be protected by constitutional law.[88] The will of the individual and of the community melted together with reference to the *state* as the instrument of the sovereign people. Sovereignty delimited its political power and led to the paradox of representation. The constitutions in America, France and elsewhere harmonised basic rights with procedures for delegating power to authorities. From then on, the constitution denoted a self-description of the systems of politics and law, dictated by the people and the Nation but practised by educated elites.

In the early 1830s French radicals continued to speak of sovereignty of the people or of the republic, and in 1842 the *Dictionaire politique* devoted more space to sovereignty than democracy itself. Sovereignty was referred to as 'the philosophical idea of democracy'.[89] In the decades following 1848, democracy continued to stand for a diffuse ideal of equality and universal suffrage. Its meaning differed: what it meant depended on its contextualisation (popular, parliamentary, liberal, socialist, direct, etc.). Its meaning swung, and continues to do so.

Conclusion

This brief tour of the early liberalist dealing with the 'problem of the people' demonstrates the centrality of a sociology of sovereignty. First, constitutional concepts appear in intellectual history to handle paradoxes of power. The invention of letting the people be the owner of sovereignty (Rousseau) led to a paradox that was addressed cunningly by Sieyès in his dual concept and by introducing the *nation* as a frame for citizenship and constitutional powers. This way of seeing conceptualisation as handling not only dispute but paradox illustrates how conceptual analysis can be put into action in sociological studies of constitutional change. Secondly, on a methodological note: concepts and reasonings must be understood within a historical context of debate and contestation, as arguments, appeals, protests and demands to prior statements and events. Thirdly, and more substantially; what Rousseau and the rationalists had in common was the notion of the people as abstract and undifferentiated: that, however, Sieyès's pair of concepts helped to alleviate. However, as Tocqueville demonstrated, each side of the controversy on popular sovereignty based its understanding on the increase and variety of *associations*, *guilds* and *classes* that was organised all over the continent during the nineteenth century. The sociological realisation that the people articulated itself institutionally later emerged in the writings of Marx, Proudhon and other radicals all over the continent.

After Napoleon, constituted power opened the gates for the expansion of a complex political domain that called itself *the state*. Political institutionalisation and the constitutionalised state powers promoted the concept of the state to be the name of not only assemblies, the government and its expanding apparatus, but also the political people of the nation, whom state bodies served. The constitution remained key. From the revolutionary years, the constitution was a medium of action and an object of reflexivity – or a mirror, with which the *notabilités* could observe the imaginary of the people from a distance and negotiate liberal values. In France, Constant's distinction between ancient and modern liberty (or between the state and the individual) and Guizot's emphasis on the intersubjective character of 'sovereignty of reason' explored and developed the political space of liberalism. With innovative and sophisticated conceptualisations, the liberals defended elite power in a society which heralded political equality. Ultimately this was only possible with the *state* as a unique, long-lasting formula by which the people, public power and the nation unite.

Notes

1 Dieter Grimm, *Sovereignty: The Origin and Future of a Political and Legal Concept* (New York: Columbia University Press, 2009), p. 1.
2 Ibid., p. 64.
3 Ibid., p. 7.
4 Skinner, *From Humanism to Hobbes*, p. 347.
5 Grimm, *Sovereignty*, p. 80.
6 Quentin Skinner, *Machiavelli: A Very Short Introduction* (Oxford: Oxford University Press, 1981/2019), pp. 62–63.
7 Ibid., p. 76.
8 See Jean Garrigues and Eric Anceau, 'Discussing the first age of French parliamentarism (1789–1914).' In Ihalainen and Cornelia (eds) *Parliament and Parliamentarism*, p. 50.
9 Grimm, *Sovereignty*, p. 23.
10 Ibid., p. 30.
11 Ibid., p. 28.
12 Quentin Skinner, 'Surveying the foundations: a retrospect and reassessment.' In Annabel Brett and James Tully (eds) *Rethinking the Foundations of Modern Political Thought* (Cambridge: Cambridge University Press, 2006).
13 Dieter Grimm, 'The achievement of constitutionalism and its prospects in a changed world.' In Dobner and Loughlin (eds) *The Twilight of Constitutionalism?*, p. 6,
14 Sophie Nicholls, 'Sovereignty and government in Jean Bodin's "Six Libres de la République."' *Journal of History of Ideas*, 80:1 (2019), 47–66, at 50.
15 Jean Bodin, *On Sovereignty: Four Chapters from Six Books of the Commonwealth* (Cambridge: Cambridge University Press, 1992), p. 3.
16 Ibid., p. 12.

17 Ibid., p. 27.

18 Richard Bourke, 'Introduction.' In Richard Bourke and Quentin Skinner (eds) *Popular Sovereignty in Historical Perspective* (Cambridge: Cambridge University Press, 2017), pp. 2–3.

19 Richard Tuck, 'Democratic sovereignty and democratic government: the sleeping sovereign.' In ibid., p. 118.

20 Bourke, 'Introduction', p. 8.

21 Thomas Hobbes, *Leviathan* (Cambridge: Cambridge University Press, 1996), p. 114.

22 Ibid., p. 120.

23 Ibid., p. 121.

24 M. P. Masterson, 'Montesquieu's grand design: the political sociology of "Esprit de Lois".' *British Journal of Political Science*, 2:3 (1972), 283–318.

25 Emile Durkheim, *Montesquieu and Rousseau* (Ann Arbor, MI: University of Michigan Press, 1965), p. 51.

26 Sharon R. Krause, 'Freedom, sovereignty, and the general will in Montesquieu.' In James Farr and David Lay Williams (eds) *The General Will: The Evolution of a Concept* (Cambridge: Cambridge University Press, 2015), p. 475.

27 Ibid., p. 480.

28 Montesquieu, *The Political Theory of Montesquieu*, p. 84.

29 Ibid., p. 82.

30 Ibid., pp. 96–97.

31 Pierre Rosanvallon, 'The history of the word "democracy" in France.' *Journal of Democracy*, 6:4 (1995), 140–153, at 141.

32 Ibid., 142.

33 William Connolly, *Political Theory and Modernity* (New York: Basil Blackwell, 1988), p. 43.

34 Durkheim, *Montesquieu and Rousseau*, p. 114.

35 Ibid., pp. 111–112.

36 Ibid., p. 122.

37 Lucia Rubinelli, 'How to think beyond sovereignty: on Sieyes and constituent power.' *European Journal of Political Theory*, 18:1 (2019), 47–67, at 48.

38 Rosanvallon, 'The history of the word "democracy"', 144.

39 Here from Martin Loughlin, 'The concept of constituent power.' *European Journal of Political Theory*, 13:2 (2014), 218–237, at 220.

40 Lucia Rubinelli, *Constituent Power: A History* (Cambridge: Cambridge University Press, 2020), p. 49.

41 Ibid., p. 19.

42 Emmanuel Joseph Sieyès writes: 'Aucune sorte de pouvoir délégué ne peut rien changer aux conditions de sa délégation. C'est en ce sens que les lois constitutionnelles sont fondamentales.' (Qu 'est-ce que le tiers état?', ch. 5, https://fr.wikisource.org/wiki/Qu'est-ce_que_le_tiers_état_%3F (accessed 1 March 2023).

43 Emmanuel Joseph Sieyès, *The Essential Political Writings* (Oliver W. Lembcke and Florian Weber, eds) (Hague: Brill, 2014), p. 88.

44 Ibid., p. 186.

45 Ibid., p. 24.
46 Rubinelli, 'How to think beyond sovereignty'; Rubinelli, *Constituent Power.*
47 Grimm, *Sovereignty*, p. 41.
48 Loughlin, 'The concept of constituent power', 219.
49 Damian Chalmers, 'Constituent power and the pluralist ethic.' In Martin Loughlin and Neil Walker (eds) *The Paradox of Constitutionalism: Constituent Power and Constitutional Form* (Oxford: Oxford University Press, 2008), p. 292.
50 Ibid., p. 293.
51 Ibid., p. 295.
52 Rubinelli, 'How to think beyond sovereignty', 50.
53 Raymond Carré de Malberg, *Contribution à la théorie générale de L'État: Tome II* (Paris: Edition de CNRS, 1922), p. 157, section 321.
54 Rubinelli, 'How to think beyond sovereignty', 53–57.
55 Emmanuel Joseph Sieyès, cited in Lucien Jaume, 'Constituent power in France: the revolution and its consequences.' In Loughlin and Walker (eds) *The Paradox of Constitutionalism*, p. 80.
56 Loughlin, 'The concept of constituent power', 220.
57 Raf Geenens and Stefan Sottiaux, 'Sovereignty and direct democracy: lessons from Constant and the Belgian Constitution.' *European Constitutional Law Review*, 11:2 (2015), 293–320, at 306.
58 Steven K. Vincent, 'Benjamin Constant and constitutionalism.' *Revista de Historia Constitucional*, 16 (2015), 19–46, at 22.
59 Brian Garsten, 'From popular sovereignty to civil society in post-revolutionary France.' In Bourke and Skinner (eds) *Popular Sovereignty in Historical Perspective*, p. 241.
60 Constant, cited in Vincent, 'Benjamin Constant and constitutionalism', 22–23.
61 Ibid., 28.
62 Geenens and Sottiaux, 'Sovereignty and direct democracy', 307.
63 Constant, cited in Vincent, 'Benjamin Constant and constitutionalism', 26.
64 Vincent, 'Benjamin Constant and constitutionalism', 22–24.
65 Geenens and Sottiaux, 'Sovereignty and direct democracy', 308.
66 Constant, cited in Vincent, 'Benjamin Constant and constitutionalism', 36.
67 Vincent, 'Benjamin Constant and constitutionalism', 34.
68 Constant, cited in 'Benjamin Constant and constitutionalism', 27.
69 See Gauchet, in Nora Timmermans, 'A positive or negative conception of sovereignty? Marcel Gauchet, Benjamin Constant and liberal democracy', in Bas Leijssenaar and Neil Walker (eds) *Sovereignty in Action* (Cambridge: Cambridge University Press, 2019), p. 201.
70 'La limitation de la souveraineté est donc véritable, et elle est possible. Elle sera garantie d'abord par la force qui garantit toutes les vérités reconnues, par l'opinion: ensuite elle le sera d'une manière plus précise, par la distribution et par la balance des pouvoirs.' Benjamin Constant, *Principes de politique* 1806/1815, 31–32, https://gallica.bnf.fr (accessed 1 March 2023).
71 'La souveraineté n'existe que d'une manière limitée et relative. Au point où commence l'indépendance de l'existence individuelle, s'arrête la juridiction de cette souveraineté.' Constant, ibid.

72 Ernst H. Kantorowicz, *The King's Two Bodies: A Study in Medieval Political Theology* (Princeton, NJ: Princeton University Press, 1957).

73 François Guizot, 'Philosophie politique: de la souveraineté.' In *Histoire de la civilisation en Europe; [suivie de] Philosophie politique de la souveraineté: depuis la chute de l'Empire romain jusqu'à la Révolution française* (P. Rosanvallon, ed.) (Paris: Hachette, 1985), pp. 305–389.

74 Ibid., p. 372.

75 Ibid., p. 372.

76 François Guizot, *The History of the Origins of Representative Government in Europe* (Indianapolis, IN: Liberty Fund, 1851/2002), p. 67.

77 Ibid., p. 69.

78 Ibid., p. 63.

79 Pierre Rosanvallon, *La démocratie inachevée: Histoire de la souveraineté du peuple en France* (Paris: Gallimard, 2000).

80 Aurelian Craiutu, 'The battle for legitimacy: Guizot and Constant on sovereignty.' *Historical Reflections*, 28:3 (2002), 471–491, at 474.

81 Luhmann, *Introduction to Systems Theory*, p. 132.

82 Luhmann, *Die Politik der Gesellschaft*, p. 279.

83 Ibid., p. 281.

84 Alexis de Tocqueville, *Democracy in America*. Vols I and II (New York: Dover Publications, 2017), p. xvii.

85 Ibid., p. 72.

86 Ibid. p. 72.

87 Luhmann, *Die Politik der Gesellschaft*, p. 349.

88 Martin Loughlin, 'The nature of public law.' In Cormac Mac Amhlaigh, Claudio Michelon and Neil Walker (eds) *After Public Law* (Oxford: Oxford University Press, 2013), p. 18.

89 Rosanvallon, 'The history of the word "democracy"', 151.

4

Differentiation: national sovereignty and the sovereign state

In the twentieth century, the state became a more clear-cut reference for people's power than in the previous century. Class struggle and the militaristic power-game internationally enhanced the understanding of the state as legitimate and centralised cohesion. National sovereignty appeared as a synthesis of legitimate force, welfare and democracy. In this chapter I address in particular the legal-political perspectives of Georg Jellinek in Germany and Raymond Carré de Malberg in France at the beginning of the twentieth century, and their attempts to synthesise the legal and the political in a theory of the modern nation-state. Again, my motive is not to cover their entire argument about the state, but rather to pursue the argument that a gradual advancement in the dealing of Rousseau's paradox continued to take place by the use of political and legal conceptualisation. From the second half of the nineteenth century, the state was seen as a manifest power apparatus to which massive power was constitutionally delegated. Sovereignty was to be dealt with by means of the concept of the state that became more than a presupposition in constitutional law. Alongside its factual expansion as a power and welfare apparatus, the state appeared as a formulaic concept.

Jellinek: the self-limiting sovereign state

In the thinking and practical examinations about politics, the nation, democracy and international relations, the concept of the state remains a key reference despite its evasiveness. Thinkers in legal philosophy have struggled with the concept. Max Weber has given his famous definition that was influenced by the historian Otto Hintze. The concept of the state appears in many parts of Weber's work. A coherent state sociology was among his plans. Weber's colleague in Heidelberg, Georg Jellinek, published the first volume of his *Allgemeine Staatslehre* in 1900. Carré de Malberg referred frequently to Jellinek on the concept of national sovereignty some years later. Jellinek is essential for other reasons as well: he not only influenced

Weber's ideas on the state and the ideal type, but he was also a central political figure on the international scene of his time. His theories on international law were well known to central political figures in the royal Sweden–Norway union from 1814, that collapsed in 1905. Moreover, Jellinek's ideas are of interest because he, more than his contemporaries, presented a theory of the state that acknowledged sociological perspectives on the social context and factual status of law. Jellinek's work influenced the discussion on the state in the twentieth century. He in many ways grounded the study of the state, a *Staatswissenschaft* or political sociology.

For Jellinek, the political refers directly to the state; when thinking of the political, the state has already been thought of, Jellinek argued. He tended to equalise the concepts of politics and the state that Carl Schmitt later separated to prioritise the political decision.[1]

Conceptions of the state in Jellinek's Germany attempted to specify distinct purposes like security and safety. It was argued that no state 'purposes' existed other than its self-assertion.[2] Weber and Jellinek did not explain in any detail why the state must be legitimate or exactly when it is sovereign. This is the question to which the notion of popular sovereignty provides an answer. State power, no matter how fundamental, rests on something that supplies legitimacy. With the formulation 'the normative force of the factual', Jellinek referred to the factual existence of a political and legal order that exists because people believe it exists. It is valid because it performs. This is Jellinek's legitimacy argument: the factual order of the state is maintained over time because law admits it to exist, independently of its reasonableness.[3] What is required by the state is not the support of individuals, but a general and historical order derived from the totality of the people.[4]

Jellinek proclaimed a statutory positivism associated with the German Empire and the interpretation of statutes as the highest expression of state will.[5] The emphasis on state *Herrschaft* distinguished it from the statist positivism at the time that emphasised valid norms and procedures of a legal state in general. Jellinek recognised the German *Sonderweg* with a closed system of state law, but saw in the acknowledgement of German history an avenue to the understanding of public law; in the factual creation of the German state and its will. What Caldwell calls Jellinek's paradox was formulated by him following the German experience: 'How can a state, conceived as sovereign, be subject to law?' This had been a question since Bodin, but as the new classes challenged the state's legitimacy, new answers had to be invented. Jellinek considered the state as sovereign in legal and factual ways that acted according to law and protected the continued existence of national and international law.[6] State sovereignty meant that it was the inventor and protector of law. It could not, as Bodin wrote, be sovereign and subordinate at the same time. Nevertheless, to Jellinek the law fulfilled two disparate functions: as guarantee of state sovereignty and its regulator.

To alleviate the paradox, Jellinek developed his *two-sided theory of the state* as a legal system and as a real, political entity. Political sociology, such as the later contributions of Weber on bureaucracy, legitimacy and leadership, could explain the workings of the state beyond the law, and why (or why not) it developed in a stable and liberal fashion. In his *Allgemeine Staatslehre*, Jellinek discussed empirical features of the state in terms of 'types'. It allowed for a separation of historical and analytical arguments that enabled him to present different state formations. The types were composites of sociological and cultural features of national developments. They gave evidence of an ever more complex development, with a diverse range of international constellations that he had addressed earlier (such as Austria–Hungary and Sweden–Norway). Legal as well as political history played a vital part in explaining the modern state as the most advanced social institution ever developed.[7] Generally, Jellinek stated that it is necessary to distinguish between law and politics to see how they interact. In his *Staatswissenschaft* he wanted to include empirical and historical reasonings alongside norms.

Jellinek viewed the state as a socially and legally developed formation that could be accounted for historically, and to be bound legally. He saw law as two things: an expression of human development, its achievements and capacities – and the heart of its self-binding character. He produced the *zwei-seiten Lehre*, in which the legal state produces a system of laws and negative rights, and on the other hand consists of a sociological landscape of groups, organisations and interests ('a function of social relations between men'). States were seen as historical forms restricted by law. The state therefore needs to be studied from two points of view: from law and from society.[8] Individuals are members of the state in the capacity of both citizens and social subjects. The state is a legal and political association, and the two perspectives need to be kept separate. Furthermore, the people, the *Staatvolk*, were formally subjects but *de facto* mere objects of state rule.[9] Jellinek saw the state itself as the sovereign power, resting on the constitutional monarchy. As in Weber, the status of the people in Jellinek's theory of the state was seen as modest as compared with later twentieth-century standards of democracy. The role of the people was essentially secured in the parliament and as bearers of rights.

The paradoxical self-limiting role of the state – as subject and object of its laws – could only be explained through the historical development of the state alongside the legal dimension. According to Jellinek, a social *Staatslehre* needed to focus on pre-juristic empirical and historical circumstances. To Jellinek, the state was the location of politics, and he considered the state as an autonomous entity that acted only upon its own norms, and was therefore meaningfully judgeable according to internal legal and political norms. Weber elaborated on this in his specification of political ethics, and Luhmann went further by arguing that the state is the conceptual self-reference of the operatively autonomous political system. For Jellinek, Weber and Luhmann politics is debate *about* the state *in* the state. Politics is the discourse and controversy about the state on the state's terms, and therefore a political struggle for power.

A new world of sovereign states

Jellinek developed a doctrine of the self-binding state with the assistance of law and the constitution, which he thought applied to both constitutional and international law. The paradoxical status of the doctrine not only places it safely in positive law, but also underlines the state as an entity that 'denies' its ultimate power. This was another paradox in the midst of a theory of the self-governing people. The paradox was made into a methodical factor in positive law. In a neo-Kantian sense, seen from the legal and social sciences, the state was a concept, a *type* referring to the ultimate integrational power.[10] The focal point for Jellinek, as it was for Weber, was *authority*, without which the state is nothing. To Jellinek, ruling power of the state was only limited by law; otherwise its use of force would be unconditional.[11] As Weber stated in his definition of power, unlike other forms, the authority of the state could overrule all other wills.

When Jellinek talked about the 'normative *Kraft des Factischen*' (that Weber specified further in his discussion of rational-legal authority), his point was to make a distinction between norms and power only to reconnect the legal-theoretical with the social-historical. Ideas and values, not necessarily reasonability, could shape legal norms that were operative as facts.[12] Together, norms and facts form a *legitimate* social and political order. In addition to the legal dimension of laws and courts, the social dimension referred to analytical accounts of states in time and space, including the role of law in popular culture (*Volksleben*). He saw social life as an undercurrent that subsequently yields norms. The analytical and methodological distinction between norms and state power in Jellinek's theory was necessary to identify their mutual influence, and a recognition of the fact that the state was a social and political power before it became a constitutional order.

On the French and American constitutions, Jellinek argued that the idealist influences of Rousseau and Locke were more modest than generally considered. In a more realist mode, he emphasised the influence of national, religious and historical circumstances. His predecessor Johann Kaspar Bluntschli's emphasis on the state as the sovereign juristic 'person' had a wide impact in the late nineteenth century.[13] His emphasis on national history clearly influenced Jellinek, particularly in his contributions to international law. Sovereignty stemmed from the state headed by the monarch and his government and legislative assembly. Legal stability and political order were connected in the concept of sovereignty. The self-binding principle of rule of law underlined the rationality of the sovereign state.

Jellinek's academic reputation was established with *Die Lehre von den Staatenverbindungen* from 1882 on international law that made a profound impression in legal environments in Central Europe and Scandinavia. Like Weber, he generally adhered to German nationalism and the expansive ideas of the German state. Jellinek acknowledged the modern state as a sovereign state in its many versions, and sought to protect the concept of sovereignty *and* international law in an increasingly complex and militarised world. Sovereignty could no longer simply mean *summum imperium, summa potestas*. No state could simply act as if it were the only state in the world. Restriction and self-limitation were necessary to act in its own interest. In this obvious view Jellinek was certainly not alone, but he made an important distinction between sovereignty as a principle which can only be limited by its own will, and sovereignty as competence, rights and duties.[14] Sovereignty as a principle can be applied to impose limits on itself by granting treaties and other institutions certain state capacities. Self-determination and self-limitation co-developed, like in the ethical development of the individual. National sovereignty could mean transferring capacities to extra-state agencies, since legislative and administrative power in principle could be exercised outside of the state. But states were still to be considered sovereign subjects, which meant that if (and only if) self-preservation of the state depended on it, they could one-sidedly pull back from any treaty at any time to regain their sovereign powers.

As argued by Stirk, sovereignty was a *fin-de-siècle* concept of considerable concern.[15] For example, the concept became acute in Norway in 1885 when the nation lost its shared foreign policy that had resided in the king to the Swedish government. Norway suddenly became a nation without international status; it almost did no longer 'exist' in the international order of states. What Jellinek called the highest duty of the state – self-preservation – became acute and required action on the part of the Norwegian parliament. After two decades of turmoil Norway one-sidedly terminated the union. International law could not sort out questions like this, nor did the principle of self-preservation cancel out international law. In general, from the 1880s European nation-states armed themselves rhetorically and literally.

Today, the plausibility of the concept is questioned by those who argue that Westphalian norms of territorial and state sovereignty belong to the past. A way out of the imagined aporia has been to suggest *versions* of sovereignty to modify nation-state power. Such strategies tend to suffer from a lack of understanding of popular sovereignty as the inherent dimension of the state. The distinction that has to be upheld in an international world of nation-states was that noted by Jellinek; between the principle of state sovereignty and sovereign capacities in the shape of *summa potestas*. While the first is indivisible and irreducible, the latter can to some extent be transferred or shared. The breach of the first is unimaginable. The extensive but gradual use of the second would limit the *de facto* power of the state only to leave a shallow façade of independence. The question is, following Jellinek's argument, at what point the people and its constitution set the limit for the state's submission under alien powers.

Jellinek's socio-legal understanding has continued to be a reference for debate concerning public law.[16] His scientific treatment of politics generated reflections on the state from philosophy to the empirical field. He distinguished the study of law and politics only to bring them together in the practical study of the state. To define the state is the never-ending purpose of *Staatwissenschaft* since purposes of the state change according to circumstances. Nonetheless, what seems to be its functions are, first, self-assertion, security and development of power; secondly, law-making and legal protection; and thirdly, cultural promotion.[17] Such key functions must be exercised by the state, for without them the state would no longer appear valid. Beside their instrumentality, the functions perform a legitimating function.

Carré de Malberg: from the people to the nation

The French scholar of law, Raymond Carré de Malberg's 1922 *opus magnum*, *Contribution à la théorie générale de L'État* viewed the distinction between national and popular sovereignty from the position of positive constitutional law.[18] With admiration for post-revolutionary rationalism and legal positivism, Carré de Malberg joined the criticism that Rousseau's formula *volonté générale* had seduced the French people despite its problematic inconsistencies and potential consequences. To Rousseau the people compose the general will, but he also stated that each citizen participates as a member in the general will and in the will of all as subjects of the laws of the state. The practical consequence of such 'atomisation', Carré de Malberg argues, is that the concept of sovereignty ends up being the sum of *volonté particuliéres*, with the effect that minorities are subjugated under the majority as the greatest sum of individual wills. After Rousseau one could not avoid that the concept was translated into individual wills in the mass of citizens, that formed majorities and minorities.[19] In Rousseau, no protection of the minority is addressed, and it is difficult to explain why a minority should subordinate itself to the majority if each individual is seen as sovereign.[20] The consequence, Carré de Malberg argues, is that all citizens are seen as completely subordinated to the state. Popular sovereignty cannot refer to the singular power of the citizen, nor to a total mass of citizens. The cardinal error of Rousseau, Carré de Malberg argues in line with nineteenth-century liberalism, is that he did not avoid, with dangerous consequences, viewing every individual will as completely subordinated to state power.

To alleviate this, Carré de Malberg argues that the concept of *national* sovereignty secures all citizens. The nation, he argues, is the fundamental concept in French revolutionary history for individual rights and powers.[21] Except for the Restauration period 1814–1830, this has been clearly stated in the constitutions. Carré de Malberg interprets the idea of national sovereignty in a liberal direction and avoids interpreting state power in an absolutist sense. Rather, as a theoretical and political concept it connects dynamically to actual historical circumstances. The concept of the nation is more defensive than Rousseau's understanding because it is governed by the constitution and the general assembly on behalf of the state, and is therefore relieved of the lurking absolutism of *volonté générale*. Still, national sovereignty is *indivisible*, and it rests only and totally in the nation. National sovereignty cannot be transferred, as was stated in the Declaration of 1789 and in later constitutions. In France sovereignty does not refer to the king in parliament as in England, Carré de Malberg notes, nor to the people as in America, but to the nation that acknowledges the rights of the people and its legislative assembly. The state is a public personification of the nation.[22]

On the classic division between types of government (monarchy, democracy, aristocracy), Carré de Malberg points out that the principle of representation was not properly developed until the king and the people respectively acknowledged that they had to delegate their sovereign power to the general assembly, according to the constitution. Sovereignty itself lies neither with the king as person or the individual citizen, but with the nation as an encompassing concept.[23] The king is a legal entity in the nation with the purpose of serving the state. The sum of the singular citizens is not what possesses sovereignty, only the people as a unity in the nation. Only the nation is the legal person, and the state is its organised principle; state and nation are *one*.[24] The state is the 'name' of the nation, and with the state, the nation receives its juridical status. It would simply be inconceivable, Carré de Malberg argues, to understand the nation as a legal entity without the state.[25]

Carré de Malberg differentiated between at least three understandings of sovereignty that became evident during the revolution: monarchical sovereignty of the old regime, Rousseau's popular sovereignty, and national sovereignty that implied a limited and indirect understanding of political authority.[26] His distinction between popular and national sovereignty, formulated as a critique of Rousseau, was in his eyes necessary to raise an international framework for stability and peace. Sovereignty cannot be associated with the individual since that would mean that sovereignty is lost when the citizen transfers it to the representative organs of the state. Building on Sieyès and post-revolutionary liberals, Carré de Malberg states that popular sovereignty, for practical and moral reasons, cannot be associated with the constituent power in any unmediated sense.

It is symptomatic of the period, with its militarisation and colonisation, that Carré de Malberg views the *state* as a sovereign and self-limiting power, in that it operates on behalf of the nation as an indivisible unity. Building on Sieyès, Carré de Malberg considers nothing other than the representative assembly as the national will of the nation.[27] The nation is the only sovereign, and its will can only be expressed by the representative assembly. He retrieves Sieyès's ideas and puts them into a theory of the legitimacy of the state. The state is the nation, its subject and personification, and its legal entity. What legitimates the state is national identity, with its culture and tradition. The notion of popular sovereignty as well is absorbed into this consolidated concept of nation.[28] The duality of state/nation constitutes a dynamic of legitimacy and power.

Following the ideas of Jellinek, Carré de Malberg and Weber, around 1900 sovereignty was differentiated into at least four contemporary meanings, coined in English and German terms as follows:

- *Sovereignty (Souveränität)*: the supreme power of the territorial nation-state independent of external control, including its history and culture.
- *State authority (Staatsgewalt)*: the monopoly of legitimate powers of the state's internal regime, such as taxation, currency, police, and so on.
- *Domination (Herrschaft)*: the quality of the state's ruling institutions such as government, parliament and the courts, based on legitimate power.
- *Popular sovereignty (Volk Sourveränität)*: the quality of that entity (the demos) in whose name sovereignty in the first three senses is exercised.[29]

Political theology

Today, national representation means uniting the abstract principle of popular sovereignty with the concrete society of groups and interests in parliament. But how can the abstract totality of society be represented in the amorphous aggregate of numerical representation? Does the concept of *the political* only exist as a myth or an imaginary, as a promise about the future never to be fulfilled? Or as something more concrete as an invisible 'constitution' and deployment base for a wide range of political conflicts? These are questions sociologists tend to leave to political philosophers. Nevertheless, the concept of political theology has relevance here because the non-political and prehistorical presupposition for the political may help in understanding the historical legitimacy of politics. Like Weber in his study on the origin of European industrial capitalism, or Durkheim in the study about suicide, early sociology looked at religious underpinnings of social phenomena. Carl Schmitt went a step further in arguing for the existentialism of politics. The secularisation of the concept of the political, he argued, emptied politics of its heritage of mysticism and potency. The liberalisation and parliamentarisation of politics diluted and undermined its ability to govern.[30] Sovereignty, particularly, is seen by Schmitt as a theological-political concept that metaphysically and historically explains the *de facto* power of the sovereign to make decisions about the state of exception.

Schmitt makes a point of the theological origins of Rousseau's concept of the general will. The concept seems to possess a godlike divinity uniting power and justice in its indestructible and infallible nature.[31] Bodin's concept of sovereignty describes the divine power of the monarch. This extraordinary quality assumed in political reflexion, distinguishes it from the will of all, the observable, empirical multitude. Similarly, Abbed Sieyès's concept of constituent power is infinite and inexhaustible, but nevertheless *constitutes* new law-giving institutions. Rubinelli argues that Schmitt reinterpreted the concept of constituent power to justify his idea of presidential dictatorship in chaotic times or when an enemy threatens the state.[32] The concept provided Schmitt with a way to retain the idea of the stable non-liberal democratic and unified *nation*, as in his 1922 work, *Politische Theologie*.

Famously, Schmitt rejected the perspective of the law of nature and positive law, and he turned away from Weber's formalist view on the state apparatus. Sovereignty to Schmitt is very radical and in effect reactionary: it is the outcome of the necessary, political and sovereign decision, beyond liberal and participative processes. In response to the, in his eyes chaotic, Weimar republic, it conceives of politics and people in one constitutional unity, where political leadership executes its orders. Contrary to positive law, there is no pure law that sets limits for political decision; it must itself form a concept of the political to legalise the necessary political defence of the constitution. Abstract legalism associated with Hans Kelsen is in Schmitt exchanged with concrete political decision. In the book *Der Begriff des Politischen*, he argued that the concept of the state conditions the concept of the political. In *Political Theology*, with reference to the conservative post-revolutionary thinker Joseph de Maistre, he famously stated that the sovereign is the one who decides the state of exception. At the centre stands the political decision amidst conflicts concerning survival. Beyond universal ethical norms, deliberation and the parliament, there is only one transcendent subject: the deciding agent. The decider must consider what is the right thing to do based on some political, left or right, criteria. Political choices are always or typically embedded in conflict that demands priority before any ideals. The decision is born out of nothing, as he writes in his work on theological-political concepts.[33] Rousseau's ideas about an encompassing and authentic community remain an illusion. What matters is a sober diagnosis of present dangers and the readiness to apply the necessary means to neutralise them and restabilise the state.

Carl Schmitt's concept of the political and its further elaborations in political philosophy throw light on the emerging concept of *popular* sovereignty as its base. Ways of handling the paradox of popular sovereignty have since Schmitt been searched for in political theology, a term that now encompasses the theological in politics and the political in theology. Since Schmitt, political theology has speculated on historical and metaphysical foundations for the idea of the political. It addresses legitimacy of politics as a practice at a general level that touches the metaphysical and the empirical in combination. Political theology is the philosophical locus of renewed interest in the post-secular, and ultimately relevant for the understanding of the energy of political power as a horizon for politics.[34] The 'theological' origin of the (modern) political concept has been associated with the early modern idea addressed by William Blackstone as late as the 1760s: the sovereign king was given divine qualities; he inhabited two bodies, the human natural body and the immortal body politic, which united human and divine powers. The omnipotence of the king was of the people and God. This construction provided him and his advisors with power over the people and the nobility.[35]

Schmitt connected the concept of *Das politische* to a basic distinction as delimitation, the one between friend and enemy, thus to the survival of the will of the people. The existence of a society necessitates a non-society, which must be kept at a distance or defeated. Schmitt's distinction indicates that the human condition cannot evade antagonism. This fact makes the society a *political* society. On this premise politics is a struggle among political forces on who the enemy is and how to guarantee national security. Schmitt's point is that antagonism is fundamental to society and constitutes politics. Weber's insistence on *Kampf* as a general characteristic of politics is for Schmitt too an ontological and inescapable foundation for society and politics. A collective is always ready to confront, if necessary, violently, another threatening collective – this is simply a political condition. Because a collective implies inclusion, someone must be considered the enemy and defeated by the means of the state.

The expansion of a state apparatus also necessitated handling of domestic conflicts. At this internal level, disagreements on how to organise society were dealt with not according to a friend/enemy distinction, but as agonism. Constitutions are themselves texts that contain 'seeds of dissonance'.[36] Politics on a variety of issues concerning decisions about society in its totality is conducted on the distinction between government and opposition that is institutionalised. To Schmitt, the point of the state is to control conflict to the extent that problems can be handled by politics. Domestic politics remains sufficiently 'political' in that a sense of unity normally prevents friend–enemy antagonism from escalating. Public law and the constitution are conditioned by the state, and their role is to serve as a normative bond for the political. The ultimate mission of law is to preserve the political unity as apolitical law addressing the political directly. But what is to legitimise this encompassing overarching political unity that supersedes conflict and maintains unity? Neither division of power and rule of law, nor individual rights. Fundamental rule of law would rather serve to limit the power of the political. Democratic representation is a question of limited interest to Schmitt. Political pluralism should not have influence on the operative politics of the state. Only the political leader, the president or chancellor, can make the decision that makes the difference.

The contrast to Weber is striking concerning liberal values, rule of law and pluralism. While Weber was not impressed by the German *Reichstag* and provided an immanent critique of liberalism, Schmitt developed powerful external rejection, to the extent that he described the total state. Schmitt represents a sophisticated reaction to modern differentiation of politics mediated by power, that had been a topic for discussion in political theory since Machiavelli. Unlike Schmitt, Machiavelli was ahead of his time in specifying politics as the handling of force politically and legitimately in a secular sense. Schmitt noted that politics cannot hide behind judicial proceduralism and Kantian reason. Ultimately politics is about being able to make decisions based on the unity and divinity of the political. Deeply concerned with the instability of the Weimar period, his diagnosis ignored the decisional power of the legal-rational state apparatus. Perhaps ironically, despite the fact that democratic politics moves from crisis to crisis, it appears normal. And possibly, as argued by Thiem, the unchangeable theological dimension underlying politics can never be entirely abolished.[37] This may throw some light on the status of the concept of popular sovereignty today, if we contrast it with another, more democratic view from the same Weimar period.

Heller: politics and law

From the critical writings on sovereignty by the less known inter-war constitutional thinker Hermann Heller, one sees even more of the role of sociology in constitutional matters. Heller was a leading German jurist in the Weimar period and published a central work on sovereignty in 1927. He was thus a contemporary of Hans Kelsen and Carl Schmitt, whose works he responded to in his work on sovereignty and in his unfinished *Staatslehre*. Heller's main target in the book on sovereignty was Kelsen, who developed a legal positivist view that went far in suppressing the legal concept of sovereignty in his understanding of an international legal order. Heller agrees with Schmitt that the attempt to completely undo the political connection between juristic theory and political value judgements is a 'grandiose self-deception'. The pure juristic German doctrine from Laband to Kelsen is revealed to be political judgements of liberalism and a 'juristic mask of liberal opposition to the dogma of state sovereignty'.[38]

Heller went back to Bodin to show that his concept of sovereignty was 'by no means limitless ... but subjected the state's individuality to the highest legal principles'.[39] Heller viewed sovereignty as a political matter in a more sophisticated and democratic way than Schmitt. A declaration of a state of emergency, he argued against Schmitt, was to be seen as a response to a political crisis but still framed by law. Heller viewed sovereignty as a product of political judgement in a historical and political context within a legal framework. David Dyzenhaus points out that Heller reached beyond both Kelsen's legal positivist approach and Schmitt's attempt to show that rule of law is, in Heller's words, a 'liberal sham'.[40] As Jellinek before him, Heller demonstrated how domestic and international law relate to the same concept of the state as a self-bound sovereign power and the same set of normative legal norms. The state is 'a decision-making unit that is universal in a specific territory, and therefore necessarily unique and sovereign'.[41] Any attempt to understand the state separately from its territory was doomed to fail.[42]

The problem of the legitimacy of the modern state is the axial point from where Heller begins to understand both popular and national sovereignty. He takes a historical approach to examine how legally regulated communities develop a modern and bounded state that can be seen as legitimate to those subordinated to political power. In many respects he followed Jellinek who, with his two-sided theory of the state, attempted to handle the paradox of state legal-political power; how state 'Wille' was subordinated to *and* constrained the sovereign. As Jellinek, Heller accepted the paradox of the sovereign state as a normative sovereign and factually constrained. Also like Jellinek (and quite different from Kelsen), he developed his ideas on international law from the fact of the legitimate territorial sovereign state. International recognition in the international society is conditioned by state sovereignty.[43] Not unlike Weber, Heller stressed the impact of judgement and social action in both politics and law. Much more than legal positivism, he emphasised political and legal practice in dealing with specific problems.

Popular sovereignty was represented through a pluralist party system and a national assembly that provided a foundation for a top-down *Rechtstaat* and attempted to compensate for its injustices.

What motivated Heller's book on sovereignty was not only the misunderstandings regarding Bodin and Kelsen's legal positivism that went too far, but also the fact that the concept of sovereignty degenerated. When it no longer could be connected to the divine powers of the king, it was without a 'home'. The depersonalised modern *Rechtstaat* was connected to 'the existence and cognizability of a natural order of the world that determines our lives with a steadfast legality over and above any personal arbitrariness'.[44] But as the universally binding political idea attributed to all dissolved with new class divisions in 1848 and the following years, natural law could no longer demonstrate objective law in a legitimate fashion. Rousseau's general will – the people as a unity of will, as Heller defines it – could no longer form a base for law beyond interpretation of this will. The principle of the division of powers did not repair the problem, since it was originally based upon the general will. With the emergence of positivist legality to save politics from itself and from the demands of the working classes, true legitimacy was exchanged with what Weber called formalist legality and rationalist impersonal forms of government. In Heller's narrative formal theory referred to a state that cannot ascribe to ideal norms because it has lost contact with the unity of will: 'On this path, the concept of sovereignty must inevitably become depersonalised if it is followed consistently.'[45] Hans Kelsen's positivist ideas were only symptomatic of this formalism.

To Heller, the state is neither to be equated with the representative government nor the people, but must be considered as the sovereign person. Sovereignty is a function of state power or the state's will. But the state can only be considered the sovereign person if 'it is seen, with objective necessity, as a unified reality of will or decision-making unit'.[46] One cannot rely only on a materialist conception of society with an added utopian element. But how can the will of individuals within a unity be understood in relation to a sovereign state authority? How are state authority and state will to be understood in relation to one another? To Heller, sovereignty cannot be an abstraction, or a fiction. Heller distances himself from logical positivist (Kelsen) and existentialist (Schmitt) concepts of sovereignty in relation to the individual will: 'The theory of pure, ideal legal sovereignty has no conception of the essential importance of individual decisions for positive laws; in contrast, the doctrine of organic sovereignty ignores the decisive role played by law in the broader sense for the sovereign individuality of the will.'[47] The latter Schmittian approach simply focused on the political reality of 'the compelled construction from a point above the state, a construction from top down'.[48]

The crises of the concept, Heller argued, which stem from its abstract or fictitious character, are grounded even more deeply in rule of law rationalism that 'denatured' or mystified the concepts of the state, sovereignty and the people. If the concept of state sovereignty is to make any sense, it must be reconnected to a legal person. The sovereign state, as the antithesis to monarchic autocracy, must be conceived of as 'a unity of will resulting from a multiplicity of wills, which is subject to no higher unit of political decision-making'.[49] Because the state is founded on an act of will by those represented: once it was the king; in a democracy, it is the people. Individual wills are unified through representation and the majority principle. The unification may rule over the people as a multitude of sovereign wills, as the sovereign person. The status of representativity marks the distinction between democracy and monarchic autocracy: 'the state of popular sovereignty invariably has only juristically bound magisterial representation'.[50] State power emanates from the people – that is the essence that legal theory indirectly attributes to, when speaking about the spirit of the constitution or the will of the state. The sovereign state cannot refer to an abstract system, nor to the government, because it encompasses the entire people.

The problem of sovereignty relates to the connection between state and law, will and norm. In rationalism this connection did not exist. But this, Heller notes, was a thinking of the state that belonged to the nineteenth century. Since then, ideas of scholars like Husserl, Rickert and Simmel noted the practical, common-sensical dimension of understanding in social life that bridges wills and norms. Heller brings in sociological and social-philosophical thought to explicate these essential relationships that throws light on the relationship between the state and law. Heller emphasises the social aspect; it is not a question of psychological motivation: 'Only will in the sense of socially correlated behaviour, that is, announced through signs, and only a meaningful will, that is, behaviour that means "something", is taken account of by every science of human society.'[51] The point is not the mind of the individual but rather 'an intersubjective meaning, a reference to something substantive, separable from the subjective course of experiences'.[52] Without this awareness of the social and objective significance of the sign, Heller notes with reference to Georg Simmel, one ends up in Kelsen's reductive theory where the ideal objectivity of law is 'liberated' from the subject. The basics are that law is 'norms, meaningful, objective norms, established, supported and destructible by acts of human will, that aim meaningfully legal effects'.[53] Law is not a mass conception of a norming, and therefore the state is not an association of a multiplicity of people. It is a structural totality that remains relatively persistent in the fluctuation of acts; the totality of effects is found even where only its parts seem to be active. The jurist challenge is to reimplement a legal structure into a historical and social order. A step in this direction is to recognise that state will constitutes law. Heller's view of the state is legal-sociological; as a social structure the state is composed by the inseparability of facts and norms within a territorial entity.

On sovereignty, Heller concluded that: 'Sovereignty is the characteristic of a universal territorial unit of decision-making and effect, by virtue of which, for the sake of law, it sometimes asserts itself absolutely against the law.'[54] Sovereignty preserves its absolute character despite international law and organisations like the League of Nations. Heller is quite clear on the impossibility of international law without autonomous states that are free to act in their own interest: 'The absolute right of self-preservation demanded by international law is the basis for the absolute character of sovereignty.'[55] To believe that state sovereignty can only be preserved through a more comprehensibly sovereign European federation, Heller writes presciently, is a grand delusion and would only present itself as political agitation. Arguments in favour of such a change of the sovereignty concept would in fact work for the dissolution of the sovereignty dogma because it implies juridication of ethics and moralisation of law, a semantic expansionism that violates both spheres. 'It is this failure to recognize the autonomy and relative independence of law that leads to a failure to recognize the sovereignty problem.'[56] Heller notes that such an idealism can be identified in the rhetoric presented by those who moralise international law, such as the League of Nations that unsurprisingly had proven useless. The point is that state sovereignty consists of politics and law as indispensable and relatively autonomous spheres. There cannot be any higher decision-making unit within a territory, but it conditions true representation of the people within a constitutional framework.

The reduction of democracy

Having discussed some 'long' nineteenth-century proposals in political and legal theory on how to handle the dilemma of 'the sovereign people', it is instructive to have a look at how practical politics operated to achieve stability. As I noted in the introduction, theory and politics are not separate worlds, they are in a sense both politics with words in their respective genres. The historian and philosopher Pierre Rosanvallon successfully integrated the two in his volumes on French post-revolutionary philosophical history. Rosanvallon argues that a persistent if implicit question in post-revolutionary France was how to reconcile rational government with popular sovereignty: 'The concept of the general will, was the principal black box of the revolutionary process.'[57] It contained and therefore concealed the paradox of self-government. The political subject had somehow to be harmonised with its limitation because of the necessity of political order. The connection to the nation was a way out. The connection of national sovereignty and the general will made anti-absolutism possible in a liberal sense, as stated in the 1789 Declaration. The sovereignty of the people was first connected to governance through Bonapartism as a particular form – caesarist rationalism, yet, as we have seen, later stimulated into liberal rationalism by Constant and Guizot. The 1848 events gave way to another combination of unity and administrative power in a celebration of the nation. The frenetic oscillation between rationalism and voluntarism continued to characterise the French political path.

Rosanvallon sees voluntarism and rationalism as equally dead ends that 'secretly' united in a 'post-political' promise about a place without conflict over interests or grounding in sociological realities. But of course, social conflict could not be dreamt away with the help of the image of the general will, and in France a tension emerged with consequences long after the revolution.[58] The revolution first did not want intermediary (representative) bodies.[59] So how was representative democracy conceived as serving the people, not distancing them from it? As we have seen, Sieyès did his part. From 1793 the term 'representative democracy' was in common use and the constitutive moment was seen as separated from ordinary governance, to ensure proper representative government. Proposals were developed by the great scientist Condorcet on how to organise assemblies and were central in the tense debate about the future of the revolution.[60] Condorcet worked to enhance several modes of representation. He saw the general will as inherent to political processes of continuous interaction and reflection. Condorcet was on the track of a way to realise the true ideas of the revolution in a more complex constellation but was effectively stopped by Robespierre and the Montagnards. In the following years democratic voluntarism and liberal rationalism contested and undermined one another in a confusing and destructive game of power.[61]

'Moderation' and 'normalisation' are Rosanvallon's terms for French democracy's balance with a liberalism that avoided absolutism after the fall of Napoleon III. A 'silent revolution in the political system' took place from 1880 to 1920. And yet it also marked a rupture. 'Le moment 1890' was a decisive milestone that implied an expansion of institutional arrangements of representation and legitimacy, beyond rationalism and voluntarism, such as professions, political parties, trade unions and proportional elections.[62] 'Le moment 1890' implied the recognition, mediated by the social sciences and sociologists like Durkheim, that society must be interpreted as composed of *social groups* whose interests must be articulated in intermediary councils and assemblies that connect the social and the political. With this, France left behind its rousseauan heritage of suspicion of intermediary bodies, and its narrow celebration of direct democracy. The party system synthesised the strands in a 'rationalised pluralism'. Rosanvallon sees the organisation of a stable system of organised identities in parties in the 1880s as a complex pluralism connecting the social and political to politics. Besides parties, syndicalism after the legalising of unions in 1864 signalled a rupture with universal voluntarism and '*démocratisme*', in that they organised particular interests and developed the idea of representation. This trend led to ideas of the welfare state as a political intervention in the economy as an alternative to syndicalist-socialist demands for industrial democracy. After the first world war, industrial democracy and nationalisation were at the heart of the programme of movements and unions.[63] Totalitarianism (Stalinism, Nazism) was seen as a pathology of democratic thought. Illiberalism was avoided by pluralism that supported parliamentarianism. The revolutionary heritage was largely rejected, and public space expanded with commentary and criticism in the political system. Politics and public opinion highlighted the connection between parliamentarianism and democracy.

After the first world war a minimalist and realist conception of moderate democracy (*démocracie moyenne*) gained ground, reflecting the ideas of Kelsen, Popper and Schumpeter, that considered democracy as a practical procedure for legitimacy.[64] Democracy referred no longer to a sovereign people, but negatively to the absence of absolutism. This minimalist realism concentrated on defeating illiberal forces by defining some absolute democratic thresholds but had in the long run little to offer in terms of empowerment and participation.[65] After the second world war a negative minimalist understanding of democracy dominated until the 1960s. *Representation* secured its position as the hegemonic formula of democracy. Rosanvallon sees the post-war period in France as in the hands of technocracy and planning agencies without innovative ideas.[66] Totalitarianism was waiting in the shadows and the establishment rarely conducted anything more than careful planification, combined in a rational government and democratic representation, by fulfilling and cancelling further need for extended democracy. But the system could not provide formulas for the human desire to take control of their collective lives for new generations, and the phase was interrupted by the events of 1968.

Reflecting on the status of French democracy, Rosanvallon considers Rousseau's theory of the general will as largely discredited today. To appear credible, the sovereignty of the people must be conceptualised in completely secular terms. The former imagery no longer works.[67] Rousseau's totality of the people, the people as principle, has already been supplemented by other forms of embodiments of the people; the people as individuals and groups, which will continue to develop the project of democracy. A minimalist negative definition of democracy, Rosanvallon believes, will retrieve the pressure towards participative and innovative forms of legitimacy. He considers the word 'democracy' as at once a solution and a problem. 'In it coexist the good and the vague. This coexistence does not principally stem from democracy's status as a distant and utopian ideal, but with disputes over its definition pertaining to questions of what means should be used to realize it.'[68] He continues: 'Far from banally corresponding to a sort of methodological indeterminacy, the fluctuating meaning of democracy reflects its history and its essence, inextricably mixing the question of popular sovereignty with that of equality.' Consequently, moral sentiments and political ideologies yielded by social and economic conjunctures lead the understanding of 'democracy' in quite unexpected, such as 'populist', directions that society needs to deal with, by inventing new concepts and their paradoxes.

The popular and the national

The tension between popular sovereignty and rational politics was essential in France in the nineteenth century, and less so in English liberalism where the Parliament played a pivotal role in bridging the principles of governing by law and the balance of state powers. In France and elsewhere in Europe, rationalism represented a doctrine and a specific form of implementation in the second half of the nineteenth century (bureaucracy).[69] However, Rosanvallon's studies of post-revolutionary France demonstrate that citizen rights did not simply emerge from the principle of reason, nor from representation, but to a large extent from the idea of popular sovereignty that constructed itself by means of exclusion (nobility, foreigners). The general will remained as an abstract foundation for law, although in public debate the *nation* was the source of sovereignty, as the Declaration of 1789 stated.

Law, rational government and state administration could not be raised on the immediate foundation of an abstract notion of popular sovereignty alone.[70] The concept of the general will and references to the people carried with it an ambiguity between the popular and the national. The equivocation, I think, could be seen as flexibility that relieved the people of its direct ruling responsibility by emphasising the nation and the state. Also, with the concept of the national, the reasonable could be mobilised alongside the popular. In the new age of democracy, science and internationalisation, the undisputed noble and revolutionary term 'popular sovereignty' was confronted with waves of political rationalism that it could not withstand. Unlike the institutional and compromising concept of democracy, it had problems dealing with international contexts and class divisions. It represented too much will and too little reason.

With liberal constitutionalism in the nineteenth century, the constitution marked the legality of the assemblies that were to take care of the future. Execution of authority through restraining denoted the idea of democracy. The French revolution and the semantics of the nation and the republic made it evident that a self-organised political system was in the making.[71] In the absence of the body politic of the monarch, the specifically political had to be addressed; its principles and semantic conditions. The combination of individuality in the idea of human rights and the reason of public opinion that emerged from Rousseau moved beyond *la volonté générale*. The will of the individual and of the community were magically melted together with reference to the *nation* as formula. The people's sovereignty delimits political power and leads to the paradox of representation. The first constitutions harmonised basic rights with the necessity of procedures for delegating power to apply force. Constitutions denoted the self-description of the political system, based on the nation, liberty and procedures for representation of government.

From the late nineteenth century, the key term is *democracy*, with the accompanying paradox, that the people now rules itself, which it cannot. Following Luhmann, the paradox could not be resolved through procedures like general elections but had to be addressed in the very definition of politics. As pointed out, from the late seventeenth century the understanding of the state began to relieve itself by referring to *public opinion* as the voice of the people. This brilliant invention increased the ability of the state to interpret its environment and was a response to increasing expectations of a paradoxical rationality. The state observed society politically and acquired increased possibility to react to movements and demands.[72] The 'people' was re-included as a generalised reference in the political system. In the nineteenth century this became basic to the understanding of democracy in a more specific sense, until universal suffrage established itself as its definitional mark. The increased expectation of society to observe and orient itself in a complex environment that it can only understand functionally encouraged a reflexive and 'democratic' phase in political history. The operative autonomy of the political system developed responsive and efficient institutions with appropriate legitimating semantics that enabled it to deal with its increased *dependence* on society. Democracy emerged as a self-description for society and served as an instrument for stability. Constitutions referring to rights and law were insufficient, as they tend to look backwards while politics is expected to operate towards the future of known and unknown demands, with new promises.[73] In the nineteenth century public opinion made opposition and democracy possible.[74] With reference to deliberation and public reason, it assisted in the production of themes and genres to attract the political agenda. The press became structurally coupled to politics as political public opinion and encouraged the notion of democracy as the self-description of politics. Parties and political movements demanded more democracy, which could mean very different things but always something positive.

The concept of democracy brought with it additional normative ideals such as human rights and social equality. To early French rationalism, sovereignty could not provide any solution to the problem of despotism or absolutism. It had an answer but no direction, and it clearly could be arbitrarily abused. Of itself, it cared little for facts and evidence, even institutions. It could be seduced but cared little for deliberation. It had to be controlled by the law and the rational state administration. In France, rationalism never saw Montesquieu's 'English' remedies as sufficient. Immediately after the French revolution common law and the parliamentary system in England were seen as less than adequate as protection against arbitrary rule, compared with rights, rules, education and debate.[75] English ideas of sovereignty of the king in Parliament were inconceivable. Nor was political representation an inherent element in the French doctrine. Freedom referred to reason, not voting and 'splitting' political parties. However, the revolution meant a new beginning, and healing of old divisions. In public debate social unity was celebrated by many and inspired by Rousseau, but often by means of exclusion. Citizenship as a fundamental political value was not kept separate from the notion of popular sovereignty. The individual citizen was seen as a member of the sovereign power, and rights originated not from representation but from the revolutionised idea of sovereignty. Rosanvallon points out a fundamental change: belonging and equality as fundamental values were integrated with the idea of sovereignty that in turn was identified with the being of the nation. Citizenship was not connected to the principle of representation but defined a distinct social status, 'that of the individual member of a people collectively taking the place of the king'.[76] Rosanvallon formulates this as a paradox: 'French democracy is not founded on a deconstruction of absolutism. On the contrary, it consists of a reappropriation of it.'[77]

The concept of democracy subsequently emerged as a formula for the political self-descriptions of society, and the political parties encouraged the conception since it allowed them the possibility of power. The democracy concept, backed by the concept of human rights, became a key referent for how to develop policies. General paradoxical and utopian expectations about freedom, equality and individual autonomy ran through its semantics. It served to consolidate the state and its politics, and to neutralise the proletarian movement. It was combined with issues of Christianity, nationalism, conservatism and reform movements. Public criticism had already established itself as a fact of politics, even if public debate was 'guided' from the elites.

The notion of democracy remains the political way of describing society as a political society, ignoring other and contradicting ways of observing it. As a description of something 'unmarked' it too constitutes a paradox, in that democracy provides politics with meaning and guides complex society. It legitimises operations at home and abroad and serves as self-legitimation. Politics in democratic states is *eo ipso* democratic politics. It therefore legitimises the potential and necessary political use of violence. The democracy concept allows for state violence such as war by introducing a distinction between our and their violence, and between legally framed democratic violence and non-democratic violence. Which is which can be decided by states and governments according to circumstance. The term 'democracy' continues to introduce semantic values that define recognised terms like 'freedom', 'equality', 'peace' and 'human rights' in new and adequate ways for the political system.[78] New interpretations of old concepts leave an impression of continuity that masks the disruptive transfusion to a modern society. Niklas Luhmann argues that these insights cannot be addressed adequately in the 'culture of suspicion' (Marx, Nietzsche, Freud) because this is not a question of true and false, liberty and oppression, but simply the transformation of a semantics of values that reflects structural problems in modern society.

In a complex and differentiated society the concept of democracy is an utterly *political* self-description, and it cannot claim to cover society irrespective of position. It makes no sense to speak of a democratic market or democratic art. 'Democracy' is society's self-image of politics, which increases its ability to produce order and legitimacy internally. Paradoxically, it is a *description* of the political system that indicates how it *normatively* operates.[79] With the formula of 'democracy', political authority is arranged or staged for itself and legitimated. The legitimating power of this evolution of semantics that projects society as a political totality is evident. By making a distinction between democracy and totalitarian rule, an external reference is formulated that unites 'negatively' by minimising internal differences.

The representative turn

Towards the end of the nineteenth century the problem of popular sovereignty in Europe had given space to questions of state sovereignty. This came to the fore in particular in the German tradition to which Jellinek belongs, and also with Carré de Malberg in France. It was a time for nation-state-building internally and international law externally. Duncan Kelly argues that 'If the nineteenth century does have a theory of popular sovereignty, it exists only with reference to the particular development of a new state theory of national, indirect and representative government.'[80] Following Rosanvallon, that conclusion goes very far. In France and elsewhere in Europe, the century experimented with various forms of popular self-rule, theorised by Proudhon and many radicals across the continent: it was apparent in the aftermath of the revolution, in the February revolution in 1848, in the Paris commune, in various socialist and grass-roots movements struggling for autonomy and political participation. Nevertheless, universal suffrage gained ground as a definition of democracy at the beginning of the 1900s. The paradox of representation had moved to the centre of political debate.

The democratic *and* elitist nature of political representation has been noted by many, not least by Bernard Manin and Hanna Pitkin.[81] Manin found a middle way to view representation, between self-rule and aristocratic elitism. He saw representation as authorisation given to a selected few by the citizens and seen as an 'audience' that more or less passively reacted to media-conveyed stimuli. Curiously, despite his critical observations, Manin never did abandon hopes of a debating and involved citizenry, although his visions are hardly concordant with his diagnosis of western democracy. What is absent in his book on principles of representative government is a way to see representation as a form of legitimation orchestrated by media-savvy political elites but nevertheless vibrant within democracies. Conversely, critics of Manin responded with a one-sided moralising of representative democracy, viewing the citizens-as-audience as out-manoeuvred and disempowered. What was equally difficult for the critics to conceive, was a democracy of spectators as one model among others.

I have remarked that a rationalist version of representative democracy is currently the hegemonic model in western democracies, to the extent that democracy is seen as identical to elective democracy. Nevertheless, democracy inhabits features that leave it incapable of filling this notion of democracy. Elections alone cannot meet expectations of a popular will. The legitimacy of elected representatives is volatile and, for reasons of functional differentiation (politics is no longer seen as ruling society any more than markets), generally sinking. It develops elites at a distance from the lives and concerns of the electorate. What is essential to highlight is that this system nevertheless works because mechanisms of *legitimacy*, like elections, are not entirely a top-down arrangement but include people being recognised as agents.

What has been called 'the representative turn' in democratic theory was largely an offshoot of John Rawls's massive influence some decades back but one that went in different directions. Mansbridge and Saward come close to seeing representation as an element of democratic politics on its own quite limited and hierarchical terms.[82] Saward allows himself to be influenced by empirical observations produced by political sociology and sees representation as events of claim-making in formal and informal political institutions, foremost the media. Representation is *performed* and claimed regularly in particular ways that need to be examined. Saward approaches a view on representation as a complex public process that produces and demonstrates politics in distinct ways. Elections regularly demonstrate and confirm a distinct *version* of democracy. His view is compatible with a perspective on election campaigns as critical constitutional moments that are social and political before they are democratic. In this view, political legitimacy comes forward in a Weberian sense as the acceptance of popular claims under given circumstances.[83]

The representative turn tended to view representation as the comparably best way of reproducing democracy. Only to a limited degree did it allow grim empirical trends to influence its theorising, and rarely did it explore other forms of democracy. In the writings of Nadia Urbinati and others, the 'turn' implied a defence for an already hegemonic but highly imperfect democratic mechanism. It viewed representation, with its sub-elements of nominations, campaigns and mediatisation, in the light of normative demo-cratic theory, rarely from the perspectives of political theory and political sociology. Urbinati connects sovereignty to the electoral process of information and judgement that both includes and disconnects the citizenry in an ongoing circulation of influence and power.[84] Sovereignty is exercised when people critically observe their contesting representatives. Unlike Pitkin's projection, representation is not seen as an expression of an absent sovereign but involves that very power as process.

However, the concepts of democratic representation and popular sovereignty are not sufficiently kept apart in this view and its ideological implications are many. To see sovereignty as the passing of judgements in and through political parties, election campaigns, social movements and protest groups, as well as in the state institutional powers, glosses over the essential point that these are *expressions* of sovereignty with their underlying ultimate source intact in the political culture. Someone must be represented; something must be expressed. Neither representation nor public opinion can be identi-fied with this *something – the political* cannot be reduced to individual practices.

An idealist position views representation as a process of congruence and correspondence between representatives and the represented. In a realist view, I think political representation can be seen as a procedure of construction and constitution: representatives attempt to constitute the represented by presenting the people with images and stories that place the representative in a preferable light. The demands of the people are constructed and made figurative in the turmoil of the political process. In democratic representation, competing stories are presented by parties and representatives that reproduce politics as processes of contestation. The undeniable distance between people and representatives is not an obstacle for democracy but a premise for the freedom of representatives and their apparatus to construct and perform their political stories. Demography, territorial expansion and class opened space for politics to constitute itself communicatively and morally and created distances that became functionally compensated by the press and electronic and digital media, which in turn reproduced and transformed representation as the prevailing mechanism of political legitimacy.

As a mechanism of separation, representation allows formal politics to reproduce itself operationally and morally at distance from the diffuse and latent sentiments of the wider political society. Political representation, then, has come to be a process of social and political construction organised by the political apparatus with the assistance of the distinct logics of the media. By way of representatives in politics, society can observe itself politically and point out directions for its future. This does not imply that political representation and legitimacy is an entirely manipulative process, only that the image of voters and their opinions is deliberately constructed in a particular and passive way. The view rather begins and ends with the paradox of representation and democracy and observes how it is tackled by elites. Political claims, performances, even the representatives and citizens themselves, ought to be seen as endogenous to the political system, and as pivotal elements in the process of generating legitimacy.

To conclude, in political theory the paradox of 'representative democracy' tends to mean simply 'democracy', and 'legitimacy' to mean the acceptance of representative politics. Democracy is seen as valid representation, through which the political can be expressed and articulated by representatives given a mandate by the citizenry. Representative democracy is a highly imperfect and often structurally biased and manipulated arrangement; nevertheless, it is seen as the most legitimate form of governance available today. It basically leaves a version of the people as multitude to institute moderate change. If other versions of the people are suppressed too long, a mismatch appears between a narrow definition of democracy and increasing expectations driven by structural conditions of stagnation. Representation is based on political equality in a society of growing economic inequality: it symbolises a growing gap between representatives and the represented. Representation is based upon participation of all, only to leave the power to some few. I have argued that this paradox of representation is not to be avoided because it is the point of representation. The paradox of representative democracy is at the same time what makes the society governable. It provides modern society with efficiency and, so long as it works, with legitimacy. This was the insight of early thinkers of modern democracy like Sieyès and Condorcet who saw representation as one necessary channel of many in the relationship between the people and the assembly.

Popular sovereignty is expressed through entangled media of political and juridical articulation, such as elections, direct participation, councils, hearings, courts and public opinion. They modify and complement one another in the bridging and translation of the gap between people and the leaders of the state. Informed by (but not identical to) Rosanvallon, we may generally speak of three main forms of relationship or articulation: *representation* (through universal suffrage, free elections, referendums), *participation* (through direct decision-making in organisations, trade unions, social campaigning, protest and public debate) and *litigation* (through the courts). They are quite differently valued in contemporary society and occur in very different shapes. They connect and detach politics and the political. They articulate constituent power. They present individual and collective stories that provide legitimacy for governmental and parliamentary power. In quite different ways they are embedded in institutional networks. As political structures, they release forms of action and opinion with foundation in the sovereign people. They circulate power and legitimacy among citizens and the powers of the state in a never-ceasing game. They rely on different kinds of performative and symbolic elements. Together they translate and convey a conception of the people's will, but even more the will of groups and classes into political opinion in a multi-democratic society.

Conclusion

Rationalism, in yet another neoliberal, transnational version, has dominated for forty years since the hegemonic social-democratic parties in many European countries joined forces with Christian-democrats in promoting mainstream liberalism. The new rationalism in a context of regional integration sees state sovereignty as in decline, and a largely redundant concept. The state is seen as predominantly a vehicle in the hands of the government. A side-effect is that its historical significance and relationship to the nation has been reduced. When we realise that the state is an all-encompassing concept beyond legal-rational administration, security and welfare, it becomes apparent that nation-states remain the principal protector of democracy. We therefore need to make sense of the state as a supreme legal-political institutional agency, with social and cultural repercussions. When the democratic state acts (or fails to act), the people act.

It is misleading to reduce the concept of popular sovereignty to an idealised notion of representative democracy. Nor does it make sense to hold that political representation makes the social political.[85] It is not representative democracy that enables popular sovereignty, but *vice versa*. People, independently of representation, will always feel obliged to question the long-term actions of our common state 'will'. Representation expresses and visualises the people, but cannot create it, since representation only sees the multitude. It cannot sense the social in the political, nor the political in its full complexity.

In place of idealist revisioning of the 'representative turn', we ought to base our understanding on the history of politics and the political.[86] Hermann Heller provided the inter-war period with some fundamental insights on the state, and his views on the dynamic and conceptual relationships between the people, the state and politics have much to offer today as well. In his perspective, as in Condorcet's, representation is not a second best, nor the best, but simply a form of articulation among others. Representation is no doubt considered as a vital articulation of popular sovereignty, but it makes sense to see political representation as predominantly an element of *constituted power*. The people pre-exist representation at the level of the political, or the *imaginaire*. It is true that representatives and their institutions shape constituencies. It is equally an ontological truth that citizens hold an ultimate authority that representation cannot capture.

Democratic representation guides and interprets people in their political orientation and makes it visible with the help of the ballot box. The people are then given shape and brought into public light as an aggregate, but not into *being*. Processes of representation are often fundamentally unfair by most criteria. The essence of representation is election, campaigns, mathematical formulas of transferring votes into mandates, and so on, that have arbitrary origins and effects that favour stability rather than change. The recurring error of celebrating representation to the point of metaphysics is ahistorical. It is true that representation is a main mechanism that formally provides individuals with equal political relevance. But it is also a historical and cultural truth that people consider themselves as the very purpose of politics.

Notes

1 Georg Jellinek, *Allgemeine Staatslehre*, Volume I (Berlin: Springer Verlag, 1900/1921), p. 180.
2 Andreas Anter, 'Georg Jellineks wissenschaftliche Politik Positionen, Kontexte, Wirkungslinien.' *Politische Vierteljahresschrift*, 39:3 (1998), 503–526 at 509.
3 Anter, *Max Weber's Theory of the Modern State*, p. 170.
4 Anter, 'Georg Jellineks wissenschaftliche Politik', 521.
5 Peter C. Caldwell, *Popular Sovereignty and the Crisis of German Constitutional Law: The Theory and Practice of Weimar Constitutionalism* (Durham, NC: Duke University Press, 1997), pp. 3–5.
6 Ibid., p. 42.

7 Kelly, 'Revisiting the Rights of Man', 514.
8 Jellinek, *Allgemeine Staatslehre*, p. 11.
9 Anter, 'Georg Jellineks wissenschaftliche Politik', 515; Kelly, 'Revisiting the Rights of Man', 520.
10 Jellinek, *Allgemeine Staatslehre*, pp. 180–181.
11 Ibid., p. 180.
12 Ibid., p. 338.
13 'The State is the embodiment and personification of the national power. This power, considered in its highest dignity and greatest force, is called Sovereignty.' Bluntschli, *The Theory of the State*, p. 493. To consider the state as 'person' with a will was, of course, not a novel idea.
14 Peter Stirk, 'The Westphalian model, sovereignty and law in *fin-de-siècle* german international theory.' *International Relations*, 19:2 (2005), 153–172, at 159.
15 Ibid., 155.
16 Anter, 'Georg Jellineks wissenschaftliche Politik', 510.
17 Jellinek, *Allgemeine Staatslehre*, p. 287; Anter, 'Georg Jellineks wissenschaftliche Politik', 510.
18 Carré de Malberg, *Contribution*, pp. 156–165.
19 Ibid., pp. 154–155.
20 Ibid., p. 161.
21 Ibid., p. 167. This is clearly stated in the Declaration of 1789: 'Les principe de toute souveraineté reside essentiellement dans la nation. Nul corps, nul individu, ne peut exercer d'autorité qui n'en émane expressément.'
22 'Le vrai souverain, ce n'est plus le roi, ni aucun gouvernant quel qu'il soit, c'est exclusivement la nation.' Carré de Malberg, *Contribution*, p. 171.
23 Ibid., p. 183.
24 Ibid., p. 187.
25 'L'Etat n'est que la nation elle-méme (la collectivité) juridiquement organisée.' Ibid., p. 187.
26 Ibid., p. 185; Rubinelli, *Constituent Power*, p. 149.
27 Carré de Malberg, *Contribution*, p. 47.
28 Olga Bashkina, 'Nations against people: whose sovereign power?' In Leijssenaar and Walker (eds) *Sovereignty in Action*, p. 173.
29 Michel Troper, 'The survival of sovereignty.' In Kalmo and Skinner (eds) *Sovereignty in Fragments*, p. 139; Neil MacCormick, *Questioning Sovereignty* (Oxford: Oxford University Press,1999), p. 153.
30 Annika Thiem, 'Schmittian shadows and contemporary theological-political constellations.' *Social Research*, 80:1 (2013), 1–23, at 9.
31 Schmitt, *Political Theology*, p. 118.
32 Rubinelli, *Constituent Power*, p. 109.
33 Schmitt, *Political Theology*, pp. 37–38.
34 Thiem, 'Schmittian shadows'.
35 Kantorowicz, *The King's Two Bodies*, pp. 3–23.
36 Martin Loughlin, 'The constitutional imagination.' *Modern Law Review*, 78:1 (2015), 1–25, at 15.
37 Thiem, 'Schmittian shadows', 11.

38 Hermann Heller, *Sovereignty: A Contribution to the Theory of Public and International Law* (ed. and introduced by David Dyzenhaus) (Oxford: Oxford University Press, 2019), p. 183.
39 Ibid., p. 63.
40 David Dyzenhaus, 'Introduction', in Heller, *Sovereignty*, p. 3.
41 Heller, *Sovereignty*, p. 134.
42 Ibid., p. 137.
43 Dyzenhaus, 'Introduction', p. 45.
44 Heller, *Sovereignty*, p. 64.
45 Ibid., p. 66.
46 Ibid., p. 96.
47 Ibid., p. 104.
48 Ibid., p. 106.
49 Ibid., p. 107.
50 Ibid., p. 108.
51 Ibid., p. 110.
52 Ibid., p. 110.
53 Ibid., p. 112.
54 Ibid., p. 173.
55 Ibid., p. 174.
56 Ibid., p. 185.
57 Rosanvallon, *Democracy Past and Future*, p. 138.
58 Pierre Rosanvallon, *Le peuple introuvable: Histoire de la représentation démocratique en France* (Paris: Gallimard, 2002), p. 31.
59 Rosanvallon, *La démocratie inachevée*, p. 201.
60 Ibid., pp. 59–61.
61 Ibid., p. 91.
62 Ibid., p. 245.
63 Ibid., pp. 353–358.
64 Ibid., p. 380.
65 Ibid., pp. 364–365.
66 Ibid., pp. 384–385.
67 Ibid., pp. 396–397.
68 Rosanvallon, 'The history of the word "Democracy"', 153.
69 Pierre Rosanvallon, 'Political rationalism and democracy in France in the 18th and 19th centuries.' *Philosophy and Social Criticism*, 28:6 (2002), 687–701, at 690.
70 Ibid., 696.
71 Luhmann, *Die Politik der Gesellschaft*, p. 349.
72 Ibid., p. 355.
73 Ibid., p. 356.
74 Ibid., p. 302.
75 Pierre Rosanvallon, 'Political rationalism and democracy',691–701.
76 Ibid., 694.
77 Ibid., 694.

78 Luhmann, *Die Politik der Gesellschaft*, p. 359.

79 Ibid., p. 358.

80 Duncan Kelly, 'Popular sovereignty as a state theory in the nineteenth century.' In Bourke and Skinner (eds) *Popular Sovereignty in Historical Perspective*, p. 296.

81 Bernard Manin, *Principles of Representative Government* (Cambridge, MA: Harvard University Press, 1997); Hannah Pitkin 'Representation and democracy: uneasy alliance.' *Scandinavian Political Studies*, 27:3 (2004), 335–342.

82 Jane Mansbridge, 'Rethinking representation.' *American Political Science Review* 97:4 (2003), 515–528; Michael Saward 'Representation and democracy: revisions and possibilities.' *Sociology Compass*, 2:3 (2008), 1000–1013.

83 Michael Saward, *The Representative Claim* (Oxford: Oxford University Press, 2010), p. 144.

84 Nadia Urbinati, *Representative Democracy: Concept and Genealogy* (Chicago: Chicago University Press, 2006), p. 3.

85 Nadia Urbinati, 'The democratic tenor of representation.' In Mónica Brito Vieira (ed.) *Reclaiming Representation: Contemporary Advances in the Theory of Political Representation* (London: Routledge, 2017), p. 196.

86 See contributions in Vieira (ed.), *Reclaiming Representation*.

5

The political, politics and sociology

Machiavelli was the first in early modern times to make a point of rule as conditioned on citizens' beliefs about the ruler. In premodern times discourse on how to rule was in principle not yet differentiated. Machiavelli leads the way into a non-traditional way of handling politics proper. In the absence of the divine, Machiavelli is sensitive to the fact that the prince must *appear* to be the sovereign. Authority is *handed* to the prince, and he must always recognise this fact in his conferences with representatives for the people, as described in *The Prince*, for instance in chapter XXI on how to earn a reputation. Throughout the work, Machiavelli stresses the space between the prince and the people, the ruler and the ruled, politics and the political, that the prince must cultivate. The abstract and yet immensely concrete concept of the people emerges as protagonist. This is observed with growing intensity as we approach high modernity. Politics is not about justice or reason, but how judgements appear in public. Politics begins with the recognition of the fact that the people are to make sense of the actions of the prince given their values and expectations. Only then can politics operate effectively.

This chapter examines the concept of *the political*. I attempt to demonstrate that the concept helps to account for sovereignty as the source of political struggle. Based on rationalisation of modernity we see a line of reasoning from Machiavelli to Hobbes, Montesquieu, Durkheim, Schmitt and Luhmann that addresses a *distinction between the political and politics*. Weber describes politics through the legitimating qualities of law, bureaucracy, tradition and political leadership at distance from citizens. Luhmann adheres to, and I think clarifies, this tradition, as he offers important insights concerning the autonomy of the political system. Pierre Bourdieu presented central insights on a theory of politics as a social field. On the basis of Claude Lefort's ideas, Pierre Rosanvallon addressed the political as a distinct and autonomous object of study that must be distinguished from the study of politics.[1] He thus joined a diverse group of scholars in operating with a concept of *the political* as opposed to 'politics'. I would like to explore that line of thinking in relation to the question of sovereignty, rather than focus on Schmitt's infamous friend/enemy distinction.

Theorists of the political ask their questions differently and they come from different disciplines and positions. Nevertheless, what seems to unite these approaches is the view that *politics* is the process by which persons and institutions deliberate or engage in conflict on who should make decisions on behalf of society, whereas *the political* is the relatively diffuse background that invests politics with purpose and meaning. It refers to the wider dimension of society that is directed towards questions of how to go on in a world of inequality, abuse of power and external threats. I view it as the political dimension of Durkheim's collective consciousness. The political consists of public and private communication on social matters in a multitude of genres voiced by civil society movements, in the shape of civil disobedience, public debates, intellectual publications, social media, riots and more. What the abstract concept lacks in conceptual specificity, it possesses in the necessity to name the self-confidence of the multitude of 'we'. Realistically inclined political thinkers from Machiavelli onwards provide us with the history of ideas about the political as the environment of politics. The political defines and reproduces politics, and in modern states its form and reference are defined constitutionally. Understanding the political implies seeing it as the legitimating source and reference for politics. To examine this argument, it is necessary to expand from political philosophy to contributions in political sociology and public law.

Although sociology and realist political theory tend to be concerned with how legitimacy is reproduced by politics, they do not necessarily reject the ontological character of the political, at least so long as we may speak of a historically constructed being.[2] It offers specific historical descriptions on what successful and legitimate politics entails, including qualities of public leadership that draws on undercurrents in the political. Realist theory would generally be concerned with politics as techniques for handling conflict, including individual leadership qualities that serve to cool down heated conflicts and keep them productive to society. But none of these observations of politics contradicts the existence of the people as more than the sum of the individuals. On the contrary, the historically produced ontology of the political in the state throws light on the concept of popular sovereignty, as I attempt to show. Society is many things; *political* society is society viewed politically – understood as a delimited collective that changes itself by means of bounded decisions in the state. To speak of political societies of course includes the public reflection on how to organise society in the context of collective power. On this second-order level we find political 'theories', imaginaries and political self-descriptions.

An empty space

The French philosopher Claude Lefort pointed out that the now secular idea of *le politique* in democratic theory cannot but remain abstract and empty. It cannot be transformed into a unified political force of itself in the hands of political leaders in politics, what he called *la politique*. Lefort addressed the political in his 1988 essay on 'The question of democracy', where he approaches it as an *imaginary*, a profound symbolic experience of openness that must not be closed or 'filled'. It must remain an empty place (*lieu vide*). It refers to the essential unpredictable, the Holy Spirit of politics, to borrow an expression from Luhmann. This, of course, needs to be understood in view of the development of modernity. Walter Benjamin once addressed sovereignty as a response to a sense of history that no longer views the world theologically, nor has put it entirely behind it. Sovereignty, in his understanding of the term, becomes a key concept when the new truth dawns, that the destiny of Europeans lies in human hands only.[3]

As already briefly touched upon, Carl Schmitt was among those who emphasised the theological dimension of political power and Lefort as well points out that the symbolic function of power is of medieval and theological origin. Society is more than anything else *historical* and its symbolism remains inherent in the time dimension of modernity.[4] After the French revolution, Lefort notes, the political and its symbolic form came closer to a secular-religious meaning where the political itself was 'sacralised'.[5] Popular sovereignty recognised itself as a social force and invented new collective symbolic modes of expression against abuse of the proper political: corruption and elitism, and other phenomena where power fails to recognise that its mandate is limited. The people were handed the secularised sovereign power of the king:

> What emerges with democracy is the image of society as such, society as purely human but, at the same time, society *sui generis*, whose own nature requires objective knowledge. It is the image of a society which is homogeneous in principle, capable of being subsumed to the overview of knowledge and power, arising through the dissolution of the monarchical focus of legitimacy and the destruction of the architecture of bodies.[6]

Lefort notes that society appears in three ways, as *the state*, *the mass* and *the people*:

> It is the image of the omnipotent state, of a state both anonymous and, as de Tocqueville puts it, tutelary. It is also, in so far as inequality exists within the boundaries of the equality conditions, the image of a mass that passes the last judgement on good and evil, the true opinion. Lastly what emerges is the image of the people that remains indeterminate, but nevertheless is susceptible

of being determined, of being actualized on the level of phantasy as the image of the People-as-One.[7]

In modern society we find the remarkable status of power – not simply as the medium for domination or oppression, but as authority. Power, so long as it is detached from the autocrat, and remains *latent* as the power of the people, will always be subjected to attempts to reduce it to technique and narrow interests. Like Niklas Luhmann, Lefort conceives power both as a medium of struggle within an area of society and a general 'instituting moment'.[8] The destruction of the latent power of the People-as-One would eradicate 'the idea of society as such, bearing the knowledge of itself, transparent to itself and homogeneous, the idea of mass opinion, sovereign and normative, the idea of the tutelary state'.[9] In democracy, the king's body politic is revitalised as the guiding and guardian state with its immense powers and its legitimate monopoly of violence, and there is no way back to any other kind of sovereignty.

Lefort's distinction between politics and the political society helps us understand how societies achieve a symbolic representation of themselves as a unity but also as divided.[10] Lefort provides a connection between the sociological thesis of the birth of subjectivity and individualism, and the political project of autonomy which enables the individual to achieve political freedom through collective efforts. Indeed, a sociological point here is that the philosophical and constitutional debate rising in Europe in the late eighteenth century constituted a new symbolic level by which communities understood themselves and formed projections of a common future. European societies were from then on 'free' in the sense that they became more widely aware that they were 'alone', no longer decided over by the king or God. Symbolic representation enabled reflexivity about the social community as a project. Constitutional debates in Europe and America since the eighteenth-century revolutions can be seen as pivotal cases of such a reflexive logic, with an underlying message that a space of freedom exists. Society stretched above itself through reflexive struggle around essential concepts like sovereignty and freedom. The political discourse in the nineteenth century continued this disclosure with the introduction of social classes and divisions that questioned the commonness of the future. Public discourse increasingly reflected a class-divided society, but it also provided society with a mirror through which social classes and interests could realise what was at stake. A unified definition of sovereignty was unavailable, and totalitarian ideas and movements could find windows of opportunity.

Political pluralism remains a definitional feature of liberal societies. In Lefort's writings, it derives from *an empty space* that must not be allowed to be filled: absolutism always wishes to prevent society from access to an empty space where it can define itself. Although an argument for liberalism, it is a critique of the failure of liberalism to acknowledge conflict beyond politics. It has accepted – and policed – the division between self-reflective politics (*La politique*) as a sphere of formal equality, and the political society (*Le politique*) situated in a society of inequality. Debates on sovereignty from the years of the revolutions to the present day constitute the core of a sphere of reflexive representation. Irrespective of its substantial arguments, the sovereignty discourse, as it has developed over more than three centuries, has become regular and accepted action in a reflexive society. The sovereignty debate constitutes human power in the form of communication that enables society to observe its own political freedom and limitations. Sovereignty has become depersonalised and disembodied into principles regarding the people and the nation. With the constitutions in the nineteenth century, power became addressed in the language of law, that provided politics with an eternal, non-dominating set of rules constructed as protective human rights. Today, law is a coded communication in society but also distinct from society. That fact enabled the social and political struggle to proceed with a common symbolic language and prevented society from closing the empty space of political freedom. No-one could take complete possession of political power, only have it temporarily delegated.

Following Lefort, Pierre Rosanvallon states that the political 'exists by virtue of the fact that there is such a thing as a "society," whose members, by acknowledging it as a totality, afford meaning to its constituent parts'.[11] In speaking about 'the political', the reference is democracy and law, state and nation, equality and justice, identity and sovereignty, and citizenship and civility: 'in short, of everything that constitutes in its essence political life beyond the immediate field of partisan competition for political power, everyday governmental action, and the ordinary function of institutions'.[12] As a project, the political is the process whereby a human collective cannot be reduced to a population. It gradually becomes a fully fledged community:

> It is constituted through an always contentious process whereby the explicit or implicit rules of what can be shared and accomplished in common – the rules which give form to the life of the polity – are elaborated. Whatever the catalogue of cultural and social facts, economic variables, and institutional rationales, it is impossible to decipher society at its most essential level without bringing to light the nerve centre from which the very fact of its institution originates.[13]

To Rosanvallon, politics (*La politique*) refers to the formal and immediate competition for political power. In contrast, the political (*Le politique*) refers to the polity or the political community. He understands it as a field where individuals constitute a collective. He also describes it as a project where the population transforms itself into a specific community.[14] He sees it as a life form at distance from the game of politics. It is constituted by everything that is political outside of politics. Rosanvallon argues that it has of itself no ontological structure but is an inherently historical category. As a screen or a medium, it is where politics looks to sense the interests and will of the political community, and where the political signals what it wants.[15]

In this view the political is the political dimension of society – its unobservable collective existence, but detectable in its multitude of collective expressions that speak about itself; about what 'we' must allow or not allow to happen. One might say it is the medium and outcome of political practice based on society as justification and subtext. Rosanvallon argues that it is 'the mark of society acknowledged by its members as a whole that affords meaningfulness to its constituent parts'.[16] It is a 'synthetic order', the self-observation of a community, which then constitutes it as a (political) society. In this constitutive and symbolic process, basic concepts like democracy and popular sovereignty comment on themselves, leading to experimentation and expression. The specific *forms* of observation and commenting appear contested, from deliberation via manifestations to Molotov cocktails.

Rosanvallon brought the concept of the political closer to the sociological by understanding it as a modality of collective action. The idea of the political that is observable only in its expressions, suggests that it can be understood in the historical contextualisation of temper and colour. It consists of a language that thematises 'our' interests and concerns, 'our' customs and ways of life, 'our' place. Taken together popular sovereignty is the overall message of the political. Historical examination to verbalise and illustrate notions about the just and fair supreme position of the people is a way to encircle the political. Rosanvallon begins his discussion with what it unintentionally brings along: unfulfilled expectations, dissatisfaction, disappointment, resentment.[17] Frustrations spread as a result of the discrepancy between the idea of the *political* and its 'fundamentals' of equality and justice, and the sociological reality of differentiation and individualisation.

Popular sovereignty had more fertile conditions as a concept in opposition to tyranny and war when it simply meant freedom from oppression. In a democratic context, where the liberal argument of majority rule defines democracy, it must justify itself differently. The development of individual rights illustrates the trend: 'It is the *juridical* consecration of the individual which leads to the rejection of substantive conceptions of the social as archaic and unbearable.'[18] The people is a constitutional and symbolic idea that has become unrepresentable. The political, following Rosanvallon, expresses itself in the tension between individual and collective self-government that are equally fundamental for democracy. Populism, particularly in the period 2010–2020, was one of the aporias of this tension. Gaps between constitutionally stated equality and growing social inequality, stirred by demagoguery, changed the political landscape of nations like France, Italy, Sweden and the US.

The political and the sociological

The political is an empirical presupposition and a *raison d'être* for politics. It is the totality of political sentiment and the discourse about 'us'. It is a social field that can be historically traced and (by way of its public expressions) sociologically mapped. Obvious examples are the struggles on national independence, on voting rights, on the heated debates on other individual and social rights. It is the ensemble of political experiments in freedom triggered by the indeterminacy of the future of society, through which groups (cohorts, minorities, classes) make claims on behalf of themselves, or of all. Their logic is not numerical, nor are they appealing to pure reason. They are simply demanding *de facto* respect for long since constitutionally accepted aims, such as the absence of violence against women, the absence of police violence, a carbon-free future, protection against corruption and nepotism, for peace, for living species, oceans, and rainforests, and so on.

In contrast, 'politics' is a term reserved for the relatively autonomous, self-referential and multi-institutional domain that draws on norms, rhetoric and agendas through contestation about making binding decisions for society. It involves policies, party manifestos, legislation. Politics is inherently concerned with the production of legitimacy that can only be cultivated in the political. The self-reference of politics must build on a contingent environment of impulses, and in this sense the political is the wider political dimension of the state as a community. The political, as it emerged with the European nation-state and then articulated in the constitutions, is a discursive dimension of the national community imagined in its political totality. It is the environment of politics, where verbal and non-verbal expressions of protest, appeal and acclamation take place among all concerned.

The political, I would say, is a philosophical concept turned sociological, because only sociology can demonstrate its existence and nature. A task for political sociology is to explain why groups of many shapes and inclinations turn their heated anger towards politics and the state, irrespective of what is moral, legal or profitable. What is the basis for resentment and desperation in civilised and comparably stable countries like Sweden, France and the US? We must turn to the political as an idea and a logic: to the political background of a foreground of politics. The political is a conceptual presumption we need to make sense about constitutional politics, because the constitution cannot write itself, and delegated politics cannot alter its preconditions, as we have seen that Sieyès made clear. Political order must rest on a *social* order. Its paradox is that it remains a 'presently absent' that marks the outside of politics. The political is an imaginary reality, the background for politics to exist and appear democratic. It is where politics originates and has its constant reference. It doesn't justify any unified ideology or regime but exists as a constant reminder of its existence; it is the historical dimension of the distinction between political power and formal decision-making that today is named democracy.

This again indicates that popular sovereignty cannot avoid paradoxical descriptions: the political is non-politics: the greater purpose of making decisions for all, the purpose of having a *legitimate* monopoly of power ensuring order and welfare. This was the insight of Rousseau. What he helped to clarify was the foundation for politics, its *raison d'être* that enables politics to make binding decisions for all. The distinction between Bodin's sovereignty and the sovereign, or Sieyès's constituent and constituted powers, shares similarities to the distinction between the political and politics in that the one cannot be explained without the other. As in Schmitt, too, there is a distinction at play: not a friend–enemy dichotomy, but a distinction between the inside and outside of politics. Whereas the inside is constituted by 'agonistic' struggle for power between government and opposition to make binding decisions, the enigmatic people constitutes its environment of latent antagonism.[19] The political provides the modern logic of legitimacy that goes beyond the principle of political representation.

One may see the political as the collective dimension of society – society seen as conflict, solidarity and will, due to a world of finite resources. It can be associated with notions of the general will and popular sovereignty, as long as we do not stick with descriptions of it as harmonious but also as conflictual. From the political, politics differentiated itself as the sphere of power of binding decisions, and the monopoly of legitimate means of violence. How formal politics operates with such principles or constructed ontologies as environment is a key question for constitutionally oriented sociology. The concept of democracy, we might say, refers to the nature of the bridging of the gap between the political and politics. There are many such bridges, representation being clearly the prioritised, and therefore vital in the definition of contemporary democracy. But, as I have argued, the medium of representation is insufficient and deficient in societies where formal political equality is embedded in growing social inequality.

Without the organisation and institutionalisation of power society will get nowhere, and this cannot happen without the political. Lefort argues that the empty space of the political that political forces wish to invade cannot be ignored or made into an abstract idiom.[20] Its latency cannot become manifest as polling, general elections or debates among elite persons on prime time TV. Nor can it vanish; it represents a never-ending, if negative, principle of legitimacy. It is always present, if only latently or indirectly, as voices involved in conflict discourses. The political never speaks with one voice; from it stem a wide variety of collective claims and demands that struggle for the interests of classes, minorities or humanity as such. They are particular *and* universal. This is what politics must relate to on the basis of the always 'absent presence' of the political.

This view on the political as the home of the concept of popular sovereignty brings the thinking about democracy back on track after some decades of misplaced neo-Kantian idealism. The approach signifies political realism without cynicism; political legitimacy is legitimation *qua* political procedure and observation, and therefore to be seen as largely self-legitimation without ambitions of being directed by universal truth and reason. It is nevertheless fundamental.[21] Legitimacy is guided by political rationality, not understood as means–ends calculations, but as the sensitivity of politics towards its environment – the political.

The political and popular sovereignty

From these considerations we see contours of what popular sovereignty means today. It is a concept that historically and normatively places citizens in an increasingly subjective or reflexive position *vis-à-vis* power. Sovereignty is the political in its self-description. From describing the God-given ruling power, political theory enabled it to be related to the popular and its representatives, and it is now a concept for arresting the erosion of state self-determination, and, with it, a functioning democracy. It is historically shaped by the relationship between the ruling and the ruled that it describes. It accepts and understands the coercive nature of power, and therefore leaves out naive delusions about its workings. It explains the role of *the people vis-à-vis* politics. Consequently, the concept is pushed out to the site of rhetorical struggle when democracy or state independence is in flux. It formulates the idea of legitimacy more specifically than notions of 'democracy' that can opportunistically be reduced to a rather thin and a-historic principle of democratic representation. Equally, the self-contradictory character of newly constructed concepts like 'shared sovereignty', 'pluralisation of sovereignty' and 'European sovereignty' evidently demonstrates their function as smokescreens covering irreconcilable entities.

Based on the work of the British philosopher Michael Oakeshott, Martin Loughlin points out three basic features of the modern state that sovereignty expresses: internal coherence, external independence and supremacy of law.[22] These features mark the distinction of the political from economic and other forms of power. In this sense sovereignty is a representation of the autonomy of the political. Sovereignty also marks the difference from the system of law, which concerns what is legal, not what is politically appropriate. Oakeshott refers to *societas* as the relationship between citizens and the state. What was called public power in the classical age referred to both unlimited power and loyalty among citizens. Hobbes stated that the representative Person was the opinion and belief of the multitude as authors. The relationship between public office and the people is a political relationship characterised as legitimacy. With the rise of public administration, constitutions and political representation, sovereignty had its meaning transferred from power to authority, and the question of legitimacy was theorised as inherent in politics and the state.

Popular sovereignty refers to the *acknowledgement* of people's power in the state. This has been commented on by thinkers of sovereignty since Bodin: 'Understood as an expression of public power, sovereignty resides in the established institutional framework of the state.'[23] It is a function of a political and public relationship between the ruler and the ruled. The ruler is formulated in the constitution as unified, despite separation of powers and a highly specialised administration. The constitution as nexus demonstrates internal coherence. Sovereignty is reproduced by the state apparatus, which ensures stability, safety and peace. It is assumed by the sovereign that the government and the state apparatus realise their obligations; that they operate on behalf of the general trust that the sovereign authorises. Sovereignty is institutionalised by constitutional law. The political is an imagined nation reproduced by welfare and protection associated with statehood. The government operates competently and coherently according to law, and its capacity rests on public acknowledgement. The two dimensions of the legally bounded state, the horizontal (competence) and the vertical (capacity), are fundamentally entangled. Sovereignty without the one or the other is inconceivable.

The political demonstrates its potency through symbolisation and representation. It cannot remain entirely abstract; it must prove its existence to itself, as in cases of collective protests and demands for democracy and equality. It relies on a different notion of power from formal politics: it mediates in Arendt's sense a power for change, in contrast to the zero-sum power game of formal politics. The power of the political is of itself generally invisible, non-institutionalised, unpredictable, ungraspable, sudden, symbolic, uncoordinated, emotional, at times violent. In each struggle it confirms its constitutional status to itself. It marks its rationality as non-economic, non-private, non-scientific, and so on. As truly political, it defends Lefort's empty place of democracy, and as what can never be observed in its entirety. It refers to a historically generated principle inherent in the Europe-modelled history of nation-states, as the territorial foundation for modern democracy. It appears as: a) a concept, b) a latent *Stimmung* or sensemaking in the people, and c) as collective action; even explicit emotional outbreaks. If this latter form of collective action reaches a certain magnitude and intensity, we speak of revolution.

Sovereignty is a reference for political unity in a political sense, but, as Claude Lefort noted, it carries an identity that remains undefined.[24] Society finds itself in constant internal conflict and can rarely come fully to terms with its own representation as a people. It has become too differentiated to keep its political identity as its priority and it must regress to a multitude in front of the ballot box and leave its will to constituted power – or to demagogues that dedicate their message to the unmediated People once more. There are always, as we know, those who feel that they have the gift to reinstate themselves as sovereign 'king' in the contemporary complex society. What passes as popular sovereignty is not always on the side of the people. The political history of constitutional democracies in Europe has narrated an opposition between unmediated democracy and representation; it has taken many forms: romanticism vs technocracy, judicial pragmatism vs formalism, socialist majority rule vs liberal pluralism, urban rationalism vs. rural populism, and so on.

Rosanvallon points to the dynamic of this fluctuation from the revolution to the present day, as constitutive for French democracy.[25] He argues that the optimal mediation between democracy and liberalism leads to a diversification of the expressions of popular sovereignty. It involves a multiplying of sites and spheres at which popular sovereignty leaves its messages, and a certain distancing from the old metaphysics of the general will. When the people took the place of the king as the sovereign, it first appeared in a liberal abstract and a democratic concrete version. Then, at the beginning of the twentieth century, it became a reference, or signification in a representative and moderate democracy. Today, the people are present in its absentness, or manifest only as multitude and as disparate segmental expressions of power.

It is necessary to distinguish even more sharply than Rosanvallon between popular sovereignty and its social expressions. While expressions constantly come in a wide and inexhaustive range of forms, popular sovereignty itself ought to be understood in a 'monist' manner.[26] This point is of importance today since some express an interest in differentiating or getting rid of the concept of popular sovereignty altogether. Today popular sovereignty expresses itself in differentiated ways. The range of groups that speak for the good society (involving national, ethnic, religious, sexual and political freedom), as well as their imaginative selection of collective means of expression, multiply. The firework of shapes and colours, for the planet, global population, nature, democracy or peace, can be attributed to a unifying and state-protected concept of popular sovereignty. Whether they are cannot be decided outside of politics, but is for the majority and the future to decide.

Expressions of popular sovereignty are rarely in line with itself. There are 'critical' moments when the popular voice in fact appears as a solid, unified and self-conscious majority expressing its will and not prepared to yield. On other occasions, like the 6 January 2021 attack on the US Congress building, action is predominantly a product of immediate demagoguery and long-term societal pathologies. The incident at Capitol Hill had a history and could be diagnosed, regardless of one's political view, as a symptom of serious defects in the relationship between the American political and politics.

Negative sovereignty

Resentment today is a product of sensations justified in a very present and concrete sense about a collective will that cannot be individualised away, transferred to foreign powers or dissolved in any other way. Society consists of individual citizens, of social groups and of a *people* beyond immediate sociological configurations. In democratic nations, an image of the people as different from the sum of its individuals exists as a motive and reference for political power. Addressed by political philosophy and philosophy of law, popular sovereignty exists as a conceptual, political projection, an imaginary of the political as a negation of politics with latent *counter-democratic* power, to use Rosanvallon's paradoxical term. People are concerned when the idea of the people or the political seems to be disregarded by those in power. Lapavitsas is probably right that 'For the plebeian classes in Europe, sovereignty has never been anathema. On the contrary, it is understood as the power to make and apply laws, to design and implement social and economic policy, and to elect and hold to account those who administer those laws and policies.'[27] It represents the right to be consulted and to reject.

Once, popular sovereignty did not distinguish between the ideals of equality and democracy. The American and French constitutional processes did not separate the society of economic and political equality.[28] In the nineteenth century, sovereignty had a concrete but plural form, as a legitimate shape of what came to be called democracy, involving a diversity of expressions in the nation, with a plurality of expressive and symbolic means accompanying claims. These were all practices to legitimate power, most evidently of the negative kind, and therefore unwelcomed by governing power. However, the emphasis on the electoral channel and the enforcement of representation tended to de-politicise culture. Later, through privatisation, individualisation, alternative channels for confidence and appropriation of society were undermined. With the growing confidence in capitalism, the ideals of equality and democracy were differentiated empirically as well as in theory. To avoid instability, democracy was operationalised as representation.

Nevertheless, negative sovereignty, the widely heard 'no thanks', constantly targets the task of prevention. Fragmented, at times violent, opposition in a complex society with grave problems leaves negative protest a viable form of action and appears today as a critical contribution to democracy. The distinction between positive and negative sovereignty is difficult to distinguish clearly. To act resolutely against police racism, harassment against women, military oppression and political neglect is to oppose the existing reality but also to implicitly demand an alternative society without systematic denigrating abuse of power. Veto-democracy or dissident democracy deriving from the political thus may have affirmative dimensions.

Party politics is increasingly challenged by pluralism based on a multitude of non-ideological and non-consistent demands and interests. Pluralisation of group identities that experience oppression implies more complex demands based on different non-traditional affiliations, and with political effects. The idea of representation is confronted with new forms of sociality and claims. The gap between constituent and constituted power, for instance measured as low election turn-out, seems unbridgeable. Representation cannot avoid its paradoxical nature. Furthermore, technocratisation of politics in liberal democracies, the 'failure to develop a comprehensive understanding of problems associated with the organizations of a shared world', causes a sense of political fatigue.[29] On the other hand, technocratic and notoriously moderate policies have lost confidence in large portions of the citizenry. A way out for politics has been to concentrate on winning elections by presenting all-in-one, short-term solutions. Cartel-like parties have been established around a front-figure, as in Holland, Italy, Britain and, most successfully, in France. Party politics relies on polls, focus groups and de-politicised 'analysis' to decode the identities and preferences of the electorate. Yet it is hardly feasible to aggregate the fluid diversity of interests and clusters into stable bases of support. Governmental politics is under the influence of the noise of spin, lobbying, political entertainment and scandal. The complexity of politics, in contrast to the simplicity of the political, causes it to frequently lose sight of the constituent power from which it is constituted. The decline of European social democracy since the 1990s is illustrative.

Popular sovereignty finds direct forms of expression for the purpose of placing particular and universal demands on politics in an age of urgency. To an increasing share of the population, sovereignty is seen as expressed through everything from petitions via civil disobedience to vandalism. The political with its sovereignty is itself quite diverse in its output, while still referring to its unity. We must distinguish between popular sovereignty as a singular and abstract entity, and its diverse collective forms of action, including its 'populist' and violent forms. The elective channel is perceived as incapable of dealing with the great problems concerning nature and human relationships. The biased electoral systems of large nations like the USA and UK are for many citizens an argument for ignoring elections as channels of democratic change.

Popular sovereignty describing the space of the political stands in a tension to electoral politics, in part because the latter is majoritarian, in part because it is *not*. Electoral systems tend to favour a narrow mainstream centre that becomes magnified. Rosanvallon argues for a mixed model of plural forms of legitimacy, that may more coherently reflect the voices of 'the people'. What Rosanvallon calls a 'sovereignty of prevention' is a *negative* sovereignty that opposes what is on the agenda of elite politics or what they must take responsibility for. This has been an inherent form of political expression in democracies for two centuries but is magnified in the process of growing symbolic representation of politics in the media and spectacle society.

In the tradition of Montesquieu, Rosanvallon addresses the possibility of 'organisations of distrust' to compensate for the erosion of confidence in representative democracy. Counter-democratic forces may compensate for the thin and distrusted electoral system and at the same time reinforce it. Rosanvallon argues that counter-democracy of distrust may 'thicken' democracy in the wake of the hollowing out of the electoral system.[30] Besides the electoral system of legitimacy that was gradually extended during the nineteenth century and provided an unambiguous direct form of leadership election, another interest in a more permanent form of control over the elected government emerged. Negative sovereignty expressed sanctions and preventions by civil society, the trade unions, the courts and the streets. History reminds us that the potential of counter-democratic action could serve as compensation for the erosion of conventional democracy.[31] The democracy of expression is another way of demonstrating sovereignty in theatrical and rhetorical forms of demands, claims, protests, and so on.

Seeing sovereignty as a general denominator for popular protest corresponds to modern sociological diagnosis of an identity-oriented and socially unequal society that can no longer be projected as a coherent totality. Its expressions may take very different routes. Resentment awakens when popular sovereignty as a principle is seen as neglected or ignored. Disrespect may appear in statements, decisions and acts on the part of the ruling elite that seem to ignore or contradict the general interest, or in any other way act according to their own 'rules'.

What Rosanvallon calls negative sovereignty refers to protests to abuse of power without suggesting alternatives. Political negation is precisely what takes place frequently in all countries. Groups form loose alliances behind a single 'no' and single out the police or public buildings as targets for their resentment. This veto-demos, this spontaneous, formless difference, often without any programme or organisation, is a product of social media and the persistence of rigid politics more than two centuries after the revolutions. To Rosanvallon, counter-democratic movements of negative sovereignty are one consequence of the distance from elite politics, their ways and arrogance. This is a democratic phenomenon that has been inherent in democratic development throughout modernity. While some waves of discontent and resentment are channelled into populist movements, others die out after letting out energies of protest. They may ground themselves in the semantics of populism, nationalism, anti-racism, feminism or socialism, but most frequently this is a matter of issue politics with no other platform than the negative.

Claims that these are anti-democratic or immoral disturbances must be sociologically addressed. Windows may be broken, and protests may need to be stopped by the police. Groups may be right-wing and racist; they nevertheless contribute to the wide variety of counter-democratic occurrences. They may be informed by conspiracy theories and demagoguery. Rather than making moral judgements, sociology needs to compare and judge even incoherent expressions in conjunction with other forms, such as political party initiatives, public media debate and elections. They are diverse expressions of portions of popular sovereignty, and one cannot assume that they express 'the people' in its totality. All existing definitions of the people address the sociological general will in a particular way – numerically based on universal suffrage, identity-based or based in *de jure* equality – none alone completely embraces the people.

Populism and the sovereignty claim

In what is now associated with populism, counter-power is absorbed into machineries of movements and parties, to energise simplified demands. Populism is an effect, and often a syndrome, in which the multi-party system seems unable to sense the identities and grievances of the people. However, the populism label is frequently used by interests that seek to 'justify a legalistic, formal conception of politics'.[32] Used as a *stigmata* the term distracts from the importance of understanding unconventional and 'popular' forms of political demands and expression. Populism describes occurrences and forms of articulation deriving from the political, as an 'infrastructure of society', on which politics is built. European societies have scarcely begun the debate on how to *benefit* from this diversity of popular sovereignty, at least not on a large scale. European nations remain relatively loyal to the risky large-scale experiment in democracy directed by the EU. However, there may be limits as to how far a multi-state union can move away from the Enlightenment conception of democracy before it departs from political liberalism in any recognisable sense. How thin can a definition of democracy be before resentment spreads even to the middle class? The imperfect ability of politics to listen to the many voices of the people has been handled by simply containing it within a greater project. The dual tendency of trans-nationalisation and juridification at the expense of parliaments is observed in several countries. When questions considered important for national sovereignty are processed as mere technicalities, legitimacy problems are likely to occur. A likely hypothesis is presented by Rosanvallon: technocratic control and populist reaction are reinforcing one another in creating obstacles for a pluralist (collective and individual) representation of the people.

Rosanvallon seems willing to invest much confidence in supra-state governance, and he understates the power of politics to play the game of self-legitimation. He makes a lot of the inherent paradox (structural gap) of democracy that might lead to crisis. In his book on sovereignty in France since the revolution, Rosanvallon argues that re-symbolisation of politics ought to imply 'the constitution of an unlocalizable people in a living community'.[33] The creating of an imaginary is envisioned in almost romantic terms, at the expense of actual social conditions. He seems to overestimate the coherent power of the political in making real political change. Of interest in a sociology of sovereignty is not so much what ought to be done to repair democratic aporias beyond the nation-state, as much as observing: 1) how society connects narrow definitions of democracy with numeric and unambiguous techniques of legitimacy into governmental technocratisation; 2) how this narrowing is applied in national and international politics and in European federalism; and 3) how such trends facilitate non-intended counter-democratic tendencies. The unintended and unanticipated consequences of narrowing the definition of democracy and increased social inequality are likely to yield counter-democratic reactions, spanning from issue-related street riots and protests to right-wing populism. The list of which became rather long from around 2007 to the present day.

Delimitations of the political

The boundary of the political, then, concerns the semantic undercurrents that may or may not bring topics on to the agenda of politics. It is reproduced in the communication of the political itself. In this sense the political is autonomous; it operates according to its own standards. It appears moral, as in both sides of the abortion debate; it may appear moral-aesthetic, as in a conflict over a public monument; and it may appear more or less scientific, as in how to combat a pandemic. It includes external criteria selectively according to the history of its own political communication. The controversies and hegemonies decide to what extent they are transformed into political criteria. The political is no sphere; rather, it is the fertile field of political communication and sentiment from which politics grows. It appears everywhere in the form of communicative distinctions between our society/not our society and public/private. It might appear as rational justification, but is generally a never-ending struggle to be heard, that simultaneously is a dispute on how politics ought to be legitimated.

The political evolved through the early modern age, and its stages have been described by the history of political theory: transformations are identified from the point of view of law (natural law, Reason of state, positive law, political jurisprudence, modern constitutionalism), as well as in politics (political representation, sovereignty, constitutional democracy, the welfare state). The complex interrelationship between the differentiated semantic domains of law and politics is acknowledged by the more politically inclined jurists, like Carl Schmitt and Hermann Heller, philosophers like Lefort, or juristically sensitive sociologists like Max Weber and Niklas Luhmann – scholars who think that politics is not legitimated simply by universal suffrage, but rests on a legal, historical and territorially defined culture that questions the unavoidable tension between politics and the political.

The political and the constitution

The new constitutions in the nineteenth century supported both ruling and oppositional sides in conflicts. They have been instruments of change, but also of stability and control, depending on the state and its crises. The Norwegian constitution of 1814 stated unfulfilled expectations of popular sovereignty and national independence and served the opposition. Generally, constitutions have since the 1860s secured the authority of state institutions; they constructed political long-term horizons for political action. Constitutions have continued to *stabilise distinctions* between politics, the political and the private sphere. They enable popular influence within constraints, and they mark the action boundaries of political institutions. They mediate, as I continue to emphasise, a paradox in that they provide power to the people *and* control the people by securing the institutional power of politics. This as a continuation of the paradox of democracy; the ultimate power of the people *and* its submission to political elites.

With the modern constitution, power is transferred from political to legal institutions, which transforms the power of a collective people to individual rights. The constitution is the liberal medium of controlled state intervention into society.

As an effect of liberalism, and then of fascist and communist totalitarianism, the turn from negative to positive constitutionalism constrained power and people, stabilised the separation between state powers and normalised a moderate conception of democracy. Generally, the constitution is no longer seen as an obstacle for political change, but as a stabilising medium for formal politics in its struggle with public debt, microbes, climate change, migration, terrorism and invasion that needs to be met by unified politics. Democratic social struggle today consists in *defending* the constitution against misinterpretation. Once, the point of political opposition was to argue from the point of view of social justice; now the crux is to be on the side of the constitution. Even radical social change must be orchestrated constitutionally, by means of the 'objective' justification of courts. Increasingly, intervening and expanding constitutionalism and legalism of political life place the constitution in the midst of political conflicts, concerning fundamentals like sovereignty and democracy. Loughlin argues that: 'The meaning of constitutionalism changes: rather than connoting limitation on government, it is a power-generating discourse. With no fixed meaning, adherence to the constitution changes through time in accordance with social, economic, and political circumstances.'[34] By this, law makes itself 'dirty' and must ultimately fall back on certain prevailing political values on how to interpret the constitution. What sovereignty is, cannot be decided legally.

Constitutions and their implicit or explicit statements of sovereignty are attributed with a particular value, but they remain contested. The need for political legitimacy is universal, while the liberal form of legitimacy construction (general elections, human rights, public deliberation) also describes the current form of democratic power. Power is explained in a way that justifies its use. State power is made into a part of the solution and not a part of the problem, as Bernard Williams puts it. This means that legitimate state power is not simply coercive power. For there to be a legitimate government, Williams argues, 'there must be a legitimate story, which explains why state power can be used to coerce some people rather than others and allow people to restrict other people's freedom in some ways rather than others'.[35] These stories distinguish societies of legitimate rule from other societies with stories that don't appear credible.

Constitutions are key actual or virtual documents of legitimation for the state monopoly of legitimate force.[36] Formally they authorise the voice of the constituent power, and in real politics they are documents for legitimation of the state. Their centrality lies in the text but even more in the discourses and conventions that circulate with the constitution as reference. With Claude Lefort, a democratic regime is 'founded upon the legitimacy of a debate as to what is legitimate and what is illegitimate, a debate which is necessarily without any guarantor and without any end'.[37] Lefort's definition fits well a perspective that emphasises constitutional communication and political legitimacy as formative and conflictual processes. When looking at the question of political legitimacy as not a moral but a political question, the constitution reoccurs in history as a locus for controversy that influences the meaning and legitimacy of politics and the state. Morality is mostly involved as a rhetorical resource.

Constitutions are thus seen as key statements of a contested kind that in conflict will yield victory for one side and defeat for another. The political domain consists of a plurality of interests, arguments and beliefs that confront one another to avoid violence. Diversity and contestation are therefore signs of a functioning political domain. Political realism parts with idealism on the question of pluralism of legal *foundations* in the political domain. Realists would argue that there can only exist one constitution, and only one sovereign. There can be only one master, or else political authority is undermined. The conflict therefore tends to be revisited and renegotiated. Contestation on constitutional questions serves to contain and resolve disagreements in a stable and formal fashion that tends to lead to new disagreement.

Conclusion

The concept of sovereignty in a world of growing international cooperation and integration, it is said, is now of marginal political and legal importance. 'Transnationalists' argue for a softening of its definition, or ignoring the concept altogether. However, through juridification and transnationalisation, a sociological hypothesis is that the concept of sovereignty is likely to attain renewed relevance as a contested political issue. As the life-course of the concept of sovereignty narrates the story of the independent nation-state, it is far from approaching its end. The dual question of popular and national sovereignty concerns the definition of the state seen in a political-legal constitutional approach. Undermining of the doctrine of sovereignty would lead to a transformation of the definition of the state, with far-reaching repercussions for its relationship with its people and the world.

Notes

1 Rosanvallon, *Democracy Past and Future*, p. 31.
2 Rasmussen, *Political Legitimacy*.
3 Thiem, 'Schmittian shadows', 9.

4 Lefort, *The Political Forms of Modern Society*, p. 305.
5 Ibid., p. 275.
6 Ibid., p. 304.
7 Ibid., p. 304.
8 Ibid., p. 305.
9 Ibid., p. 305.
10 Natalie Doyle, 'Democracy as socio-cultural project on individual and collective sovereignty: Claude Lefort, Marcel Gauchet and the French debate on modern autonomy.' *Thesis Eleven*, 75:1 (2003), 69–95, at 74.
11 Pierre Rosanvallon, 'The political theory of democracy.' In Oliver Flügel-Martinsen, Franziska Martinsen, Stephen W. Sawyer and Daniel Schulz (eds) *Pierre Rosanvallon's Political Thought: Interdisciplinary Approaches* (Bielefeld: Bielefeld University Press, 2019), p. 24.
12 Lefort, *The Political Forms of Modern Society*, p. 305.
13 Rosanvallon, 'The political theory of democracy', pp. 24–38.
14 Rosanvallon, *Democracy Past and Future*, pp. 12, 36.
15 'une ércan et un moyen': Pierre Rosanvallon, *Pour une histoire conceptuelle du politique*. Leçon inaugurale faite au Collège de France le jeudi 28 mars 2002 (Paris: Editions du Seuil, 2003), p. 20.
16 Rosanvallon, *Democracy Past and Future*, p. 34.
17 Rosanvallon, 'The political theory of democracy', p. 28.
18 Ibid., p. 29.
19 See Chantal Mouffe, *The Democratic Paradox* (London: Verso, 2005).
20 Claude Lefort, 'The permanence of the theologico-political?' In Claude Lefort, *Democracy and Political Theory* (Cambridge: Polity Press, 1988), pp. 213–255.
21 Rasmussen, *Political Legitimacy*.
22 Martin Loughlin, *The Idea of Public Law* (Oxford: Oxford University Press, 2003), p. 75.
23 Ibid., p. 82.
24 Lefort, *The Political Forms of Modern Society*, p. 166.
25 Rosanvallon, *Democracy Past and Future*.
26 Ibid., pp. 199–200.
27 Costas Lapavitsas, *The Left Case Against the EU* (Cambridge: Polity Press, 2019), p. 130.
28 Pierre Rosanvallon, *The Society of Equals* (Cambridge, MA: Harvard University Press, 2013), p. 4.
29 Pierre Rosanvallon, *Counter-democracy: Politics in an Age of Distrust* (Cambridge: Cambridge University Press, 2008), p. 22.
30 Ibid., p. 12.
31 Ibid., p. 9.
32 Michael P. Crozier and Adrian Little, 'Democratic voice: popular sovereignty.' *Australian Journal of Political Science*, 47:3 (2012), 333–346, at 343.
33 Rosanvallon, *La démocratie inachevée*, p. 250.
34 Martin Loughlin, *Political Jurisprudence* (Oxford: Oxford University Press, 2017), p. 167.

35 Bernard Williams, *In the Beginning Was the Deed: Realism and Moralism in Political Argument* (Princeton, NJ: Princeton University Press, 2005), p. 95.
36 Gray, *Enlightenment's Wake*, p. 74; Sleat, *Liberal Realism*, p. 170.
37 Lefort, 'The permanence of the theologico-political?', p. 39; see Paul Blokker, 'Politics and the political in sociological constitutionalism.' In Blokker and Thornhill (eds) *Sociological Constitutionalism*, p. 185; Ingram, 'The politics of Claude Lefort's political', 43.

6

Constitutional symbolism

Democratic societies constantly communicate about what norms ought to be legitimate. The representation of society as a nation-state is itself a work of communication and symbolism. Its task is to maintain the construction of unity despite diversity. This is the work of constituent power, which mirrors itself in *the state*. The state is what the constituent power achieves. The concept of the state refers to an objective and symbolic reality. The latter is associated with imaginaries of freedom, democracy, self-determination and justice. Symbolism underpins social cohesion and integration and occasionally social conflict.

A constant challenge for political power is to handle the split between the actual and the potential that makes policies appear insufficient and deceptive. The gap between present facts and expectations every so often leads to resentment. The discrepancy is inherent in the hierarchy of representative democracy and must be made invisible or trivial with political techniques for generating sufficient legitimacy through symbolist politics, political leadership, stylisation, TV charisma, social media presence, and so on. Such mechanisms of trust may discourage others from using their freedom to protest. This means that the relationship between the political and politics is always a symbolically mediated relationship. We cannot make our judgements on politics without the symbolically mediated in mind.

In this chapter I address symbolic aspects of constitutional politics with emphasis on popular and national sovereignty. I discuss 1) the relevance of the constitutional symbolism of Rousseau; 2) the typification of constitutional cultures; and 3) Bourdieu's concept of symbolic violence, and more generally sovereignty as story. My intention is to show that constitutional disputes are deeply connected to past and present culture, and to affective identification through symbols as power. I will not fully enter the debate on the practice of symbolism and the comparative character of constitutional cultures. The point is to bring further understanding to the multidimensional dynamics of sovereignty as societal communication in and about the nation and the state that include symbolism filled with stabilising and oppositional powers.

Alongside its instrumental functions, the constitution is itself a symbol. Although rarely actually seen or read by citizens, it nevertheless symbolises the existence of the nation as a political society. It is a focal object with references to grand ideas that otherwise is only conceptualised in political philosophy and history, and only at certain moments through constitutional moments and social manifestations. A dual legal–political symbolism operates here: a legal reference point for politics and a political reference point for law, that together provide legal identity to a political subject. The constitution is a programme for the norms of a political order, providing foremost the legitimation of basic values of personal liberty, division of powers and popular sovereignty. It runs through history as an anchoring for innumerable rituals, celebrations and other manifestations; it serves as the negation of sarcasm about the perfect democracy. In Scandinavia, for instance, premodern sagas narrated the unification of the nation, and provided national identity through centuries of dependence and suppression. In all nations one can find non-instrumental collections of 'the political' within a historical nation-state context.

Rousseau's symbolic constitutionalism

As is evident from the subtitle of Rousseau's *Du Contrat Social: ou Principes du droit politique*, he was concerned with the study of *political law*, which controls the relationship between governmental institutions, and acquires its legitimacy from society. *Droit politique* was to become the philosophical study of sovereignty, with its frame of reference in Rousseau rather than in Hobbes on law as the prerogative of the sovereign. Rousseau's republican view of freedom is not the opposite of law, because freedom is not absence of force or constraint. Rather, it is enabled through the legal effort of the collective. The general will is an enhancement and expression of liberty. Law is the medium of self-government, and the necessary expression of people's collective will. When law is grounded in the will of all, it enhances liberty and political equality under the condition of solidarity. On this the general will rests and constitutes the state and its government.

As noted earlier, the general will cannot be invented out of nothing. Rousseau is very conscious in *The Social Contract* and other political writings of the sociological and cultural conditions that need to be in place for the general will to fulfil its task. For law to heal the tension between the sovereignty of the people and the sovereign state, it must reflect the beliefs and customs of the people in a wide sense. Rousseau's concern about the community's ability to promote collective sentiments and civic participation was reflected in his attention to customs and mores. To reproduce solidarity as the foundation for the moral order of a collective will, rituals, ceremonies and symbols were seen by Rousseau as ingredients in the making of citizens – and above all in producing a public space.

The centrality of the symbolic is thus evident in Rousseau's writings on constitutional affairs.[1] What creates citizens even more than laws are institutions and rites that demonstrate for every community member their mutual interdependence. In his discussion about Poland, he notes that bonds inherent in religious ceremonies, games, exercises and spectacles attach citizens to their fatherland and to each other through their hearts and spirits.[2] He was sympathetic to religious practice because of its quality to make the individual love his or her duties. In his recommendations for new constitutional constituencies, substantial weight was put on simple rituals and ceremonial practices.[3] It was essential to Rousseau that emotions and rituals were not hidden away in the private sphere, leaving a gap for abstract and non-emotional reasoning to flourish. Laws must be produced by representatives that are able to reason with the hearts and minds of citizens.

Rousseau's notion of self-government based on the general will rests on symbolic public practices that allow for both individual freedom and legal authority. To be effective, Rousseau recommends small communities where the horizontal ties reach the biggest number of people. In *The Social Contract* he makes clear that egalitarian and fraternal communities are best equipped to withstand particularistic interests and loosening of social bonds, and to assist the general acceptance of political right.

It is evident from Emile Durkheim's lectures on Rousseau that early sociology was indebted to Rousseau concerning solidarity and integration.[4] A sober approach to sovereignty today should not lead us to ignore Rousseau's notes on the cultural aspects of constitutionalism. It is perhaps a weakness that despite its emphasis on political legitimacy, historical sociology and non-ideal political theory tend to focus on political domination and conflict, while integrational factors concerning culture and symbols appear of secondary importance. In sociological constitutionalism factors of solidarity or unity are not addressed with as much caution as structural differentiation. Due weight needs to be given to the symbolic and identity-shaping dimension for reasons of legitimacy. Constitutions and their institutions of power have instrumental *and* symbolic significance, or structural and 'super-structural' implications. The ambition of sociological constitutionalism is to reflect on more than just instrumental dimensions. This implies a closer look at the role of the constitution beyond politics in *the political*. As was underlined above, to understand the stability of politics, a notion of the political through which politics is legitimated needs to be included. As approached in related ways by scholars like Arendt, Schmitt, Lefort and Rosanvallon, the political refers to a dimension of meaning that acknowledges society as symbolically organised.

The idea of the political necessitates a wide variety of sociological-constitutional studies about social facts that *ipso facto* carry legitimacy as subtext: political representation and political culture, values and self-descriptions, leadership, collective identity, social integration and social order, non-violent conflict, inter-political cooperation, and so on. Operationalised, these themes can be observed in personalities, sentiments of a 'we', in belonging, deliberation, traditions, constitutional texts, images, myths and narratives, civil society participation, TV debates, election campaigns, symbolic procedures, celebrations and ceremonies, rituals and memorial moments that reproduce political society by re-entering distinctions of meaning in the ongoing communication, which by this is precisely defined as 'political'. Taken together, this means that the bases of legitimacy of the constitution go beyond its legal and political character. Symbolic communication brings the legal and political into a historical frame of reference that adds to its social value and helps us understand in what ways the constitution and its key principles are reproduced.

Constitutional culture

Under the heading 'constitutional culture' different regions and nation-states have since Montesquieu been compared as to how their dynamics of legitimation of political power takes place, with what benefits and sacrifices. During the nineteenth century the revolutionary processes in several countries and regions interacted, and transfers of political ideas like sovereignty and democracy took place. Constitutional semantics circulated and was adapted to very different political and cultural circumstances, enhancing stability *and* change.[5] As Hensel writes, 'In their enactment these constitutions as fundamental laws were meant to set up a new, completely different order, but at the same time they laid claim to future legitimacy and to continuity.'[6] At the outset constitutional cultures are, as Paul Blokker argues, entangled with different cultural ideas and national constitutional traditions.[7] He argues that constitutionalism-in-practice should be understood in a pluralistic fashion: 'Constitutions are open to a number of interpretations, and hence are always contestable, as constitutional actors interpret constitutions by taking recourse to different mindsets.'[8] Across cultures and social specificities, constitutions and their political institutions are always involved in circulations of legitimacy beyond politics and law in a narrow sense.

Constitutional culture includes symbolically invested discourses on political matters that refer to the constitution. 'Symbol' is here understood in a wide sense as those non-instrumental aspects that are somehow inscribed into the ongoing constitutional discourse, whether at the service of conflict or unification. What makes the discourse 'cultural' is precisely the symbolic mediation of constitutional meaning, whether it is National Independence Day celebrations, the annual opening of the parliament or monumental buildings inhabiting state powers. With varying community-building force, they articulate and underline the powerful nation-state. By this, 'the political' is imagined and framed, and political institutions legitimated.

Legal constitutionalism focuses on the constitution as a collection of legal norms on which juridical decision-making is based, while political constitutionalism sees the constitution as an expression of political struggles underpinning the organisation of the state. Brought together, these approaches and disciplines cover substantial aspects of constitutions. The constitution's legitimating resonance, however, cannot be fully grasped within a legal-political framework. Basic is also the construction of a political community and its institutions through constitutional discourse. To what extent and how constitutions muster legitimacy vary among constitutional cultures. Cooperation is at play between, on the one hand, the constitution as a set of formal rules to be interpreted, and, on the other hand, meaning that enables some form of unification of the constitution, political institutions and the people. The constitution connects the political and the legal, and the structural and the symbolic, the latter with centripetal and centrifugal powers. Hans Vorländer states that 'the condition for the instrumental function and also the integrative dimension of the constitution is always the successful symbolic representation of the guiding principles.'[9] After all, only when the constitution is represented and makes an impression in people's experience, can governmental structures assume their legitimacy. The authority of the constitution is not a given but lies in its historical inheritance – that can be distorted and abused. It must reproduce the expectations directed towards it or attributed to it. It must prove itself in the practices of collective life.

We should not confuse constitutional legitimacy with democracy, nor legitimate constitutions with the simplified idea of bottom-up legitimation. I think historical evidence shows that citizens and their political constellations serve as a resonance for political initiatives of legitimacy. A lesson to be learned from European history is that political and constitutional legitimacy takes place based on historical trajectories of rule that draw on the citizenry in the legitimation process. The constitution, with its key concepts and norms, symbolises a legitimate relationship, and is nurtured by central institutions, notably the government, parliament and the High Court. The ruled must 'be brought to' legitimate the system of government, and the constitutional culture of a state is in large part mobilised to assist the legitimation process. In this non-ideal sense can we most reasonably interpret Sieyès's principle of the constituent power today. It is a resonance board, an acoustic space for politics. However, as I have discussed, it also serves as the base for protest from below, of negative sovereignty.

Constitutions change and adapt through change of wording, amendments and new interpretations. In this sense they can be regarded as social structures; they are the medium and outcome of political practices framed legally – reconfigured through revolutions, mundane modernising and reinterpretations of written or conventional form. A comparative view on the US, French and British debates on constitutional power confirms constitutional diversity even within the European-liberal tradition: in US conventional constitutionalism, constituent power generally signifies the power of the people to change the constitution through an article V amendment process.[10] However, studies of constitutional change in the US by Ackerman and others have noted that changes have occurred outside of the formal process – change can of course be constitutional without being formally legalised.[11] Constitutions, including in the US, interact with political institutions that create legality in the process. At certain points in history constituent power intervenes in a more direct fashion, as was the case during the civil rights struggles in the 1960s.[12] I have discussed this related to Ackerman's 'constitutional moments'. Griffin points out that changes take place more often than Ackerman noted, even if they are not so decisive. What he calls informal constitutional change occurs through the political process as the Supreme Court takes notice of what is legislative and executive practice.[13] As we know, a conservative reversal took place during the Trump presidency, that underlined the US *Sonderweg*. The fundamentalist or originalist changes in the wake of the Trump years have been formal and consequential, such as the upending of the landmark Roe vs Wade case from 1973 thus rejecting abortion rights as constitutional.

In France the status of 'the people' was subject to controversy during the Constituent Assembly 1789–1791 and handled by turning to the symbolic reality of 'the nation'. The distinction between constituent and constituted powers was to ensure foundation of legitimacy while allowing for representative government.[14] Jaume notes that 'this conflict between "the sovereignty of the people" and "representation" has reverberated across two centuries of French history'.[15] Sieyès was clear on the separation of the two powers for recognising the people as constituent power (and to protect individual rights) and for the governing of the nation as a cultural and symbolic totality. Constituent power was to ensure both the revolutionary and the protective gospel of the revolution. In French constitutional debates, constituent power was seen as the basis for legitimate government, but also in its *ad hoc* forms as a potential threat against constitutional democracy. The debate recognised, in Jaume's words, a sense of distance from the notion of the sovereign people *vis-à-vis* parliamentary powers. While integration was central for dialogue and legitimacy, political instability was for obvious reasons seen as a threat: 'In France, the legitimacy of representation and parliamentarianism as well as the force of executive power, came to foment an upsurge in disagreement and create constitutional instability.'[16] The people as constituent power has demonstrated its symbolic power at several critical constitutional moments. To somehow handle the tension between constituent power and its constitutional *form*, the idea of the Nation was applied as a justificatory device. The separation of the people from its power was justified and compensated by the symbolic prerogative of the territorial and cultural nation. The idea became a key principle in Gaullism after the second world war. It was of course fundamental to Mussolini's and Hitler's regimes.

National symbolism remains noticeable in contemporary French politics, but it is worth noticing that President E. Macron follows a firm European track, opening a gap between national and 'European sovereignty'. At the beginning of 2020 Macron presented his ten-year vision for Europe. What he called 'A sovereign Europe' implied a common defence, a common area for border management and migration, a common foreign policy *vis-à-vis* Northern Africa and a common strategy for sustainable development. Macron stated that Europe's middle classes will only remain reconciled to the European Union if it becomes more integrated, with an effective defence policy, a larger budget and integrated capital markets, and is shorn of vetoes that slow decision-making. The continent, he said, was reaching the hour of truth, the moment when it must decide about 'greater integration and commonality'. He warned: 'If the Franco-German tandem do not come up with a perspective for the middle classes, that will be a historic failure.' European sovereignty thus means further integration and building power.[17] Already in November 2018, when marking the centenary of the end of the first world war, Macron was quite clear that France and Germany together were the nations that had to build EU sovereignty:

> Too many powers today want to exclude us from the game by attacking our public debate, our open democracies, and stirring up our divisions. ... Our strength must also become our sovereignty. If we want to guarantee to our fellow citizens that we're putting ourselves in a position to protect them against the new risks and to choose our future, we must be more sovereign as Europeans. ... That's why Europe must be stronger. That's why it must have more sovereignty because it won't be able to play its part if it becomes itself the plaything of powers if it doesn't take more responsibility for its defence and security and makes do with playing secondary roles on the global stage.[18]

These official and polemical statements signalled a wish for change in the constitutional culture and were not surprisingly criticised from both left and right during the presidential and parliamentary elections in 2022.

The British constitutional culture differs from the French in several respects. By the beginning of the nineteenth century, the British doctrine of parliamentary sovereignty had come to be taken for granted by jurists.[19] The notion of 'The king in Parliament' was established during the Reformation and central in Whig ideology after the revolution of 1688.[20] In the second half of the eighteenth century English political circles agreed that Westminster possessed unlimited legislative authority within Britain, and by the beginning of the nineteenth century parliamentary sovereignty was no longer questioned in British constitutional debate. S. T. Coleridge stated in 1830 that the omnipotence of Parliament could no longer be objectionable. Tocqueville observed in the second volume of *Democracy in America* of 1840 that the English Parliament had an acknowledged right to modify the constitution. Historian of the English Parliament T. E. May asserted in 1841 that the legislative authority of Parliament was subject to 'no limits other than those which are incident to all sovereign authority – the willingness of the people to obey, or their power to resist'.[21] Through several parliamentary reforms during the nineteenth century the House of Commons was associated with popular rule. John Stuart Mill was close to stating a fact when he argued in 1865 that the House of Commons ought to be 'omnipotent in the sense that it can make whatever laws it pleases'.[22]

Expressions like 'sovereignty of the people' entered a contested field in the British Parliament and parliamentary reports throughout the eighteenth century.[23] On the basis of Pasi Ihalainen's examinations, it appears that as a modern notion of popular sovereignty evolved, new paradoxes of loyalty and legitimacy followed. When new arguments were brought into the Parliament by radical representatives (inspired by the French revolution) who distanced themselves from the classic view, notions of the rulers and the ruled had to be reinterpreted. The House of Commons was emphasised as the voice of the people, whereas other interpretations were ignored. The king could proclaim himself as the sovereign of a free people in 1781, because the people remained represented by the Commons.[24] In the 1790s, the phrase 'sovereignty of the people' was used in close connection with 'democracy', and English parliamentarians evolved into a dispute between radical (French) and moderate conceptions of democracy, the latter emphasising Houses of Parliament as the most representative institution conceivable.[25]

Based on legal-historical inquiries, Hans Vorländer distinguishes between three ideal types of constitutional cultures that have emerged since the late eighteenth century.[26] First is *historical-evolutionary* constitutionalism strongly based on tradition, morals and laws, which codifies what already exists and has little or no precedence over politics. England is the prime example of this sort. The *rational-voluntaristic* type of constitutionalism can be traced to a distinct point in history when the constitution was explicitly created.

It has little binding power on politics but carries an instrumental function as a prescription for law-making. The French constitution is an example of this type. The *rational-juridical* type of constitutionalism entails a new political order which is strongly constitutionally controlled. The legal aspect of the constitution is emphasised more strongly than in the other two types. Constitutions of this sort are often created in the wake of revolutions and involve a new stage of political development. Popular and parliamentary sovereignty must give precedence to the constitution, which provides politics with legitimacy. It has a strong symbolic power in the constitutional community. In these constitutions the legal dimension provides politics with validating force and symbolic character. The US- and the Federal German constitutions, along with the new constitutions in the former communist states in Eastern Europe, are cases of this type, according to Vorländer.

Vorländer was not the first to think in terms of constitutional ideal types. In a well-known talk and article from 1962, Giovanni Sartori presented a simple categorisation of constitutions, against the background of what he saw as recent confusion about their purpose.[27] Until the first world war, the constitution meant a fundamental set of principles and some institutional arrangements. Sartori uses the term '*garantisme*', the unambiguous substantive fundamental law that was to ensure limited government and restrict arbitrary law. The constitution mediated a clear frame of government and a list of formal rights. Then, Sartori argues, the legal terms came to be abused and corrupted by demagogical politics. Political exploitation in the unstable 1920s took advantage of the constitution's status. After the second world war it was no longer clear what role the constitution had in a political system.

Sartori makes a distinction between a proper *garantiste* constitution, a *nominal* constitution that only confirms political power, and a *façade* constitution that is largely disregarded as a true constitution. Proper '*garantiste*' constitutions unambiguously define rights and limited government. They are constitutions in the true, modern sense. Gradually however, Sartori argues, nominal constitutions that are fully applied but offer little more than formalisation have become prevalent. They lack the '*garantiste*' quality of setting limits for parliaments and carry little other than reference to governmental organisational arrangements. They describe the political system, but their words seem irrelevant to the idea of constitutionalism. The third type of *façade* constitutions may have the appearance of constitutions but with modest authority. Sartori calls them 'trap-constitutions' and probably had the state communist nations in mind. Generally, Sartori argues, constitutions have lost status in that they have become political instruments rather than authorities that institute politics. Sartori's three types of constitutions were not accompanied by examples, but during the cold war constitutional law was in name only for the sake of national security. In the Soviet Union and other communist countries, the constitution was little more than window-dressing. In West Germany, Greece and other countries civil rights were ignored when seen as necessary in the ideological struggle that divided Europe.

Instructive today is to clarify the turn from Sartori's *garantiste* constitution to a nominal status of the constitution in many European states. Returning to Vorländer, constitutionalism takes place in the US and Europe that indicates the need for reassessment of his three types. They tend to blend into hybrid forms in the wake of constitutionalism.[28] In Britain and many other European states, the constitution went through considerable changes from the 1990s, primarily in the areas of human rights and European integration. Underlying the two interlinked changes, other transformations took place: textualisation and juridification under the umbrella of positive constitutionalism. The historically given constitution was tested by norms propagating in international courts, and what Vorländer calls rational-voluntarist constitutional acts. Differences between constitutional cultures certainly remain, and the British resistance to European integration marked a particular feature. And yet a tendency in France towards what Vorländer calls rational-juridical consti-tutionalism of the US American and German type takes place, opening up more autonomous jurisdictional supervisory powers. A convergence of the constitutional ideal types takes place that leads to

> Textualization of the constitution and the acts in which it can be revised, supremacy of the constitution over ordinary statutory law, the prevalence of fundamental- and human rights, limitation of political power by judicial mechanisms in the state, and last but not least the establishment of an authorita-tive and binding authority for interpretation of the constitution in the case of conflict – in other words, of a constitutional jurisdiction.[29]

The convergence or 'hybridisation' towards a modified rational-juridical type is not necessarily at odds with constitutional state sovereignty and does not automatically lead to transnationalism. Vorländer argues that 'The compatibility of historically distinct constitutionalisms, which through their development have converged, does not yet mean there has been a qualitative leap to a genuine European constitutionalism.'[30] Vorländer adds that the trends can be reversed particularly as an effect of political anti-European sentiments in the member states. This was evident with the failed constitution process of a European Constitutional Treaty that was nevertheless largely consolidated in the Lisbon Treaty. More recently legitimacy problems have been evident in Italy, Poland, Hungary and Greece, and of course Britain. However, the EU funding transfers to member states are considerable. Brexit smouldered for twenty years or more and was given oxygen by several EU constitutional interventions, such as the Human Rights Act in 2002 and a series of transnational human rights acts that were reluctantly implemented in the English constitutional tradition.

The symbolic violence of the state

Pierre Bourdieu provided studies of political and constitutional cultures with a more distinct emphasis on the symbolic power of the state. He typically argued that one cannot analyse concepts like sovereignty without understanding the social reality that provides them with meaning. Bourdieu notes the ambivalent status of the *Parlement* in the seventeenth century that was seen as legitimating and controlling the king's power. Bourdieu supplements Weber's well-known definition of the state by adding the legitimate monopoly of *symbolic* violence, which enables him to capture a range of legitimating features of state power. Bourdieu argues that 'A *fictio juris*, the state is a fiction of jurists who contribute to producing the state by producing a theory of the state, a performative discourse on things public.'[31] European nation-states have, in their historic formation since long before the French revolution (which did not signify any notable disruption in this regard), developed legitimating features of symbolic kinds that allow them to be exercised in effective ways.[32] Physical force, taxation and sending young persons to war require justification and social recognition, and preferably ought to be seenas a taken for granted responsibility. Through its historical emergence, Bourdieu writes, the state 'has all the appearances of the natural'.[33] The official state discourse, involving law and the constitution, is to perform 'a diagnostic, that is, an act of cognition, which enforces recognition and which, quite often, tends to affirm what a person or a thing is and what it is universally, for every possible person, and thus objectively'. Bourdieu argues that it is 'an almost divine discourse, which assigns to everyone an identity'.[34]

Bourdieu argues that from the various forms of capital that the state possesses, a special type of statist 'meta-capital' emerges that enables the state to exercise power in fields of society and over the special forms of capital in particular fields.[35] In this, the state manages its historical and paradoxical function of protecting economic, scientific and artistic powers in society, and at the same time it functions as a neutral 'referee' among contesting powers.[36] It constructs 'a field of power defined as the space of play within which the holders of capital (of different species) struggle in particular for power over the state i.e. over the statist capital granting power over the different species of capital and over their reproduction'.[37] Bourdieu thus emphasises, in the context of the centralised French state authority, the objectified nature of symbolic capital codified and guaranteed in bureau-cratisation and all its symbolic forms that assume submission to the established order. The recognition of legitimation, Bourdieu argues in a comment to Weber's theory, 'is rooted in the immediate, pre-reflexive, agreement between objective structures and embodied structures, now turned unconscious'.[38]

To apply symbolic capital is to institute distinctions, Bourdieu writes. It

> is to consecrate, that is, to sanction and sanctify a particular state of things, and establish order, in exactly the same way that a constitution does in the legal and political sense of the term. An investiture ... consists of sanctioning and sanctifying a difference (pre-existent or not) by making it *known* and *recognized*; it consists of making it exist as a social difference, known and recognized as such by the agent invested and everyone else.'[39]

This kind of exercising of symbolic power in the political field implies confirming transforming a vision of the world, and thereby the actions upon it. Bourdieu notes that representations of various forms cannot *not* avoid appearing symbolic; what is explained functionally and instrumentally (the flag, monuments, the parliament building) functions as signs, emblems or stigmata. Conversely, symbolic properties are used strategically according to material or symbolic interests. Representations, imaginary or objective, would mediate structural features but also the subjective relations to those structures; they will always to some degree influence the political reality and its future.[40] They might appear harmless and unnoticeable, until the political wind changes, and public monuments of 'great men' appear unacceptable. Contemporary society may juggle with time; and reselect its ways to remember and forget.

Bourdieu retains and refines important aspects in Weber's sociology on political power and conflict, as well as supplementing sociological analysis with a view on symbolic power. He emphasises the historically constituted power of the state to concentrate coercive and *symbolic* and *discursive* power within a territory. It can be argued that Bourdieu, in light of the French case, overly stresses the state as a product of concentration. The functional differentiation behind the generalised and specialised powers of politics and law was addressed by Bourdieu only to a certain point and he never achieved analysis of the 'horizontal' position of sectors in society (including politics and the state) and their normative interfaces.

To handle its paradoxes, I have argued, society runs itself with operative ontologies in the shape of political theories, of which popular sovereignty and more widely 'the people' is politically pivotal. Only a sovereign power can provide sufficient legitimacy to representative politics and political leadership, and thereby provide an essential prerequisite for the reproduction of democratic politics. Such concepts preserve and re-tell the story that 'the people' rules irrespective of governments that come and go. Hobbes noted the existence of the story of an abstract and invisible people that only becomes a meaningful entity through the sovereign person. Popular sovereignty emerged as an ideal vision of a unity as the ultimate purpose of society, that however could only be observed in its negativity, as a partial and interest-based representation. Sovereignty, with its emphasis on the popular and the national, remains a necessary 'fiction', and my own claim here is that if it is undermined over time, democracy suffers. Bourdieu reminds us that the story of sovereignty is told by the state, including the folk culture of the nation. Attempts to replace territorial popular stories of sovereignty with a diffuse transnational story of the Enlightenment run the risk of appearing unconvincing.

Sovereignty as performance and story

Weber argued in *Economy and Society* that a concept like 'nation' always carries a certain history with it and cannot be used independently of forms of political and cultural organisation. Unlike sociological concepts, 'nation' expresses a *value judgement*. In Raymond Geuss's interpretation:

> What Weber means by calling 'nation' a value-concept is that using the term 'nation' is expressing a demand on the social world: that membership in a certain group, characterised in a certain way, *ought to* give rise to feelings of solidarity and positive identification with other members of the group, and these feelings should be of a kind that would in principle lead to some potential form of collective action.[41]

This tendency can be observed in terms of what Luhmann calls prescriptions. The political system operates with legitimation semantics concerning values, to influence, or narrow down, its unknown future.[42] The mobilisation of values through the constitution or other media handles contingency without mastering it. Through the appeal to values like sovereignty, welfare and international cooperation, future possibilities are imported into the political system, which inform the internal debate on what ought to be done. Openness and insecurity about the future are acknowledged and narrated in certain directions and reflect the paradox of democracy: the people governs itself through an asymmetric power structure that excludes the people from governing. Only through values such as sovereignty can the paradox of observing society in its *totality* through *the political* code be legitimated.

The sovereignty discourse must refer to prescriptions for it to generate trust and accountability. This however is done by emphasising very different aspects, and juxtaposing with other national and democratic values, such as securing non-domination and international cooperation, and installing super-national treaties and courts. One of the most pressing questions today is how external sovereignty in an inter-dependent world has implications for popular sovereignty. To approach the problem, it must be remembered that from Hobbes on, it has been a point of ambivalence that sovereignty is a matter not solely of reason but of aesthetics and passions, not of the future but of the past, not of politics but of the political. Sovereignty is a projection, a collective and illustrated story to be constructed and told in a never-ending process of imagination. To provide a political subject with supreme power is hard labour – stories, images and imagination are put to work. From the sixteenth century a plethora of symbolic beauty and glory was mobilised to confirm and ensure the divine sovereignty of God and the king, that can only be understood at least partially theologically. Symbolisation has continued in more secular constitutional cultures as an inherent societal process. The stories of popular and national sovereignty are media and outcomes of symbolic and figurative elements that since early modernity have played their part in socialisation and cultural integration within the framework of the nation-state.

This well-known sociological insight has had modest impact on recent theories of constitutions and sovereignty. Often the sovereignty claim is viewed as outdated romanticism that causes problems for super-national integration, or it is confused with immature populism and aggressive nationalism. I view sovereignty as a set of operative stories connected to nations and states. The view oscillates between an immediate and a second-order view on sovereignty: sovereignty is the story of sovereignty – it performs what it promises. It is a collective speech-act involving performance, sound and street fury, fireworks, candle lights and roses. In the view of deliberative democracy this ensemble of multi-vocal sentiments is hardly seen as at all politically potent. And yet the constructed ontological formation of a unified political subject is highly rational in its emotional authenticity and consequences, as a protective arrangement for democracy. Politics constitutes its own normative base in the political, through which positions and representatives can justify their contestation. Theoretically, the combination of first- and second-order views implies that the history of affective collective action cannot be seen as separate from political history.

Living in a society that reproduces itself in part symbolically involves experiencing oneself as embedded in a collective subject that authorises and is authorised by the transcendent power of the state. In the spirit of Hobbes: by authorising the state, citizens are constructing, visualising, imagining and identifying themselves as the political subject. The state is represented symbolically by the capacity of citizens to build such an artificial but real power as Commonwealth or Civitas. By objectifying state power, the people in and of the political makes itself into a subject, descriptively and symbolically. The political is an image and a story with the state as mirror. Reflected by the state, the political reproduces itself as an ontological and ideological principle that wants to understand itself as democratic.

The reproduction of democracy in popular culture and education is intended to reproduce a cultural and political consensus. However, it may form the substance of protest, such as the burning of a nation's flag. It may divide, disrupt, and open old wounds. As we learn from the theorist of the sign, Ferdinand Saussure, symbols are conventional but essentially arbitrary, and their status for new generations and minorities of citizens remains principally open.

To spectators, politics is a theatre to make sense of in daily life. It is a *political* theatre with real consequences. It is a mix of ritual and events ('moments'), of the foreseeable *and* unexpected.[43] It is about visibility and appearance; telling and doing in the one and same act, whether in parliamentary deliberation or political street manifestations. As Saward points out, it is about making occasions into public significant moments. The performative complexity of political representation is a symbolically mediated apparatus dedicated to political legitimacy within the framework of the constitutional state.

What remains unsatisfactorily explained is how differentiation of political symbolisation is developing into deeper resentment and conflict between culturally anchored positions. In industrial society, symbols were seen as an aspect of class struggle. In a complex post-industrial media society, the situation calls for simplifying stories. As I have indicated, 'populism' is a term for a set of explicit cultural-political responses to political centralisation, urban arrogance and elitist networks under the condition of experienced deprivation. The attraction of populism is that it simplifies by making binaries, often with friend/enemy symbolism. By celebrating images of an undivided people, populism stands in danger of making Caesarism into an ideal. Populism feeds on the distinction between the political and politics by showing contempt for politics as non-violent contestation. As Claude Lefort pointed out, the determined rhetorical attempt to mobilise the people may cause harm if it considers democratic representation the enemy of the people.[44]

The advantage of representative democracy is not that it *replaces* popular sovereignty as Urbinati and others argue, but on the contrary that 'the people' *remains* the historically constructed sovereign that presents itself through articulation and symbolisation. Not only the king was conceived of as having two bodies as analysed by Kantorowicz.[45] The people, Rosanvallon points out, inhabited a dual status as, on the one hand, a demographically shifting multitude, aggregate or 'mass', and on the other hand as an 'immortal' imagined and symbolised sovereign. In the latter sense it constitutes what must pass as the foundation of a secular democracy. Because the sovereign people from the nineteenth century on no longer appeared with a divine 'body' but in the shape of social classes and constantly shifting populations, 'the people' transmuted into an abstract and imagined form. The obligation of the king to act as sovereign was exchanged with the reference to the secular image of 'the people'. The future of the people was left to conceptual innovations like the general will, constituent and constituted powers, and a new logic of representation. The people-as-one, following Claude Lefort, remained a narrative: its physical-empirical status was absent, it only demonstrated its existence through representation and symbolism outside formal politics.[46] As democracy evolved, indeterminacy and vulnerability gave way for the stable reproduction of the 'people', as a resonance for politics.

Legitimacy is a question of enhancing sufficient tailwind from the people of social groups to produce politics by means of communication. It is the process by which political actors and institutions gather acceptance or consent to anticipate and bypass resistance. The reference for democracy is 'the people' as a dependant on a self-constructed foundation. But this fact, as we have historically learned, makes it susceptible to attacks from anti-liberal forces in the name of the people. Politics therefore cannot rest in its search for ways to produce acceptance or consent to sustain democracy. Legitimacy is the foundation for democracy, rather than *vice versa*. Democracy is no unfinished project: rather, it is the never-ending quest for keeping its self-constructed base alive in the midst of unrest and crises.

Symbolism plays a pivotal role for political leadership, and for this reason populist movements are unstable; they tend to be either routinised into political parties or dismantled. Even more than conventional party politics, they demonstrate the relevance of Weber's discussion of political charisma as a base for legitimacy. Charismatic legitimacy may be of the inexplicable kind Weber addressed, but is also about fulfilling strategic qualities – of scripting and staging a leadership of authority with the help of political marketing expertise and what Saward calls performative technologies.[47] Symbolic and performative elements are cogs in the complex machinery of political legitimacy. It is insufficient to simply ascribe performative representation to individual or even organisational motives and interests. Rather, performative elements are the medium and outcome of a historical and structural arrangement inherent in the moral nature of politics. To generate legitimacy for politics in the public is the prime function of parliamentary politics, but this fact tends to be ascribed to personalities and events in politics. They front an intricate system of legitimation in the political system itself, involving the construction of the public. Interests and preferences are not fixed prior to politics but are formed in interaction between politics and the political, from conditions laid out in party processes, opinion polls and the media. Conversely, the notorious opportunism of political pluralism implies that preferences and sympathies can be led, rhetorically and otherwise, in distinct directions by the apparatus of politics.

Conclusion

Claude Lefort stressed that the symbolic function of power of medieval and theological origin remains inherent in modern constitutional society.[48] In democracy, the king's body is revitalised as the guiding and guardian state with its immense powers. The people now possess the secularised sovereign power of the king:

> What emerges with democracy is the image of society as such, society as purely human but, at the same time, society *sui generis*, whose own nature requires objective knowledge. It is the image of a society that is homogeneous in principle, capable of being subsumed to the overview of knowledge and power, arising through the dissolution of the monarchical focus of legitimacy and the destruction of the architecture of bodies.[49]

Political society, Lefort argued, reappears in the image of the people that retains the theological aspect.

In the image of the political society, power is not simply the medium for domination or oppression, but for the agency of legitimacy and identity. Political power is a medium of struggle within an area of society.[50] The *latent* power of the people is subjected to attempts to reduce it to representation, or to specificity and narrow interests. However, the destruction of the latent power of the people would eradicate what such threats build on; the democratic force of the reflexivity of the people, of 'the idea of society as such, bearing the knowledge of itself, transparent to itself and homogeneous'.[51] In the image of the people, political society symbolises and reflects itself as indeterminate and therefore promising.

Notes

1 See Jean-Jacques Rousseau, *Jean-Jacques Rousseau: Political Writings* (New York: Thomas Yelsen, 1953); Eoin Daly, 'Ritual and symbolic power in Rousseau's constitutional thought.' *Law, Culture and the Humanities*, 12:3 (2016), 620–646.
2 Rousseau, *Political Writings*, p. 10.
3 See Daly, 'Ritual and symbolic power', 623.
4 Durkheim, *Montesquieu and Rousseau*.

5 See Silke Hensel, Ulrike Bock, Katrin Dircksen and Hans-Ulrich Thamer (eds), *Constitutional Cultures: On the Concept and Representation of Constitutions in the Atlantic World* (Cambridge: Cambridge Scholars, 2012).
6 Ibid., p. 5.
7 Blokker, 'Politics and the political', p. 192.
8 Ibid., p. 192.
9 Hans Vorländer, 'Constitutions as symbolic orders: the cultural analysis of constitutionalism.' In Blokker and Thornhill (eds) *Sociological Constitutionalism*, p. 215.
10 Stephen M. Griffin, 'Constituent power and constitutional change in American constitutionalism.' In Loughlin and Walker (eds) *The Paradox of Constitutionalism.*
11 Ibid., p. 56.
12 Bruce A. Ackerman, *We the People: Transformations* (Cambridge, MA: Harvard University Press, 2000).
13 Griffin, 'Constituent power and constitutional change', p. 60.
14 Lucien Jaume, 'Constituent power in France: the revolution and its consequences.' In Loughlin and Walker (eds) *The Paradox of Constitutionalism*, p. 67.
15 Ibid., p. 68.
16 Ibid., p. 72.
17 *The Guardian*, 15 February 2020.
18 Emmanuel Macron, speech at the commemorative ceremony in the Bundestag, Berlin, 18 November 2018, www.dw.com (accessed 1 March 2023).
19 Jeffrey Denys Goldsworthy, *The Sovereignty of Parliament: History and Philosophy* (Oxford: Oxford University Press, 1999), p. 221.
20 Ibid., p. 157.
21 Ibid., p. 224.
22 Ibid., pp. 227–228.
23 Ihalainen, *Agents of the People*, p. 57.
24 Ibid., p. 485.
25 Ibid.
26 Vorländer, 'Constitutions as symbolic orders'.
27 Giovanni Sartori, 'Constitutionalism: a preliminary discussion.' *American Political Science Review*, 56:4 (1962), 853–864.
28 Loughlin, *Against Constitutionalism.*
29 Vorländer, Constitutions as symbolic orders', p. 229.
30 Ibid., p. 231.
31 Pierre Bourdieu, 'From the king's house to the reason of state: a model of the genesis of a bureaucratic field.' In Loïc Wacquant (ed.) *Pierre Bourdieu and Democratic Politics* (Cambridge: Polity Press, 1997/2005), p. 46.
32 David L. Swartz, *The Political Sociology of Pierre Bourdieu* (Chicago: University of Chicago Press, 2013), p. 129.
33 Pierre Bourdieu, 'Rethinking the state: genesis and structure of the bureaucratic field.' *Sociological Theory*, 12:1 (1994), 1–18, at 4.
34 Pierre Bourdieu, in Swartz, *The Political Sociology of Pierre Bourdieu*, pp. 138–139.

35 Bourdieu, 'Rethinking the state', 4.
36 Swartz, *The Political Sociology of Pierre Bourdieu*, p. 136.
37 Bourdieu, 'Rethinking the state', 5.
38 Ibid., 14.
39 Pierre Bourdieu, *Language and Symbolic Power* (Cambridge: Polity, 1991), p. 119.
40 Ibid., pp. 225–226.
41 Raymond Geuss, *History and Illusion in Politics* (Cambridge: Cambridge University Press, 2001), p. 11.
42 Luhmann, *Die Politik der Gesellschaft*, p. 363.
43 See Michael Saward, 'Performative representation.' In Vieira (ed.) *Reclaiming Representation*, p. 82.
44 Lefort, 'The permanence of the theologico-political?', p. 30.
45 Kantorowicz, *The King's Two Bodies*, pp. 3–23.
46 Lefort, 'The permanence of the theologico-political?'.
47 Saward, 'Performative representation', p. 84.
48 Lefort *The Political Forms of Modern Society*, p. 30.
49 Ibid., p. 304.
50 Ibid., p. 305.
51 Ibid., p. 305.

7

Human rights versus state sovereignty

A wide range of issues that used to be considered political are increasingly being articulated as moral-legal questions of international rights and judged by international courts. With the growing influence of international conventions and courts *vis-à-vis* state authorities, concern has been raised from governments and political agents.[1] This is prominently the case with the European Convention of Human Rights (ECHR) and its enforcement by the court in Strasbourg (ECtHR). The court plays a central part in coordinating human rights work in the member states of the European Council. The court began to operate in 1959 and has since become the human rights court with the greatest significance. It has however long been criticised by countries such as the UK, Denmark and Russia for intervening into national democratic decisions. The court principle of subsidiarity (the priority of national human rights interpretations) does not, it is argued, function in practice. The legitimacy of international human rights law and international law in general seems on shaky ground when state autonomy and self-determination are seen as not sufficiently respected.[2] Voiced concern grows when judicial intervention on behalf of human rights is politically questioned, with the potential effect that political legitimacy of international law is seen as undermined. This debate is arguably shaping current conceptions of sovereignty.

In this chapter I proceed to address theoretical and historical backgrounds for the tension between current understandings of state sovereignty and international moral jurisdiction. With europeanisation and juridification of politics, sovereignty is differentiated into various transnational regimes: trade regulations, energy, defence and security, and notably human rights. The new trend was initiated after the second world war and accelerated in the 1990s. Regimes developed inherent tensions between forces that resisted this development due to loss of sovereignty and forces that promoted a post-national understanding of sovereign power. Despite its early modern origin and its increasingly marginal status in a globalised world, sovereignty resurfaced as contested concept.

The chapter concentrates on international human rights law in relation to ideas of sovereignty, and the purpose is to approach that relationship as a sociological problem. My aim is not to question human rights as norms, but to address the public tension between transnational human rights regimes, and national and popular sovereignty. Through analysis of parliamentary and public debates it is possible to identify more clearly the historical implications of 'rightsification' of politics and democracy. Human rights are a key issue area that has energised the sovereignty debate and challenged its contemporary validity. A point here is that human rights emerged from the state and do not threaten the concept of sovereignty as such. However, as a medium for international politics, they have come to put considerable pressure on national sovereign power. A general purpose is to bring further understanding as to how democracies develop through constitutional debate and change. As I have stressed, my framework distances itself from prevailing democratic theory in that it is grounded in a non-normative view on its subject matter, and thus refrains from being informed by models that begin with justifiable normative principles. Instead, I address politics as an ongoing social process reproduced by contestation and unintended consequences. Constitutional change is a product of distinct legal and political conflict. A descriptive and analytical perspective will bring substance to what representative democracy is beyond normative principles, when such principles-as-descriptions (representation, sovereignty, democracy, welfare, rights) and their influences are objects of analysis, not theory for it.

Again, I argue that constitutional communication revolves around the theory of authority as a set of paradoxes: between participation and effective rule, between universal rights and parliamentary rule, and between domestic and transnational governance. *Paradoxes challenge legitimacy* and must somehow be handled in and through negotiation and contestation, with the unintended effect of energising the dynamics of democracy as a political and legislative process. In late Enlightenment, the image of the citizen was formed as a legal figure and emerged as the ultimate source of legitimacy that combined private rights and public political rights, leading to the normative pillars of legitimate rule. The inclusion of the image of the citizen in politics, with attached values of freedom, equality and independence, implied a more unsettling and unpredictable situation on legislative and constitutional matters. When rights were fixed in the first modern constitutions and connected to a society of free and equal citizens, power was in a sense externalised from politics as conflict. Rights were declared, seemingly independent of a national collective. With rights, argued Claude Lefort, a fiction arises of 'man' without determination. Rights move beyond any historical period since they cannot be circumscribed within society and its history.[3] Rather, they became an external constitutive element of political society. Particularly in the 'mass society' of the first half of the twentieth century, constitutionalism was connected to rights and sovereignty as undisputable sources of legitimacy. However, the citizen also saw itself as a member of classes and groups with vested interests, and social forces have since been implicated in the political dimension of society. After the second world war international right regimes consolidated themselves. Another generation of social (but apparently universal, de-politicised) rights evolved, guaranteeing equal inclusion into the welfare state.

Human rights co-evolved with the modern state in the shape of contractual constituted rights from the late eighteenth century and were instrumental in legitimating the expanding state as the manifestation of popular sovereignty. Today the situation is totally changed: human rights are universalised and now justify the overturning of state authority. Niklas Luhmann argued that rights can be seen as an institution that originated from the political system and played consolidating and warning roles *vis-à-vis* other function systems.[4] With the functional differentiation of society and the concentration of political power, mechanisms to regulate citizenship and basic rights co-developed; they limited political power by emphasising freedom and equality of citizens as rights-holders. This is a prime example of what political rationality is today: politically induced rights assist the political-legal apparatus in setting limits for itself based on complaints. Rights formalised the separation of powers and obstructed politicisation and collectivisation of society. Rights were constructed as the symbolic core of the state and thus became judicial, formal, procedural, de-politicised, territorialised. They kept politics at distance from general social power, and at the same time facilitated political power to be monopolised, legitimated and applied securely.[5] Furthermore, rights regulated expectations towards individualism induced by the logic of 'citizenship', through emphasis on freedom and equality. The law made itself available for politics as a medium for the regulation of its power and evolved co-evolutionarily with politics.

The rights discourse

The American and French constitutions were products of civil society movements and upheavals, while the Norwegian constitution was founded in a seized momentum after the Kiel Treaty in 1814. It was a given in the American and French constitutions that the rights of man were to be protected by the nation. Popular sovereignty and national sovereignty were inherently connected. Human rights were practically non-existent in international politics until after the second world war, when the first human rights laws were agreed. The UN Charter from 1945 stated a general 'faith in fundamental human rights, in the dignity and worth of the human person, in the equal rights of men and women and of nations large and small'. In 1948 the UN declaration of human rights (UDHR) was ratified by the General Assembly. The debate and growing scholarship on human rights in the decades that followed focused on social issues, women's rights and minority rights.[6]

The definition of human rights also became a strategic resource in decolonisation struggles. New postcolonial states in Africa and Asia advocated self-determination of peoples as a human right, as was already indicated in the 1945 charter. In the greatest wave of national sovereignty in world history, collective rights (housing, education, medical care, etc.) were essential to third world nations with another history and experience than Europe.[7] However, the demand for collective rights of self-determination and anti-colonial – African and Asian – internationalism were not in sync with the universalism of *individual* human rights. The focus of the west was on what Isaiah Berlin in 1958 called negative liberty. In many ways the post-war emphasis on individual rights was a European attempt after the colonial period to export anti-fascist and anti-communist civilisation in a modern democratic form.[8] Self-determination of *peoples* was still not accepted by western countries as a fundamental human right.[9]

Nevertheless, in the 1960s new non-governmental organisations in the west, such as Amnesty International, engaged in struggles for rights of children, women, refugees and victims of torture. In the Helsinki Accord and the conferences on Security and Cooperation in Europe, human rights statutes were implemented as a condition for the west to accept the Eastern European post-war borders.[10] Non-European nations have questioned the expansive definition of human rights from the 1960s regarding the rights of women and gays and freedom of speech. What came to be known as Asian values in the early 1990s criticised the UDHR for being a western export product. After the fall of the state communist regimes, efforts to enforce human rights laws were established with the Criminal Tribunal for the Former Yugoslavia in 1993 and the International Criminal Tribunal for Rwanda in 1994. In 1998 several UN states (excluding the US and Israel among others) created the permanent International Criminal Court.

By the 1990s human rights were established as a global discourse, a *lingua franca* between nations, organisations and the UN. It became a standard for talking about civilisation, democracy and humanity. This has been labelled 'the rights revolution', and as in all revolutions there are unanticipated effects and victims. In translating oppression and poverty into a question of human rights, paradox appeared. Of particular interest in our case is how the human rights revolution has been seen to affect the self-determination of the nation-state.

Generally, rights allowed for functional differentiation against attempts at totalisation from the state, markets or religious movements.[11] Rights distanced themselves from natural law in the nineteenth century and had to present themselves as state-sanctioned.[12] Human rights repositioned themselves to be grounded in the state of nature and expanded to be seen as a broader moral category that constructed the public image of the individual. Through bills of rights, human rights were grounded in positive law to resolve Rousseau's paradox of the origin and validity of the contract. This only posed new problems: 'The problem of human rights has remained. It now finds itself in a new, conflicting paradox and identifies its solution in the textualization and eventual positivization of the pre-positivized rights.'[13] The management of paradoxes concerning rights thus 'oscillates' between positivisation and naturalisation to have them appear valid measured by their violation. In sociology one does not have the luxury of seeing rights ontologically. Sociology is the reflexive discipline that views this tendency to draw upon diverse forms of moral communication as platform for criticism of the state. Only in a second-order view can we see their social and trans-forming power appear as responses to previous paradoxes. International rights regimes, we might say, are ways to avoid paradoxes at state level, primarily the problem of the state-arresting state. This means that paradoxes at state level are replaced with paradoxes at a higher level at distance from the state and its public opinion.

The language of rights

The dramatic expansion of the human rights discourse in the latter half of the twentieth century has its origin in political upheavals, war, genocide and discrimination that seemed to require more than a conventional political response. The positive evaluation of 'democracy' in the 1900s had already implied a gradual inclusion of a notion of the citizen into representative democracy. In post-war Europe, a principle was to be celebrated that had to reach beyond the nation-state. The eighteenth-century principle of human rights was made constitutional but also formulated in conventions beyond the state. The institutionalisation of rights in politics gradually transformed negative rights of guaranteeing personal autonomy and safety to a vehicle for state-building and social rights, such as the right to work. Basic rights moved from subjective rights to objective law.[14] Law and politics entwined and brought hitherto political issues to international courts on behalf of rights-bearing clients. If the constitutional protection of rights had continued the path from Kant, Locke and Montesquieu, rights would probably have been reserved for exposed areas of human life that needed protection.

However, rights have intervened directly and concretely into all dimensions of politics, and in part replaced it. Political rights claims are now directed internationally as a political mode to defend interests in many aspects of life.

The sources of constitutions and law have thus come a long way from the revolutionary declarations of fundamental rights to the contemporary situation, where rights are cast as non-political resources. Human rights and transnationalism gave new energies to a more extensive and technical mode of governance. As Thornhill and Loughlin argue (but draw very different conclusions from), rights became a new political language, and therefore were fundamentally absorbed into the pragmatic interpretation of law and the agonistic nature of politics.

The consequences for conventional and non-individualistic constitutional values, such as sovereignty, became apparent. The concept had to give way to a post-conventional semantics of rights and transnationalism. The trend towards 'rightification' of politics had consequences for the political and societal authority of the constitution. The conceptual and political consequences of European integration require analysis of a transdisciplinary character that goes beyond political idealism. After all, normative idealist forms of knowledge have paved the way for the trans-European trends under investigation. Rather, the explosive turn towards the semantics of rights must be found in the history of nation-states. Human rights are far from non-political bearers of some transcendental spirit; they originated as products of a state and its constitution that have appreciated their existence. Rights and liberty cannot exist without the state.[15] The terror of the twentieth century moved the idea of suffering and abuse beyond politics and paved the way for a *second* political language (after power) that was alien to the conventional distinction between law and politics. When the Christian-democratic and social-democratic hegemony gave way to alternate governments, rights advanced to a political imaginary or self-description. Today, rights tend to be communicated as if they were above politics when they operate *de facto* as a transnational mode of politics involving *rights claims* against states that are considered to disrespect the meaning of freedom and equality in their constitutions or in international treaties. How will their constitutionalisation beyond the state affect state capacity to act convincingly and legitimately?

International legalism and sovereignty

Universalisation of human rights took place through different agencies (UN, World Intellectual Property Organisation, Wold Trade Organisation, EU).

After the inclusion of Eastern Europe into a democratic and capitalist Europe from 1990, the moral and legal language of rights got definitive prominence, as a response to long-term dissident activity in Eastern Europe. In the new Europe, rights were conveniently seen at distance from the infected model of political and ideological law in communist countries.[16] The search for a position far from the contamination of political ambition was linked to growing transnational and global constitutionalism. New democratic constitutions, former communist countries' inclusion in the EU and the foundation of rights as a source of legitimacy beyond the nation-state – these were basic ingredients in reformed constitutionalism: transfer of power from representative institutions to judiciaries.[17] The judiciary domain expanded as political controversies were translated into judicial ones.

Consequently, democracy has become rights-based to the degree that legislative politics and the political public sphere have directed their attention towards citizens as primarily rights-bearers and thus operate as guardians of rights. Social struggles increasingly take the shape of rights struggles, no longer in the language of oppression, exploitation or class domination. With transnationalism, the authority of rights presents an image of the individual as self-managed and autonomous at the expense of the significance of the individual of the collective.[18]

We may distinguish between two ways of seeing the relationships between national sovereignty, rights and transnational constitutionalism.

One position argues that there is indeed a mutually reinforcing relationship between rights and the nation-state in that free individuals transfer sovereign power to the historically given power of the state for the protection of their rights.[19] The state with its demos is seen as a unique institution that manages to reconcile freedom and determination, because rights are connected to citizenship and the collective identity of the nation. Legitimacy problems occur when superior rights-regimes are established outside of the nation-state. This position underlines the legitimating and popular dimension of the concept of sovereignty, and stresses that it stands for something different from government: 'Sovereignty is absolute, perpetual, and illimitable.'[20] The normative arrangement and the legitimating anchoring of public law and constitutions rest on parliamentary representation that resists being marginalised by transnational 'constitutionalisation'. This transnationalisation, successful or not, is not seen as affecting sovereignty as such. In 2013 Loughlin argued that 'Those who believe that sovereignty is compromised by, for example, supra-national governing arrangements, make the mistake of failing to maintain the distinction between sovereignty and government – a distinction that both Bodin and Rousseau recognized as being a constitutive feature of public law.'[21] The civil, political and constitutional rights of citizens are protected and recognised by law in an arrangement that is intimately connected to state law, and need to be constrained by law and other rights claims: 'Those who assert the foundational character of universal rights are directly challenging the modern imagery of the political pact.'[22] Rights are *products* of sovereignty.

Another position claims that the term 'sovereignty' is outdated, anachronistic or loosely metaphoric, because the transnational development renders it empty of significance. Instrumental governments need not take state legitimacy all that seriously since the language of fundamental rights dominates constitutional discourse and makes transnational courts more powerful and conventions more encompassing. Teubner goes far in applying the term 'constitution' to systems of rules governing global function systems, and Thornhill suggests that rights have taken over as the medium of politics. For Brunkhorst, post-national constitutions are in place in various shapes, and drain the traditional meaning of the term. Nation-state constitutions will be deeply affected by trans- and post-national differentiation, as indicated by the ambitions of organisations like the World Trade Organisation, EU and courts like the ECtHR, resulting in overlapping legal and political orders. A process of uncoupling of the nexus between sovereignty and legitimacy takes place in connection with the emphasis on rights. This position sees politics as the capacity of producing and mediating political power, partly delivered in a normative semantics and legal code that avoid conflict by securing sufficient legitimacy. 'Politics', understood functionally and communicatively, may therefore be situated as much at super-state level, as at state level. Legitimacy may derive from international as well as national sources, and thus beyond national institutions like the parliament and High Court. The view opens for drastic expansion of the judicial (courts, conventions) at the expense of political, national and public norms. In Thornhill's version of system-theory, rights seem to have the capacity to evade, absorb or distance themselves from legislative power.[23]

This view argues further that the very purpose of international rights regimes is to limit state sovereignty. Therefore, the human rights of citizens need not be grounded in national sovereignty and the state. With the differentiation of rights and national sovereignty, rights achieve stronger legitimacy backed by international authorities.[24] Transnationalisation of human rights may even contribute to the reconfiguration of sovereignty by relieving it of some of its rights responsibilities. The state anchors its legitimacy not only in the nation but also in the international community of states and their human rights regimes. The widening gap between the historically given sovereign state and the future space of politics needs, then, to be bridged by transposing procedures of representative government to an international level. From this approach the sovereignty concept has differentiated into different issue areas and levels. Pierre Rosanvallon speaks of *pluralisation and complexification of sovereignty* as an effect of sources that influence democracy.[25]

Juridification of rights and the nation-state

The transnational juridification of human rights has raised a variety of criticisms of ideological and institutional kinds. Institutional scepticism focuses on the expansion and intervention of court rulings into economic and political subject areas, and the diminishing role of parliaments. Generally, this criticism points to the fact that judicial protection of human rights currently implies that unelected, unaccountable and irremovable judges are set to qualify decisions made by elected politicians of parliament on behalf of the people. In effect this power of judges to refashion legislation according to moral abstractions in rights acts is seen as undermining parliamentary sovereignty. Such criticism questions the autonomy of juridical authority in the form of judicial review and other forms of intervention, occasionally in alliance with the government, and argues for greater parliamentary power over the process.[26] Campbell et al. remind us that 'The lessons of the past are thus important for reinforcing the view that the protection of human rights ultimately depends on the capacities of political institutions, such as parliaments, political parties, the trade union movement, and interest groups.'[27] Critics have proceeded to address alternative human rights mechanisms that can protect citizens and employees in an international, neoliberal world order. The route forward, critics argue, is not further de-politicised 'juristocracy', but preservation of parliamentary sovereignty. Particularly in the UK, the implementation of rights acts caused heated debate. For instance, James Allan concluded before Brexit on the Human Rights Act:

> The first decade of operation of this statutory bill of rights has been even worse for the majoritarian democrat than anticipated. Opting to hand over to a self-selected, insulated lawyerly cast the deciding of society's highly debatable and contested rights-based issues ... seems to offer little basis for the majoritarian democrat to feel optimistic about the future.[28]

Sociological constitutionalism sees human rights not as products of law but of politics in a wide sense, and they are therefore, as Morgan argues, inherently contestable.[29] To replace political interests and party-political conflict with law as a vehicle for declaring rights and 'principle' is itself a political move. It involves a shift from legislative to judicial and executive power that effectively neutralises political contestants that seek a balance between individual and collective norms. In a realist view, human rights as they are protected by the ECtHR represent judicialisation of politics and will tend to expand the scope of rights-thinking that is politically difficult to halt. Precisely because appeals to human rights invite idealistic enthusiasm, one needs to be observant of the side-effects in state politics. Human rights may in some instances elevate and secure values connected to a distinct model of society, while appearing value-neutral. Again, this concerns not so much human rights as such, as their constitutional and legal grounding – 'the decision to make something supra-legislative, to elevate it to the constitutional plane and to that extent to disable the legislature'.[30] Because certain rights are viewed as basic rights, they are given a fundamental or supreme status. Collective rights connected to labour are not conceived as such, which raises the suspicion of its political purpose. Nicol argued before Brexit that: 'Neoliberals have done much to fashion today's supra-constitution: a higher-order law prevailing de facto over traditional British parliamentary sovereignty, by force of increasingly powerful supranational regimes.'[31]

The topic of international human rights is shaped by domestic tensions between on the one hand ideals of internationalism and humanism, and on the other, arguments for international relations based on national sovereignty. It has been voiced as a problem that the juridical understanding of human rights is empowered and extended to the degree that they come into conflict with national decisions concerning the political organisation of society. A former Norwegian minister of justice has argued that the ECtHR wastes time and effort on issues that are conventional political questions that ought to be resolved nationally.[32] In this way has the concept of human rights been watered down, and no longer exclusively protects the weak and underprivileged. Three cases may illustrate this. First, in 2012 the court concluded that Norway had offended the property rights of landowners by giving property leasers certain protection. The court overruled political decisions and Norwegian appeal courts, and in effect protected the strongest land-owning part in the controversy. In another case from 2010, the argument of owners of large Norwegian shipping companies was given priority by the court in a tax case. In this typical political conflict, the court found that the rights of the owners had been discriminated against. In a third case in 2008, the court decided that the Norwegian prohibition against political advertising on TV, as stated in the Norwegian Broadcasting Act, was a breach of international conventions on freedom of expression.[33]

Fundamental human rights in the European Council member countries have been strengthened since 2000, and the leeway for sovereignty and human rights is continuously contested. In particular, the expansion of transnational rights and the parallel uncertain status of nation-based popular sovereignty have been debated for three decades. And yet the up- and downturns of their constitutional discourse, their arguments and resistances, remain unaddressed in several nation-states. Some states have expressed their concerns. The argument is that human rights work ought to return to central and fundamental rights that were codified in the 1960s. Other cases ought to be subject to debate and decision in the national High Courts and legislative assemblies. The current juridification and de-politicisation, it is argued, simply come into conflict with the democratic decision-making of nation-states. For the last two decades Nordic ratification of international treaties has slowed down.[34] Norway has turned from being an early ratifier to the ECHR and a comparably high commitment to human rights norms, to being more hesitant. It has been argued that the legal activism of the ECtHR is in conflict with the Nordic constitutional culture based on sovereignty as exercised by parliament.[35] Against this background, a sociological path forward is to examine views as articulated in public discourse and the political-legal debate on the influence of the ECHR.

Rights as the medium of politics?

Niklas Luhmann defined power as the medium and code of the political system and connected it to the contestation between government and opposition about the prerogative to make binding decisions.[36] Building on Luhmann's theory of the political system and his discussion of rights, Thornhill presents a specification of the theory of power as the medium and code of politics, where rights have come to occupy the position as the medium of politics.[37] After the great revolutions, European states were obliged to view citizens increasingly as rights-holders. This provided the state with legitimacy, and it was able to explain its dispositions with reference to rights and rights claims of citizens. State legitimacy, according to this theory, was translated into a language of rights that was intimately connected to the differentiation of the political system. Approaching citizens formally as holders of rights assured foreseeability and stability by marking the limits of state responsibility. In the modern nation-state, it domesticated and categorised immense pluralism in the population onto more uniform sets of politically relevant features. Rights were increasingly adapted as a medium of generalisation, thus referring not to the individual as such, but to politically selective aspects of individual life in combination with an increasingly growing and consolidating political system based on rights as self-reference. This trend solidified legitimacy *and* efficiency of the state and gave way to a self-understanding of society as a liberal democracy. With the use of rights as a sensory device, the state could multiply and expand in importance, so long as it let itself be guided by rights and obtained legitimacy for its expansive and intrinsically *political* power. This arrangement made it possible for the political system to adapt to new and unpredictable objects for legislation and inclusion. It could establish legitimating principles and procedures *from within* that could be used to secure legislation in even the most rapidly changing environments of an increasingly complex society.[38] The political system came to rest its operative autonomy on the medium of (increasingly public) rights, which politics itself authorised and defined *vis-à-vis* other rights in a recursive, self-referential circulation of communication. Thornhill concludes that the public-legal coding of power through rights 'is the primary articulation of power adapted to society needing to generate and preserve its political resources, not through large volitional declarations, but in highly unfounded and internally self-referential reproduction'.[39] However, the tendency to 'rightify' politics could be seen as a juridical 'colonisation' of a pseudo-objective language into politics, replacing the productive agonism of politics with administration based on non-refutable criteria of human rights.[40] Politics is then reduced from deliberation to negotiation between contradictory rights-claims.

If negotiations of rights increasingly pervade all aspects of politics, it may have to, as a site of contestation between social interests, find other, if not more meaningful forms of *legitimacy*. This concerns the relationship between politics and the wider category of the political. In general, people expect politics to work for the social welfare of citizens and its legitimacy depends on the fact that this is demonstrated by everyday politics. If politics is displaced to international courts that operate according to abstract international conventions, the distance between politics and the citizenry widens even more. A sociological potential lies in pointing out the paradoxes that appear in the wake of 'rightification', particularly affecting the relationship between the political and politics. If all interests are translated into rights claims, and political power is replaced by judicial efficiency, political collectivity is likely to be affected.

This has an operative aspect as well: the tension between governments and transnational companies in the digital media sector has I think demonstrated that rights to privacy and freedom of expression cannot be sufficiently protected in and through the language of rights. Only *collective* values can match the immense power of international digital capitalism. The argument cannot simply be that digital media intrude and abuse individual rights. Such rights disputes go on for years and put the companies with their legal resources on parity with the nation-state. Rather, the message needs to come from governments that the core business idea of transnational companies (based on personal data) simply runs against the national interest, and that the companies need to be extensively regulated or nationalised. Such state action can only legitimate itself in the popular and national sovereignty that the state is medium and outcome of. This does not exclude the EU or any other organisation from coordinating state interests *vis-à-vis* the companies, but states must act if international action paralyses. One should have in mind that despite the increasing influence of rights regimes, they will never conquer nation-state power. The collective ideas of sovereignty and their manifest expressions in state power co-evolved, and they cannot yield entirely to other kinds of power since that would undermine state authority. To repeat, we must remember that rights are historical products of the modern state, and their rationality lies not in abolishing state cohesion, but in enforcing and balancing state powers.

Political realism and rights

In previous chapters I have discussed the sociological thesis that the early modern out-differentiation of a political system implied expansion of an advisory apparatus and government in the service of the king. Monarchical sovereignty increasingly implied delegation and differentiation of authority, as a medium and outcome of modern political rationalisation. The concept of sovereignty signalled that ultimate authority was ascribed to the public power of the nation. Sovereignty became a self-description not only for the relationship between people and the king, but also between the king and the parliament. To rule was, according to the new ideas, to anticipate future reactions. Politics came to mean to govern the nation legitimately. Legitimate power became the medium of state politics. This is presently the situation, or has been until recently. Political theory and sociology of the more cool-eyed kind tend to consider juridication of politics – that courts turn political and moral questions into legal-doctrinal problems – as a political move. Politics, in the shape of representative party politics surrounded by public opinion and civil society, concerns the struggle between interests in society about who is to be granted extraordinary status through the label of human rights. The rights discourse becomes an instrument of power in political conflict. The variety of these controversies, when human rights is confronted with notions of parliamentary and national sovereignty, is precisely a topic for a sociology of sovereignty.

Importantly, realism in sociology and political theory would not dismiss the idea of human rights but examine the effects of its strong transnational entrenchment. Given the atrocities of Nazism and the following (re)building of welfare states, the UN Declarations and the proliferation of international organisations, the expansion of the rights discourse in Europe could probably be expected. It has nevertheless proceeded with quite astonishing force since the 1990s. From the view of political sociology and realist political theory, human rights can be seen as *norms* expressed in a semantics that can be protected and used instrumentally by legitimate institutions to which particular legislative attention should be given. Then they appear as political *rights claims* that can be treated as such. In this light, human rights are based on social and moral foundations that cannot easily be treated legally based on abstract treaties and other legal mechanisms, but negotiated by parliament, within reach of concerned parties.[41] Constitutionalism of this political kind would imply a concretised and responsible institutionalisation of their further processing. General basic values can be processed transnationally and legally or protected by elected representatives in parliament and national High Courts. One can observe this normative and public 'human rights–sovereignty debate' as contestations concerning claims and interests. In a long-term view, the rise of transnational constitutionalism in the area of human rights can be seen as a process to bring stability to nation-states of conflict, and freedom for citizens under pressure from state control and repression. The emphasis on rights is then seen as an aspect of *rationalisation*, which however never evolves in any determined and uniform way. While transnational constitutionalism has been an undeniable trend since the 1960s, it is met in different semantic and practical ways by nation-states and groups. It makes sense for a sociology of constitutions to address responses among people and states that hide behind simplistic notions like 'populism' and 'nationalism'.

With a struggling welfare state after the second world war period, political representation came under pressure. Signs of national legitimation problems have been apparent in Europe particularly since the 1990s that are deeply connected to constitutional questions: the collapse of the Soviet Union and the reunion of Europe, the centralisation of the EU, social-democratic embrace of liberalist ideas in the 1990s, European and trans-European financial crises, dark climate change prospects, increasing migration and a pandemic – it all came with great human cost. Then came the war in Ukraine, during which the term 'sovereignty' was mobilised on both sides.

When the political space of representation widens for new players that advocate diffuse protest, liberal democracy interprets it as a sign of weakness. When major mainstream parties no longer muster capacity to lead a largely resentful population towards solidarity, democracy tends to turn against itself. For some decades now the terrain has been laid open for 'populist' currents with a dual (reasonable and unreasonable) message. A series of legitimation problems demanded non-normative constitutional backing for an emphasis on social equality, national protection and sovereignty. Transfer of national constituted power to a super-national body questioned the credibility of the nation-state narrative. Blokker addresses 'populist constitutionalism' and legal resentment as counter-currents to transnational liberal constitutionalism that leads to centralisation of legal and political power in Europe.[42] Populist constitutionalism would support and exploit forces that resist what is seen as undermining of national sovereignty. This is 'We the People' in a quite different appearance from that addressed by Bruce Ackerman in his work on US constitutional change, but cannot simply be dismissed as illegitimate.

A sociology of constitutions and sovereignty looks for delegations and expressions of what one may see as constituent power in decisive, authorising moments of constitutional change – historically from the first modern constitutions to current tendencies towards a federalised EU. Such a sociological approach examines the social and political significance of constituent power. It would trace the sovereignty debate as it has evolved in and through specific constitutional conflicts and connect it to EU and international organisations with super-national pretensions. While the one pillar of national legitimacy turns to international law and so (presumably) strengthens transnational relations, the other stabilising and legitimising pillar (conceptions of sovereignty) is affected by the weight of the same transnationalism. A thesis might be that the growing identity-based traditionalism and right-wing populism in Europe is a signal of this tension. Popular sovereignty in any other shape than state sovereignty finds it problematic to guide the responsibility of legitimacy.[43] The contradictory developments that constitutional decisions and norms have placed on nation-states (particularly those, for social and historical reasons, with a strong sovereignty-based legitimacy) lead to legitimacy problems and resentment (as in Greece, UK, France, Poland, Hungary, Catalonia).

In the early 1990s, Luhmann addressed denationalisation, deterritorialisation and transnational societal disintegration, with consequences for the nation-state to provide political and legal self-reference.[44] Following Luhmann, Grimm uses the terms *Entstaatlichung* and 'denationalisation' for the transnational juridification of the state through constitutional change, which reduces manoeuvring space for nation-state politics.[45] Other terms in the German debate are *Entparlamentarisierung* and *Informalisierung*.[46] They imply that ruling authorities are detached from the state and transferred to non-state and trans-state agencies. Domestically, these trends refer to participation of private agents in exercising public power, while internationally they refer to treaties and agreements of supra-national organisations that claim validity within nation-state territory. The trends affect elected assemblies since negotiations are conducted by experts on behalf of the government, with consequences for transparency and control. While domestically the weakening of the state monopoly of force and privatisation of basic welfare are central issues in political debate, the international discussion refers more explicitly to constitutional change. From this Grimm asks what social context and semantics gave away to supra-national executive legislation that currently entails a transfer of policies from deliberation among legislators to bargaining among bureaucrats – and with what consequence for national democracy?[47]

Constitutionalism and democracy

Hobbes's sovereign was replaced with a constitution that could successfully symbolise its real authority. A modern democratic society without a constitution cannot be imagined. How can a document or a conception possibly represent the authority of the sovereign? Constitutions allowed for building modern state *institutions* in their geo-political existence, which in return provided the constitution with its 'higher' qualities of validity and authority. The state could exercise self-limitation of its power and acquire legitimacy through procedures of representation according to the constitution. The constitution marked a unique formula for legitimacy of the political system. Only since the 1990s, has the idea that constitutions are basic to the authority of a democracy gained fundamental and world-wide support. The principles of popular sovereignty and the rule of law that were laid down in the first constitutions have successfully been adopted elsewhere in Europe to rebuild the political system and its legitimacy, as recently as Greece, Spain and Portugal after the dictatorships in the 1960s and 1970s, and the Eastern and Central European countries in the 1990s.

Martin Loughlin notes that state constitutions were rarely meant to be more than general frameworks for resolving governmental issues precisely through their gaps and vagueness of their formulations. They had to be interpreted against the background of the state's historically grounded values around human dignity, equality and freedom. Although constitutions were discussed among parliamentarians and interpreted by legal scholars, they were historical facts embedded in the nation's political culture or simply the political. Loughlin argues that the liberal dimension gained ground at the expense of the republican dimension. This had consequences for constitutional legitimacy: 'Constitutionalism is no longer treated as some evocative but vague theory which expresses a belief in the importance of limited, accountable government, to be applied flexibly to the peculiar circumstances of particular regimes.'[48] What is often not appreciated is that constitutions 'are replete with gaps, silences, and abeyances'.[49] Unaddressed issues are products of unsettled contestations and often functional because it is left to politics in its context to navigate the issue to a shore. In this light, constitutions were seen as legal-political instruments for settling political problems in a legitimate fashion. Loughlin argues that the emphasis now tends to be on the norms as rational principles, rather than on the abstract and authoritative *sources* of the principles.

Of course, a constitution can never evaporate conflict about issues, such as the contentious question about transfer of sovereignty. But it can narrow the alternatives for political deliberation because the constitution itself is not viewed as a political fact. This has to do with the dominance of, to use Loughlin's term, 'negative constitutionalism'. Locke and Montesquieu reasoned in terms of checks and balances, between government and society, and between powers of government. To Locke the government guarantees private property to attain its authority. Montesquieu is noted for his answer to the problem of abuse of power, by using the constitution to restrain the exercise of power to protect private autonomy. This is in contrast to Rousseau, who draws on an affirmative, outreaching concept of power according to the great human and utopian ideals. The stability of a definitive legitimate authority of a government was conditioned on the will of the people, rather than on law alone, or on a balancing act as in Locke and Montesquieu. These thinkers had enormous influence on the first ground-breaking constitutions, and those that followed as imageries, self-descriptions or ideologies. None of them escaped the paradox of a sovereign and unitary people obeying itself.

The 'rights revolution' appeared as inherent in a new wave of constitutionalism. It marked the beginning of a democratic phase of critical or constitutional moments in and for the state. Political power is today defended and challenged in the name of the constitution. We live in what Loughlin calls a constitutional age, with constitutionalism as a winning formula.[50] It is important to remember here that autocracies are often as attracted to constitutionalism as are democracies. In the last decades, regimes in Russia, Turkey, Hungary and Poland, as well as in the Middle East and Africa, have moved towards authoritarian modes of government, while retaining and even celebrating their constitution. Nevertheless, in more nation-states than ever, it is assumed that those in power will restrain themselves according to constitutional law, irrespective of the fact that law might be centuries old and that the power of constitutional interpretation is left to a non-elected judiciary. For an autocrat to remain in power, he can have the constitution changed but he cannot dismiss it.

Conclusion

Rights originated in national political systems that themselves were rooted in popular sovereignty. Despite its intended meaning to locate the exact formal supreme authority, the concept of sovereignty points to the territorial nation-state in relation to the people as constituent power. Thus, sovereignty refers to political relations within a political domain, expressed in legal terms. Parliamentary sovereignty means the primacy of legislation or the political use of law. It means the legal-political in continuous interaction, because either a one-sided weight on the political or a primacy of the legal would cause an unconstitutional and undemocratic state of affairs. This was stated by the great legal scholars Georg Jellinek and Hermann Heller, and it continues to be a perfectly valid position. In parliament the political and the legal constitute limits for one another, an arrangement which functions as restraining but also enhancing. In a similar manner Loughlin and Tierney state that the political dimension is power-generational and the legal dimension is power-distributive.[51] The task of politics is to produce legitimate power whereas the task of law is to keep private and public power under control.

In the nineteenth century parliamentary sovereignty reached a status as a legal doctrine resting on a political dimension that now comprises the people conceived of as an entity of the state. Sovereignty is inherently connected to the state, and its legitimacy is bound with constituent power that constitutes parliamentary power. Sovereignty is not a feature of government, but of the independent, indivisible ruling authority of the state. While there can be many forms of government, there is only one state, and thus sovereignty cannot be limited or divided. There may be some confusion about this, since concepts like 'administrative sovereignty', 'divided sovereignty' and 'European sovereignty' appear in legal circles, presumably to adapt the concept to what is seen as politically preferable or unavoidable. But the tendency renders incoherent the idea of the concept itself, and may undermine its authority, which is fundamentally connected to the nation-state.

As the legitimacy of sovereignty is anchored in the assembled expression of constituent power, the question is to what extent real politics is created in the parliament in relation to international rights regimes and the EU. To explain the changing character of politics towards rights regimes and Europeanisation, part of the answer is probably to be found in the changes of national politics over the last decades. In the wake of the social-democratic turn to mainstream liberalism since the early 1990s, for example, the Norwegian state has transferred extensive legal authority to the EU without being a member. The question is how long the bypassing of popular and national sovereignty stated in the constitution can continue.

Notes

1 Tom Campbell, K. D. Ewing and Adam Tomkins (eds), *The Legal Protection of Human Rights: Sceptical Essays* (Oxford: Oxford University Press, 2011); Andreas Føllesdal, Johan Karlsson Schaffer and Geir Ulstein (eds), *The Legitimacy*

of *International Human Rights Regimes* (Cambridge: Cambridge University Press, 2014).

2 Samantha Besson, 'The legitimate authority of international human rights.' In Føllesdal, Schaffer and Ulstein (eds) *Legitimacy of International Human Rights Regimes*, p. 71.

3 Lefort, *The Political Forms of Modern Society*, pp. 258–259.

4 Niklas Luhmann, 'The paradox of human rights and three forms for its unfolding.' *Journal of Law and Society*, 49:3 (2022), 567–576.

5 Thornhill, 'State building', p. 36.

6 Samuel Moyn, 'Imperialism, self-determination, and the rise of human rights.' In A. Iriye, P. Goedde and W. I. Hitchcock (eds) *The Human Rights Revolution: An International History* (Oxford: Oxford University Press, 2012), p. 6.

7 Ibid., p. 161.

8 See contributions in Stefan-Ludwig Hoffman (ed.), *Human Rights in the Twentieth Century* (Cambridge: Cambridge University Press, 2011).

9 Kenneth J. Cmiel, 'The recent history of human rights.' In Iriye, Goedde and Hitchcock (eds) *The Human Rights Revolution*, p. 33.

10 Ibid., p. 9.

11 Gert Verschraegen, 'Differentiation and inclusion: a neglected sociological approach to human rights.' In Madsen and Verschraegen (eds) *Making Human Rights Intelligible*, p. 71.

12 Luhmann, 'The paradox of human rights'.

13 Ibid., 576.

14 Loughlin, *The Idea of Public Law*, p. 127.

15 Ibid., p. 87.

16 Paul Blokker, 'Dilemmas of democratization: from legal revolutions to democratic constitutionalism?' *Nordic Journal of International Law*, 81:4 (2012), 437–470, at 444.

17 Ibid., 446.

18 Lefort, *The Political Forms of Modern Society*, p. 267.

19 This is a central argument in Habermas's normative reconstruction of democracy. The conclusions are, however, different here.

20 Loughlin, 'The nature of public law', p. 23.

21 Ibid., p. 21.

22 Ibid., pp. 23–24.

23 Chris Thornhill, 'Public law and the emergence of the political.' In Mac Amhlaigh, Michelon and Walker(eds) *After Public Law*, p. 42.

24 Daniel Levy and Natan Sznaider, 'Sovereignty transformed: a sociology of human rights.' *British Journal of Sociology*, 57:4 (2006), 658–675, at 658.

25 Rosanvallon, *Democracy Past and Future*, p. 204.

26 Campbell, Ewing and Tomkins (eds), *The Legal Protection of Human Rights*, p. 4.

27 Ibid., p. 9.

28 See James Allan, 'Statutory bills of rights' and other 'sceptical' contributions in ibid.; quote is p. 126.

29 Jonathan Morgan, 'Amateur operatics: the realization of parliamentary protection of civil liberties.' In ibid., p. 428.

30 Danny Nicol, 'Business rights as human rights', in ibid., p. 233.

31 Ibid., p. 243.

32 Knut Storberget, '17- mai og alle de andre dagene' ('17 may and all the other days'). In Andreas Føllesdal and Morten Ruud Geir Ulfstein (eds) *Mennesk-erettighetene og Norge: Rettsutvikling, rettsliggjøring og demokrati* (*Human Rights and Norway: Development of Law, Juridification and Democracy*) (Oslo: Universitetsforlaget, 2017), pp. 91–111.

33 Ibid., pp. 100–110.

34 Malcolm Langford and Johan Karlsson Schaffer, *The Nordic Human Rights Paradox: Moving Beyond Exceptionalism* (paper) (Oslo: Norwegian Centre for Human Rights, 2014), p. 17.

35 Ibid., p. 6.

36 Luhmann, *Political Theory*; Luhmann, *Die Politik der Gesellschaft*.

37 Thornhill, 'Public law and the emergence of the political', pp. 33–43.

38 Ibid., p. 38.

39 Ibid., p. 42.

40 See Loughlin, 'The constitutional imagination'.

41 Tom Campbell, 'Introduction.' In Campbell, Ewing and Tomkins (eds) *The Legal Protection of Human Rights*.

42 Paul Blokker, 'Populism as a constitutional project.' *International Journal of Constitutional Law*, 17:2 (2019), 536–553.

43 See Thornhill, *The Sociology of Law* for a similar argument, although Thornhill does not seem to consider the normative drift of the concept of sovereignty as a sociological problem.

44 Luhmann, *Law as a Social System*, ch. 12.

45 Grimm, 'The constitution in the process of denationalization', 582.

46 Martin Morlok, *Soziologie der Verfassung* (Munich: Beck, 2014); Grimm, 'The constitution in the process of denationalization', 582.

47 Grimm, 'The constitution in the process of denationalization', 588.

48 Martin Loughlin, 'What is constitutionalisation?', in Dobner and Loughlin (eds) *The Twilight of Constitutionalism?*, p. 61.

49 Ibid., p. 61.

50 Loughlin, *Against Constitutionalism*, p. 3.

51 Martin Loughlin and Stephen Tierney, 'The shibboleth of sovereignty.' *Modern Law Review*, 81:6 (2018), 989–1016, at 999.

8

Federal sovereignty?

The EU project would like to be associated with legal liberalism, while it is more likely to navigate between Carl Schmitt's political imperative and Hans Kelsen's legalism. Alexander Somek has drawn on Hermann Heller's concept of 'authoritarian liberalism' to describe the EU's liberalist governance structure without parliamentary democracy.[1] One the one hand, the Commission and to some extent the Council make decisions based on a notion of crisis management, or emergency rule. Jonathan White's term 'emergency Europe' captures political EU development after the debt crisis well.[2] To handle crisis after crisis, the EU needs to possess legally framed political power despite the risk of undermining the reproduction of legitimacy. Things are too urgent to be discussed in member countries, and there is no distinct European polity to present them to. In the short term, this ancient mode of keeping executive and administrative power in place by presenting exceptional circumstances may strengthen the internal social bond of the union. On the other hand, a legal-positivist 'pure' system of law separated from the state, morality and solidarity has proven imperative to legitimate law beyond the nation-state.

I have addressed the tension between the nation-state and the international preference for human rights. This final chapter continues to address the connection between nation-state historical ontologies and the EU, asking if it is at all possible for a European state to pursue democracy, self-determination and regional sovereignty at the same time. Voices of concern have been raised. For instance, Petra Dobner argues: 'The transformation of statehood shatters the former unity of territory, power, and people, and challenges the constitution's ability comprehensively to encompass the political entity of the state.'[3] I will not address the voluminous research on European constitutionalism here. Rather, I simply ask: Can the democratic nation-state survive within growing federalism? Is a post-nation-state democracy possible?

The state as the medium of popular sovereignty

In most writings on popular sovereignty the concept is presented as an abstract principle, while more rarely and sociologically it is reflected upon as a concrete source of collective action. In the normal state of affairs, it rarely presents itself as power in a manifest sense beyond regular electoral processes. However, exceptions occur in history and in the present, where a grand 'we' expresses demands for freedom, social equality and self-determination, often as demands for constitutional change. To be sure, the concept of popular sovereignty lost some of its recognisability during the post-war years; its references retracted from a republican sense of the fraternity of the people to the more operative and narrowed concept of representative democracy. However, as threats against human life continue to transcend national borders, this might change. Today its presence in debates is modest but when autonomy is negated and denied, the story of freedom and independence of the people reoccurs forcefully. The concept of popular sovereignty finds itself normally in an abstract and latent position, until it becomes awakened and manifest. The differentiation of societies and the corruption of power in the shape of poverty, racism, the degradation of neighbourhoods, and so on, did not finish the story narrated in national constitutions.

Manifestations constantly disrupt the image of a stable constitutional democracy. Counter-power appears frequently in European democracies, where the underlying claim is that one has the constitution on one's side accompanied by the argument that legislative politics is more than anything about *legitimacy*. The imperative of representation as decision-making alone is seen as deficient. In romantic terms: sovereignty sleeps but never dies. It may not serve mainstream liberal values – or take a uniform shape and gather around a unified message. Many ideologies motivated Brexit and the French *mouvement des gilets jaunes*, to mention two examples. When large masses turn to the streets as a unified force, they are recruited from corners of society equipped with different versions of the past. The demands may be more or less rational, seen from liberal, scientific or reasonable points of view. Yet they bring with them a conception of the popular. Seen as an expression of the political, Brexit was a perfectly rational conclusion from the voting majority against changes for the worse that they faced in their lives and towns that the political wisdom in London preferred to ignore.

The external side of the concept of sovereignty remains a constitutional problem in Europe today. Can international law based on the doctrine of national sovereignty still be regarded as the foundation for a normative framework of inter-state relations? Or is national sovereignty evolving into norms of regional governance? What is left of national sovereignty when it has incessantly been used to 'export' state power? Is it true that international agreements and obligations cannot be based on national sovereignty and that transfer of sovereign power to international agencies is a means to reproduce national sovereignty? Or will international order in the twenty-first century continue to be dependent on relatively stable and evolving sovereign nation-states?

After the first world war, the international diplomatic scene was largely negative to the notion of national sovereignty because it was seen as an obstacle to international treaties on disarmament. The concept went through a complete transition after the second world war, with decolonisation and a new map of the African continent. New nations barely fulfilled the criteria of statehood, but were morally and judicially acknowledged as sovereign, based entirely upon external acceptance. The external aspects of sovereignty came to dominate (non-interference) at the expense of internal effectiveness and democracy. A gap opened between norm and fact that still poses a problem in international law.[4] One could say that loss of internal democratic features was a cost that the people of some (African) nations had to pay for independence. The motto seemed to be: strong boundaries for weak states. Ironically, in Europe today the situation is the exact opposite. Strong and stable states are asked to export sovereign power. Ongoing debates on transfer of competence to the EU concern who holds the final authority within the state to make such decisions.

In principle *external* sovereignty cannot be clarified without a conception of *internal* sovereignty. So, who speaks for the nation? An emphasis on national sovereignty could mean that weight is given to the deliberations of the national assembly whereas referendums play a minor role. A liberal realist version advocates this approach to ensure stability and competent rule. This view provides arguments in debates on the power of the parliament and the government in vital questions concerning international relations. Parliament and government would be the only or most suitable material expression of the nation. For instance, when Common Market membership was on the agenda of the Norwegian parliament for the first time in 1961, the governing social-democratic party leadership was divided on whether this was a proper question for a national referendum. To the sceptics the EEC question was seen as too complicated for the public to decide on. An over-concentration on *popular sovereignty* could lead to an unfortunate decision on what served the national interest.

Sovereignty and federalism

Richard Bellamy has advocated a middle ground between independent nation-states and EU transnationalism.[5] His approach is among the most advanced attempts to reconcile the EU project with the normative idea of state sovereignty. On the basis of the republican value of non-domination, Bellamy advocates the EU as an association of sovereign nation-states. He seeks to reconcile state sovereignty and the EU by defining state sovereignty and then state interconnectivity on these grounds, and he concludes with a model where sovereign states delegate selected competences to supranational institutions that regulate the states' interactions under their mutual control.[6]

Recent definitions of sovereignty have concentrated on finality (the final word in an issue), supremacy (supreme *vis-à-vis* alternative sources of authority) and comprehensiveness (comprehensive jurisdiction over all state activities). Bellamy notes that associated with a state this gives the following qualities: 'it forms a territorially defined *polity*, with its own system of governance or *regime*; its own *ruler* comprising the agent(s) or agency(ies) forming the highest and decisive organ within the regime and its own *people* (the *demos*)'.[7] Sovereignty is seen as the product of the interaction between the four features. The concept has an internal (domestic) and external (international, EU) dimension, and a *de facto* and a *de jure* condition – the capacity to rule and the right to rule over those who are subject to the sovereign's authority. Furthermore, sovereignty can be understood negatively as freedom from other sources of power and authority, and positively as freedom to act according to one's own decisions. Finally, it can, according to this understanding, refer to agents, agencies, the regime and the people: 'It refers not only to the sovereignty of the rulers but also of the regime whereby their rule is implemented and legitimated by the polity and the people to which and over whom it applies.'[8]

This understanding of sovereignty essentially barricades against domination and interference in any political form irrespective of increasing interdependence and common challenges. It also requires that the citizens see themselves as a collective and a public with a background of a common political culture and shared history. European history gives evidence of the fact that the state has provided the framework for democracy which has been able to develop. It has not been an undisputed success, given the great catastrophes of the previous century. In some cases, state sovereignty protected tyrants against intervention; in other cases sovereignty was the norm on which struggle against tyranny was fought.

No-one questions the need for states to cooperate to meet immense global and international challenges. As Bellamy writes, 'to secure certain global public goods in ways that are equal and fair'.[9] However, Bellamy's external sovereignty based on international cooperation requires a number of features listed in his definition of sovereignty that can hardly be satisfactorily fulfilled, such as a demos with a European public sphere, and genuinely European political parties (rather than aggregates of the national). For these historical (political, legal, cultural, economic) reasons, constituent power manifests itself only at state level. Bellamy's republican intergovernmentalism ends with a supranational political structure of federal, double delegation: citizens delegate their sovereignty to their representatives, who delegate power to supranational entities. It is based on the view that all parties must show each other 'equal concern and respect', being aware that

> any agreement among themselves must also be capable of being agreed to among their respective peoples. The net result of this double delegation is to preserve both popular and polity sovereignty of the contracting states to any international agreement, including one – like the EU – which involves the creation of supranational institutions.[10]

With this model, Bellamy insists, the final, supreme and comprehensive sovereign authority of the people remains intact. However, state sovereignty has been eroded by an arrangement not very different from the one Bellamy proposes. To be sure, Bellamy's model is less centralised than that suggested by Habermas, without any direct link between citizens and a supranational state. It is not a question of constitutionalising the EU, as it is with Habermas's invention of dual citizenship and his concept of a post-national 'constitutional patriotism'. Nevertheless, Bellamy's model and the criteria he formulates for it to work properly remain within an arrangement broadly of the type that the EU currently represents, with Treaty changes that require unanimity and increasing power of the European Council. State governments and their parliaments have the formal opportunity of vetoing EU regulations. Regarding legitimacy it seems sufficient to Bellamy that the states that delegate power upwards to the EU are democratic. Bellamy concludes that 'The normative legitimacy of such a supranational delegated authority involves its policies according to equal concern and respect to each of the contracting states as popularly sovereign polities and so being capable of obtaining the long-term endorsement of their peoples.'[11] The simple logic seems to be that as long as the member states are democratic, their governments' transfer of basic state responsibilities is legitimated by the citizens in each member state. However, this form of legitimacy dramatically contrasts the centralisation of power in terms of capacity and competence that the EU 'troika' and other central institutions now possess.

Although more specific than John Rawls, Habermas and others in the 'normativist' tradition, Bellamy applies a descriptive-normative language in explaining how status quo is the optimal, as a middle ground between disparate demands to cosmopolitanism, federalism and state sovereignty. The obvious demand for sovereign powers to the member states as demonstrated by Brexit is seen as a backward returning to an imperfect situation. Bellamy demonstrates superbly, if unintentionally, the limitations of normative political theory when dealing with practical questions of power and conflict. His model belongs to the tradition of ideal principles of non-interference and mutuality. It prefers ideal models to real questions of power; structural as well as normative. It remains a *de jure* exercise in reconciling what probably cannot be unified.

In a different descriptive-analytical mode, Signe Larsen argues that the EU is a political union of states founded on an inter-state agreement of a constitutional nature, that neither absorbs the member states into a new super-state or empire, nor protects member state sovereignty. The European federation is a territorially bounded political association, with a particular constitutional form, and as such a third constitutional constellation alongside the state and the empire. She argues that the federation is incompatible with the concept of sovereignty.[12] The state conception of sovereignty is grounded in both a legal concept of competence and a political understanding of right and capacity. Sovereignty involves the constitution of forms of government. This political dimension of sovereignty was grounded in a territorially defined people and its political authority. The state became the foundation for sovereignty, and the fate of states has since had direct effects on the principle of sovereignty.

In line with Loughlin, Larsen argues that sovereignty is relational: 'Sovereignty expresses the supreme authority of the state to make law and as such sovereignty underpins the modern idea of law. The public power of the state is product of the *political power* that is channelled through the institutionalization of authority.'[13] What unites the legal and political conceptions of sovereignty 'is the idea that sovereignty signifies the ultimate power or authority of the state as a political association to self-legislate and decide on its own destiny. Authority and power, competence and capacity are inextricably linked to one another.'[14] In the case of the EU, its authority derives from the constitutional member states, but Larsen argues that the union nevertheless is a constitutional constellation independent of the member states and develops a constitutional theory that frames the federation as a discrete political form: 'There is a fundamental antinomy between *both the legal and the political conceptions of sovereignty* and the federation. The federation calls into question the ultimate power and authority of the state not merely with regard to ultimate legal competence – that is *Kompetenz-Kompetenz* – but with regard to *political right*.'[15] She concludes that sovereignty is impossible to reconcile with the legal and political reality of the federation: 'The federation is a discrete political form characterized by the *internal absence, contestation, or repression of sovereignty*.'[16] The basic point is that the concept of sovereignty *cannot* allow any form of divided or shared sovereignty because it cannot be divided to refer to both member state level and federal level. To the extent that state sovereignty continues to be wished as the preeminent constitutional norm, the EU in its present form cannot be the answer. This conclusion is the federation's 'elephant in the room', or its public secret, but nevertheless influences state politics. It has consequences for cultural and moral concerns about belonging, influence and trust. A federal strategy is to balance member state self-respect and EU integration, a balancing act that is every now and then disturbed by international crises. Social and political tensions and conflicts have frequently appeared between member state populations and EU emergency policies, particularly since the financial crisis of 2008.

Politically the EU is regularly facing severe crises that it finds difficult to handle well for reasons of diversity. The Commission therefore constantly addresses the union's internal cohesion and 'solidarity'. The Euro debt crisis (2007–2008), with the humiliation of Greece in its wake, the immigration crisis in 2015, Brexit in 2016, the pandemic crisis in 2020–2021 and the energy crisis in 2022–2023 are contested moments of occasional paralysis and internal disagreement that only confirm the state as the sovereign power that decides in exceptional times.[17] European Monetary Union, the failed constitutional process in 2001–2005 and the Schengen agreement have only decreased the transnational responsibility and revealed growing diversity in political and economic expectations. Member states learn repeatedly that only the nation-state can take care of its citizens. In the mid-2020s, the EU's purely economically driven process towards federalism is on a temporary halt and consolidation takes place against a common enemy (Russia). The union rests on a mixture of intergovernmentalism and supranationalism that can be labelled pseudo-federalism, not least through the activism of the European Court of Justice.

Of interest here is not so much the vulnerability and liberalist bias of the union, but its political legitimacy. Ironically, the 'democratic deficit' has so far probably been the saviour of the legitimacy of the union since legitimacy can only flow through the parliaments of member states in a two-step process. It is highly uncertain in what ways the European Parliament could have provided sufficient legitimacy. It has however become apparent that member states respond very differently to further integration in policy areas that are considered core state responsibilities such as welfare, public finance, immigration and police. Negative response to the pace of integration is labelled as 'Euro-scepticism' rather than Euro-criticism, as if to suggest that it stems from right-wing populism and lack of solidarity. A more analytical way to see this is that critical views on EU integration are expected reactions to market 'freedoms' that outmanoeuvre the state as protector of rights and interests. In this light, 'lack of trust and solidarity' is really acknowledgement of trust and solidarity at state level.

Constitutionalisation

For some years the production of state trust in a two-level or federal game has been the unintended 'plan B'. This seems to be viewed as the continued way forward among observers of the EU process. Citizens of EU (and EEA) states are expected to legitimise the EU integration project through continued support to major Christian-democratic and social-democratic parties. Although crises indicate problems associated with such a process, a return to a constellation that does not pose a threat towards state self-determination seems not yet to be an option. The EU will have to deal with the dilemma of federal inter-state commitment on the one hand, and legitimacy and sovereignty on the other, the latter of which can prudently justify only *some* delegation of competences. This boils down to a contradiction between federalism and sovereignty that can possibly be handled through a re-mix of intergovernmentalism and supranationalism – or result in further exits.

Kaarlo Tuori argues for a weaker constitutional process at the EU level than in the member states. His emphasis is on the union's evolutionary and process-like nature, its multidimensionality comprising selected policy fields, and its dependence on the state constitutionalism of the member states. To Tuori, stressing the history and features of state constitutionalism (as in Grimm's critical analysis) forms only obstacles to the specificity of European constitutionalism.[18] We should accept that certain features of national constitutions would be absent at the European level, Tuori argues, and generally avoid 'thick' concepts that tend to stress the part of the state, and are therefore unsuitable in the European case.

Tuori suggests that we should not burden our basic constitutional concepts with too demanding normative assumptions: '"Constitution" and "constitutionalism" can and should also be used in a thinner, normatively more neutral sense, which detaches them from the state template and allows for examining the particularities which mark out European constitutionalism'.[19] It appears sufficient for Tuori that EU constitutionalism is connected to thicker state constitutions. 'The concepts of revolutionary constitutionalism are not applicable to the European constitution, which has not resulted from the exercise of constituent power by a European *demos* at an identifiable constitutional moment.' Therefore, the term 'constitutionalisation' is an evolutionary alternative to the revolutionary concept of constituent power, its subject demos and its critical *chance*, its constitutional moments.[20] Tuori, too, searches for a polity: 'What is needed is a civic constitutional culture forging individual citizens into a European citizenry; a source of communicative power controlling European political institutions and infusing them with democratic input legitimacy.'[21] However, since only a thin definition of constitutionalism is feasible in the EU, Tuori opts for federalism: a two-stage legitimation process on the basis of a complementary relationship between transnational and national constitutionalism. The former will always, in some vital respects concerning democratic legitimacy, be parasitic on the national constitution.[22]

Dieter Grimm, on the other hand, finds that the object of contemporary constitutions is state power, and therefore cannot regulate public power stemming from non-state sources like the EU comprehensively and exclusively. He argues that 'The constitution still emanates from, or is attributed to, the people. But it can no longer secure that any public power taking effect within the state finds its source with the people and is democratically legitimised by the people.'[23] Public power outside the state may now have decisive influence. Along with statehood, Grimm concludes, the significance of the constitution is in decline: 'It shrinks in importance since it can no longer fulfil its claim to legitimise and regulate all public authority that is within its realm.'[24] For most European states, transfer of sovereign power is permitted by the national assemblies, which prevents this process from being openly unconstitutional. Interpretations of the constitution and what the constitutional courts say about such transfer tend to confirm existing policies. However, legitimacy problems may arise irrespective of constitutionality since the expansion and intensiveness of legal transnationalisation is seen to continuously exceed widely shared constitutional norms. Grimm points out that the EU Treaties blur the boundary between constitutional law and ordinary substantial laws on particular sectors by making, for example, social welfare and economic views into constitutional law. The European Court of Law itself is a hybrid with constitutional duties such as judicial review, guarding lower-level law and fundamental rights in many member states.

Tuori on his part argues that the features of the union only demonstrate the need not to apply state constitutions as 'template'. As with 'sovereignty', when a key normative concept does not fit an argument well, work is needed to change it. Tuori therefore comments that Grimm's arguments remain rigidly anchored to the state. In Tuori's opinion, Grimm wrongly grounds his understanding of constitutionalism on the distinction between constituent and constituted power because there is no constituent power to ground EU democracy. Obsession with the concept of constituent power, Tuori argues, only leads to a downplaying of the EU's evolutionary character. When Grimm points out that social, cultural and legal requirements for a European demos are absent, Tuori's response is that this 'thick' definition of constitutionalism does not hold in the EU case. He advocates a 'thin' requirement of union legitimacy at the expense of state legitimacy. Tuori judges Grimm's requirements for the EU too strict for the simple reason that the EU political system cannot be assessed from conventional democratic criteria like a territorially defined popular sovereignty and division of powers. Legitimacy claims are not directed towards the EU but to member state governments. There is no European statehood. Rather, the EU (at a super-state level) operates with a self-referential and self-legitimating circulation of legal and political communication that is highly vulnerable. Jiří Přibáň argues along these lines.[25]

Public power

A first phase of economic integration established the European Coal and Steel Community and then the Treaty of Rome in 1957. At this point the question of legitimacy was no issue, and governmental ratifications of the treaty were sufficient.[26] Then the foundation of the Council and the Parliament marked the beginning of the present two-stage model of legitimacy, which remains vital to the EU project. Without the contribution of national constitutional procedures to the legitimacy of European system and policies, the EU would evaporate since the EU Parliament has no genuine cultural and political base. The union must rely on the interaction between national and transnational levels involving oversight and control since there are no other pillars of legitimacy but the rhetoric and tactics from the Commission and other EU organisations. When EU enthusiasts argue that legitimacy solidly flows from parliaments to the central EU organisations, they operate with an idealised concept of legitimacy that may backfire.

Political legitimacy, as I have argued, is predominantly self-legitimation in that the state produces and circulates its legitimacy. The political society, with the state as its self-reference, legitimises itself by observing and influencing its public opinion and more generally the political as a force. After more than two centuries of European state-building, only the state can provide a robust self-understanding of the political.

The political is a potential. In times of exception, the political exposes itself. Privatisation, transnationalisation and other forms of self-inflicting and emptying of state power constitute a challenge to the legitimacy of the state. If the political system undermines its own delicate system of power and self-legitimacy, consequences occur as legitimacy problems. Strategies that work against the nation-state are likely to reduce its capacity to operate flexibly *vis-à-vis* its sources of legitimacy.[27] The political system must retain its power *qua* political power by keeping control of state power and its responsibilities to its public. To absorb insecurity and enable planning horizons, the state needs to observe its political environment.

Recent European experience demonstrates that stable circumstances are disrupted when versions of 'the political' come forward in self-conscious and collective formations as the result of political resentment. When the public observes governmental attempts to reduce democracy and national self-determination by transferring essential power to organisations outside sovereign state control, the political raises its voice above the usual voting procedure. However, criticising the state is fundamental self-criticism, and dependent on the existence of liberal democracy. When power is transported away, when the political find no Other to which to attribute political responsibility, people's protest has little purpose and may easily fall victim to simplified agitation.

Can sovereignty be transferred?

As we have seen, the concept of sovereignty makes present what is otherwise difficult to observe sociologically. It asks questions that can only be answered paradoxically. By its description it creates a relationship, and it constitutes a demand: you rule but the people are sovereign! As a constitutionally essential and contested concept, sovereignty stands at the centre of political dispute when transnational power replaces state power.

   Is popular sovereignty eroding or simply melting into another federal 'demos'? We may distinguish two kinds of replies to such questions. First, a cosmopolitan position argues that the concept of sovereignty must adapt to political and economic change, globalisation and transnationalisation. The concept must be redefined, because the shifting of sovereign capacity to the EU provides a means for increasing state control on international and global issues. This position seems to be hegemonic although it suffered a defeat in Britain. Secondly, a statist position argues that sovereignty can only prescribe the relationship between the constituent and constituted powers in the state. EU integration would if driven too far undermine the capacity of citizens to influence policies and provide legitimacy to the state. This view dismisses as inadequate the idea of the federation when it is not historically formed, as in the US, Germany and Switzerland. It rejects the call for a post-sovereign age where sovereignty is divided and transferred in favour of cosmopolitan values. European integration rather implies that the political lifeline of legitimacy is breached or only weakly connected. The accumulation of power in EU law and its agencies escapes true accountability. Constituent power, one might say, fails to locate and withhold a connection to its constituted power. Popular sovereignty cannot reach its true opposite and self-referential power. The state itself can no longer realistically veto many of the intervening policies of the EU. If the right to veto formally falls as an effect of integration, the member states cross a constitutional line.

As Beetz and Rossi argue, 'By giving up on the institutional veto, member states can no longer guarantee the sovereignty of their people. In effect, they have placed a "gifted resource" – the status of sovereignty – beyond their control.'[28] The peculiar combination of transnationalism *and* self-declared sovereign peoples triggers legitimacy problems ('populism') and endangers stability, even exits. What was called the EU's 'democratic deficit' is a problem of lasting legitimacy deficit grounded in confusion about what or who can be attributed to the term 'sovereignty'.

This position emphasises the essential distinction in the European path of political ideas, between sovereign power and sovereignty. Jean Bodin and Thomas Hobbes stressed – but tried to bypass conceptually – the perpetual indivisibility and transferability of sovereignty. The poet and government secretary under Oliver Cromwell, John Milton made clear in the mid-seventeenth century that the sovereignty of the people could never be entirely renounced and transferred, only delegated to a governing council.[29] He saw institutions of the state as a necessary means of expressing the powers of the people. Writers at the time saw the commonwealth or civitas 'to be nothing more than a reflection of, and a device for upholding, the sovereignty of the people'.[30] As I have shown, thinkers of the state like Jellinek and Heller have pointed out that sovereignty can delegate power but not itself. I propose that this historical-ontological distinction ought to serve as an epistemological base for sociological studies of political legitimacy.

Today, supranational institutions like the EU may accumulate sovereign power but, according to the history of European origins of democracy, they cannot undermine *sovereignty* as such. From Bodin on, the social-ontological point is that sovereignty is inherently connected to the evolution and manifestation of the state. Loughlin states that 'as long as the relationship between citizens and state is effectively managed, developments such as the emerging governing framework of the European Union do not impinge on sovereignty'.[31] Loughlin here simply bases the argument on a convention fundamentally implanted in European history: sovereignty refers to the public capacity of constituent power that enhances its representation and the state. As an idea and constitutional fact, sovereignty cannot be administered away or transferred to a quasi-constitutional entity. The constitution that declares the existence of sovereignty cannot impose limitations on constituent power because the constitution is its medium and outcome. To speak of 'European sovereignty' (E. Macron), for instance, would require a European constituent power with the capacity to generate its representation to govern a European state. Concepts that regionalise the understanding of sovereignty tend to rely on a notion of formal competence rather than capacity to generate representation. They ignore the social ontology of sovereignty.

Final remark

Machiavelli asked how the prince was to perform to generate support among people in his city state. Hobbes attempted to sort out the relationship between the authors in the multitude and the commonwealth, the state. Montesquieu later noted the significance of size of territory and population for an effective state formation. Republics could survive as small entities, and monarchies as medium-sized territories. He addressed proper social distance as a means of legitimacy. From the infancy of the continuing narrative about political power, the paradoxical relationship between the ruler and the sovereign ruled has been addressed. In most of Europe today, democratic political systems provide society with an elite that makes binding decisions on the state as a legitimate monopoly of many kinds of power. Neither general elections nor the public sphere but the *state* as concept and fact continues to be the absolute key element in the European democratic formula. It provides itself with self-descriptive semantics about the future, as a rule with sufficient legitimating effects.

The term 'democracy' is not an exception to the rule that even noble principles ought to be employed where they are suitable. Only the state with its territorial control has any reasonable possibility to create and achieve sufficient legitimacy to make binding decisions for the people concerning 'the necessary' (taxes, etc.) and 'the exceptional' (crises). All we know about the future is that it is going to be troubled and warmer. What needs to be ensured, normatively and constitutionally speaking, is state controllability. State facticity continues to make the constitution pivotal. Conventional constitutionalism seems to have given way to a proactive form of constitutionalism, in the wake of intensified internationalisation. As we have seen, from the 1990s nation-states tended to revise their negative constitutionalism towards a more affirmative and expanding use of the constitution to intervene more directly into the politics of the day and especially accommodate normative ideals of world society.[32] Whether this constitutional intervention into politics erodes the political authority of constitutions remains a sociological and empirical question. Analysis of the transition towards a contested post-conventional quasi-constitutionalism cannot be left to historical and political studies because state legitimacy is not only a legal and political matter.

Unsatisfactorily understood in normative theory is how the authority of the state is carried further to ensure a stable and democratic development. The concept of a legitimate state cannot rely on rationalism or voluntarism, but needs a sense of 'sociological realism' that appreciates the scale of the social, economic and cultural significance of the state as a 'person' with agency. State power goes far beyond previous stages of state development concerning practical and imaginative dimensions of people's lives. What we do collectively as citizens the state does. Our role as citizen increasingly includes what we do as clients, patients and consumers. When citizens take to the streets against inflation, budget cuts, police racism or energy prices, they claim legitimate power in the state. This is not to equalise state and society as this would entail a total state. It is to acknowledge the beginning and end of the state for democracy.

Constitutions are political documents with normative authority that cannot be suspended without long-term revision and amendment. They are the people's way of enhancing and restraining democratic political power. The constitution takes a predominant part in the normative story of political society. It is told by society, in society. As structure the constitution addresses tasks and functions of the state in the form of public law, and when approached sociologically gives evidence of conflict on its paradoxical status and function in contemporary society. Despite their structural rigidity constitutions are occasionally put into action outside the legal sphere, in defence of what is seen as the good society.

The sociological history of the political, or a sociology of constitutions that I have sketched out, is a position from which constitutional conflicts of society can be observed, without being absorbed into it as ammunition in conflicts. In observing how society applies its semantic distinctions, sociology has the benefit of a second-order position. Rather than beginning with the dogmas of reason, private property or freedom of speech, the sociology I have advocated asks how such concepts emerge, what they do when entering the political battle, what paradoxes they handle, what controversies they initiate or silence, and what new self-descriptions eventually replace them. The case of sovereignty that I have concentrated on here is a historical-ontologically informed line of struggle and contestation regarding the foundation of democracy and self-determination.

Research needs to examine paradoxes and their handling that push problems and dilemmas towards the future, in this way drafting self-descriptions of a good society. As Niklas Luhmann writes,

> The paradox prevents observations and descriptions, the future being unobservable by itself anyway. The future becomes the grand excuse for all the misdeeds of the industrial society, the grand excuse for applying the law which the society itself produces according to a calculus of interest and, increasingly, as a reaction to its own self-created problems.[33]

Society must continuously invent deparadoxification, which hides apparent inconsistencies, or replace them with others. Positive law was such an effective invention, which allowed politics pragmatically to change the law, including the constitution. Precisely for this reason sociology needs the paradox as approach or theory. Asking what Luhmann calls 'the third question' (having asked what and how), is to ask for the paradox.[34] Sovereignty is a discourse that has made itself genuine and legitimate through war and crisis. It is as real as any other dominating fiction, such as 'democracy', and with real effects and objectified in constitutions.

Elsewhere I have addressed legitimation of state and politics as self-legitimation, drawing upon political and sociological realism.[35] Such necessary legitimation may of course engage several other stabilising concepts and stories, for instance rule of law, democracy, human rights and the welfare state. Sovereignty remains an axiom for the self-legitimation of the state since it handles paradoxes of power by seeing itself as democratic and independent. It is the triadic character of the state as people, apparatus and nation that enabled it to be accepted as fundamentally paradoxical as servant and master. One could say with reference to Sieyès that the state constitutes itself. The term 'the state', then, refers to a mutually supporting circulation of communication in the political about the people, the administration and the nation, protected by the constitution. This relational character explains why the term 'sovereignty' has not withered away in the wake of internationalisation and European integration. France's President Macron wishes to apply the term in a legitimation strategy for the EU, but I think with little success. The identification of sovereignty as a description of the self-reflexive state took place in the nineteenth century, and the theories I have addressed in the previous chapters are examples of theoretical explorations towards the liberal and democratic state. With the state, popular sovereignty reached a peak of legitimate self-management. Paradoxes associated with a continent of sovereign states led to the idea of regional sovereignty that is on its way towards fully fledged federalism. The European Union is therefore a contemporary stage in the history of the paradox of sovereignty that must be dealt with, either by the union or its member states. It remains to be seen whether the union will be successful or end at the ash heap of history alongside the fascist and communist state.

Notes

1 Alexander Somek, 'Delegation and authority: authoritarian liberalism today.' *European Law Journal*, 21:3 (2015), 340–360.
2 Christian Kreuder-Sonnen and Jonathan White, 'Europe and the transnational politics of emergency.' *Journal of European Public Policy*, 29:6 (2021), 953–965; Cecilia Emma Sottilotta, 'How not to manage crises in the European Union.' *International Affairs*, 98:5 (2022), 1595–1613.
3 Petra Dobner, 'More law, less democracy? Democracy and transnational constitutionalism.' In Dobner and Loughlin (eds) *The Twilight of Constitutionalism?*, p. 141.

4 Gerard Kreijen, *State Sovereignty and International Governance* (Oxford: Oxford University Press, 2002), pp. 45–109.

5 Bellamy, *A Republican Europe of States*; Richard Bellamy and Albert Weale, 'Political legitimacy and European monetary union: contracts, constitutionalism and the normative logic of two-level games.' *Journal of Public Policy*, 22:2 (2015), 257–274.

6 Richard Bellamy, 'A European republic of sovereign states: sovereignty, republicanism and the European Union.' *European Journal of Political Theory*, 16:2 (2017) 188–209.

7 Ibid., 191.

8 Ibid., 191.

9 Ibid., 198.

10 Ibid., 204.

11 Ibid., 206.

12 Signe Rehling Larsen, *The Constitutional Theory of the Federation and the European Union* (Oxford: Oxford University Press, 2021), p. 7.

13 Ibid., p. 42.

14 Ibid., p. 42.

15 Ibid., p. 43.

16 Ibid., p. 47.

17 Sottilotta, 'How not to manage crises'.

18 Kaarlo Tuori, 'European constitutionalism' In Roger Masterson and Robert Schütze (eds) *The Cambridge Companion to Comparative Constitutive Law* (Cambridge: Cambridge University Press, 2019), p. 522.

19 Ibid., p. 529.

20 Ibid., p. 544.

21 Ibid., p. 534.

22 Ibid., p. 549.

23 Grimm, 'The achievement of constitutionalism', p. 16; Loughlin, *Against Constitutionalism*.

24 Grimm, 'The achievement of constitutionalism', p. 16.

25 Jiří Přibáň, 'The self-referential European Polity, its legal context and systemic differentiation: theoretical reflections on the emergence of the EU's political and legal autopoiesis.' *European Law Journal*, 15:4 (2009), 442–461.

26 Tuori, 'European constitutionalism', p. 550.

27 Luhmann, 'The paradox of human rights', 80.

28 Jan Pieter Beetz and Enzo Rossi, 'The EU's democratic deficit in a realist key: multilateral governance, popular sovereignty, and critical responsiveness.' *Transnational Legal Theory*, 8:1 (2017), 22–41, at 28.

29 Skinner, 'The state', p. 113.

30 Ibid., pp. 114–115.

31 Loughlin, *The Idea of Public Law*, p. 160.

32 Loughlin, 'The constitutional imagination'; Loughlin, *Against Constitutionalism*.

33 Luhmann, 'The third question', 159.

34 Luhmann writes typically: 'An answer to the third question is a way to put a basement under the building, a basement in which the secrets of the system

can be preserved, or, as some would rather suppose, the corpses. We need this basement as the rule without exception that is as the exception to the rule that there are no rules without exception. We need it as the paradox' (ibid., 161).

35 Rasmussen, *Political Legitimacy*; Jiří Přibáň addresses sovereignty as self-legitimation drawing on Foucault in 'Power in sovereignty and its self-legitimation: on the autopoietic semantics and contingency of popular sovereignty.' *International Journal of Law in Context*, 11:4 (2015), 481–495.

Select bibliography

Ackerman, Bruce (1989) 'Why dialogue?' *Journal of Philosophy*, 86 (1) 5–22.

Ackerman, Bruce A. (2000) *We the People: Transformations*. Cambridge, MA: Harvard University Press.

Aitchison, Guy (2018) 'Rights, citizenship and political struggle.' *European Journal of Political Theory*, 17 (1) 23–43.

Albrow, Martin (1975) 'Legal positivism and bourgeois materialism: Max Weber's view of the sociology of law.' *British Journal of Law and Society*, 14 (2) 14–31.

Anter, Andreas (1998) 'Georg Jellineks wissenschaftliche Politik Positionen, Kontexte, Wirkungslinien.' *Politische Vierteljahresschrift*, 39 (3) 503–526.

Anter, Andreas (2014) *Max Weber's Theory of the Modern State: Origins, Structure and Significance*. Houndmills: Palgrave Macmillan.

Anter, Andreas and Stefan Breuer (eds) (2016) *Max Webers Staatssoziologie: Positionen und Perspektiven*. Berlin: Nomos.

Austin, John (1962) *How To Do Things with Words*. Oxford: Clarendon Press.

Ball, Terrence (1988) *Transforming Political Discourse*. Oxford: Blackwell.

Ball, Terrence, James Farr and Russell L. Hanson (eds) (1995) *Political Innovation and Conceptual Change*. Cambridge: Cambridge University Press.

Bashkina, Olga (2019) 'Nations against people: whose sovereign power?' In: Bas Leijssenaar and Neil Walker (eds) *Sovereignty in Action*. Cambridge: Cambridge University Press.

Beetz, Jan Pieter and Enzo Rossi (2017) 'The EU's democratic deficit in a realist key: multilateral governance, popular sovereignty and critical responsiveness.' *Transnational Legal Theory*, 8 (1) 22–41.

Bellamy, Richard (1992) 'Liberalism and nationalism in the thought of Max Weber.' *History of European Ideas*, 14 (4) 499–507.

Bellamy, Richard (2007) *Political Constitutionalism – A Republican Defense of the Constitutionality of Democracy*. Cambridge: Cambridge University Press.

Bellamy, Richard (2017) 'A European republic of sovereign states: sovereignty, republicanism and the European Union.' *European Journal of Political Theory*, 16 (2) 188–209.

Bellamy, Richard (2019) *A Republican Europe of States: Cosmopolitanism, Intergovernmentalism and Democracy in the EU*. Cambridge: Cambridge University Press.

Bellamy, Richard and Albert Weale (2015) 'Political legitimacy and European monetary union: contracts, constitutionalism and the normative logic of two-level games.' *Journal of Public Policy*, 22 (2) 257–274.

Benjamin, Walter (2002) 'On the concept of history' In: *Selected Writings Vol. 4: 1938–1940* (Howard Eiland and Michael W. Jennings, eds) Cambridge, MA: Harvard University Press.

Besson, Samantha (2014) 'The legitimate authority of international human rights.' In: Andreas Føllesdal, Johan Karlsson Schaffer and Geir Ulstein (eds) *The Legitimacy of International Human Rights Regimes*. Cambridge: Cambridge University Press.

Biersteker, Thomas and Cynthia Weber (eds) (1996) *State Sovereignty as State Construct*. Cambridge: Cambridge University Press.

Blokker, Paul (2012) 'Dilemmas of democratization: from legal revolutions to democratic constitutionalism?' *Nordic Journal of International Law*, 81 (4) 437–470.

Blokker, Paul (2013) *New Democracies in Crisis? A Comparative Constitutional Study of the Czech Republic, Hungary, Poland, Romania and Slovakia*. Abingdon: Routledge.

Blokker, Paul (2014) 'The European crisis and the political critique of capitalism.' *European Journal of Social Theory*, 17 (3) 258–274.

Blokker, Paul (2015) 'The European crisis and constitutional claims from below' In: H. J. Trenz, V. Guiraudan and C. Ruzza (eds) *Europe in Crisis: The Unmasking of Political Union*. Basingstoke: Palgrave Macmillan.

Blokker, Paul (2016) 'Constitutional reform in Europe and recourse to the people.' In: X. Contiades and A. Fotiadou (eds) *Participatory Constitutional Change: The People as Amenders of the Constitution*. London: Routledge.

Blokker, Paul (2017) 'Politics and the political in sociological constitutionalism.' In: Paul Blokker and Chris Thornhill (eds) *Sociological Constitutionalism*. Cambridge: Cambridge University Press.

Blokker, Paul (2018a) 'Constitutional mobilization and contestation in the transnational sphere.' *Journal of Law and Society*, 45 (1) 52–72.

Blokker, Paul (2018b) 'Populist constitutionalism.' In: Carlos de la Torre (ed.) *Routledge Handbook of Global Populism*. London: Routledge.

Blokker, Paul and Chris Thornhill (eds) (2017) *Sociological Constitutionalism*. Cambridge: Cambridge University Press.

Blumenberg, Hans (1983) *The Legitimacy of the Modern Age*. Cambridge, MA: The MIT Press.

Bluntschli, Johann Caspar (1875/2000) *The Theory of the State*. Ontario: Batoche Books.

Bodin, Jean (1992) *On Sovereignty: Four Chapters from Six Books of the Commonwealth*. Cambridge: Cambridge University Press.

Boltanski, Luc and Laurent Thévenot (1999) *On Justification: Economies of Worth*. Princeton, NJ: Princeton University Press.

Bourdieu, Pierre (1991) *Language and Symbolic Power*. Cambridge: Polity.

Bourdieu, Pierre (1994) 'Rethinking the state: genesis and structure of the bureaucratic field.' *Sociological Theory*, 12 (1) 1–18.

Bourdieu, Pierre (1997/2005) 'From the king's house to the reason of state: a model of the genesis of a bureaucratic field.' In: Loïc Wacquant (ed.) *Pierre Bourdieu and Democratic Politics*. Cambridge: Polity Press.

Bourdieu, Pierre (2014) *On the State: Lectures at the Collège de France 1989–1992*. Cambridge: Polity Press.

Bourke, Richard and Quentin Skinner (eds) (2017) *Popular Sovereignty in Historical Perspective*. Cambridge: Cambridge University Press.

Brunkhorst, Hauke (2002) 'Globalising democracy without a state: weak public, strong public, global constitutionalism.' *Millennium: Journal of International Studies*, 31 (3) 675–690.

Brunkhorst, Hauke (2017) 'Sociological constitutionalism: an evolutionary approach.' In: Paul Blokker and Chris Thornhill (eds) *Sociological Constitutionalism*. Cambridge: Cambridge University Press.

Brunner, Otto, Werner Conze and Reinhart Koselleck (1997) 'Staat und Souveränität.' *Geschichtliche Grundbegriffe*. Vol. 6, St–Vert. Stuttgart: Klett-Cotta.

Burchell, Graham, Colin Gordon and Peter Miller (eds) (1991) *The Foucault Effect: Studies in Governmentality*. London: Harvester Wheatsheaf.

Caldwell, Peter C. (1997) *Popular Sovereignty and the Crisis of German Constitutional Law: The Theory and Practice of Weimar Constitutionalism*. Durham, NC: Duke University Press.

Campbell, Tom, K. D. Ewing and Adam Tomkins (eds) (2011) *The Legal Protection of Human Rights: Sceptical Essays*. Oxford: Oxford University Press.

Canovan, Margaret (2005) *The People*. Cambridge: Polity.

Carré de Malberg, Raymond (1922) *Contribution à la théorie générale de L'Etat: Tome II*. Paris: Edition de CNRS.

Castiglione, Dario and Iain Hampsher-Monk (eds) (2001) *The History of Political Thought in National Context*. Cambridge: Cambridge University Press.

Chalmers, Damian (2008) 'Constituent power and the pluralist ethic.' In: Martin Loughlin and Neil Walker (eds) *The Paradox of Constitutionalism: Constituent Power and Constitutional Form*. Oxford: Oxford University Press.

Chilton, Paul (2004) *Analysing Political Discourse: Theory and Practice*. London: Routledge.

Choudhry, Sujit (2008) 'Ackerman's higher lawmaking in comparative constitutional perspective: constitutional moments as constitutional failures.' *International Journal of Constitutional Law*, 6 (2) 193–230.

Cohen, Jean L. (2012) *Globalisation and Sovereignty: Rethinking Legality, Legitimacy and Constitutionalism*. Cambridge: Cambridge University Press.

Colliot-Thélène, Catherine (2009) 'Modern rationalities of the political: from Foucault to Weber.' *Max Weber Studies*, 9 (1–2) 165–187.

Colón-Ríos, Joel I. (2016) 'Rousseau, theorist of constituent power.' *Oxford Journal of Legal Studies*, 36 (4) 885–908.

Connolly, William E. (1974/1983) *The Terms of Political Discourse*. Oxford: Martin Robertson.

Constant, Benjamin (1806/1815) *Principes de politique applicables à tous les gouvernements représentatifs*. Paris: Gallica.

Constant, Benjamin (1988) *Political Writings* (Biancamaria Fontana, ed.). Cambridge: Cambridge University Press.

Corsi, G. (2016) 'On paradoxes in constitutions.' In: A. Febbrajo and G. Corsi (eds) *Sociology of Constitutions: A Paradoxical Perspective*. Abingdon: Routledge.

Corsi, Giancarlo (2017) 'Legitimating reason or self-created uncertainty? Public opinion as an observer of modern politics.' *Thesis Eleven*, 143 (1) 44–55.

Craiutu, Aurelian (2002a) 'Introduction.' In: Francois Guizot (ed.) *The History of the Origins of Representative Government in Europe*. Indianapolis, IN: Liberty Fund.

Craiutu, Aurelian (2002b) 'The battle for legitimacy: Guizot and Constant on sovereignty.' *Historical Reflections*, 28 (3) 471–491.

Crozier, Michael P. and Adrian Little (2012) 'Democratic voice: popular sovereignty.' *Australian Journal of Political Science*, 47 (3) 333–346.

Daly, Eoin (2016) 'Ritual and symbolic power in Rousseau's constitutional thought.' *Law, Culture and the Humanities*, 12 (3) 620–646.

Deluna, D. N. (ed.) (2001) *The Political Imagination in History: Essays Concerning J.G.A. Pocock*. Baltimore, MD: Owlworks.

Dobel, Patrick J. (1986) 'The role of language in Rousseau's political thought.' *Polity*, 18 (4) 638–658.

Dobner, Petra and Martin Loughlin (eds) (2010) *The Twilight of Constitutionalism?* Oxford: Oxford University Press.

Doyle, Natalie (2003) 'Democracy as socio-cultural project on individual and collective sovereignty: Claude Lefort, Marcel Gauchet and the French debate on modern autonomy.' *Thesis Eleven*, 75 (1) 69–95.

Drolet, Michael (2011) 'Carrying the banner of the bourgeoisie: democracy, self, and the philosophical foundations to Francois Guizot's historical and political thought.' *History of Political Thought*, 32 (4) 645–690.

Dunn, John (2000) *The Cunning of Unreason: Making Sense of Politics*. London: HarperCollins.

Durkheim, Emile (1913/1992) *Professional Ethics and Civic Morals*. London: Routledge.

Durkheim, Emile (1965) *Montesquieu and Rousseau*. Ann Arbor, MI: University of Michigan Press.

Durkheim, Emile (1983) *Durkheim and the Law* (Steven Lukes and Andrew Scull, eds). Oxford: Martin Robertson.

Durkheim, Emile (1986) *Durkheim on Politics and the State* (A. Giddens, ed.). Cambridge: Polity Press.

Dyzenhaus, David (1997) 'Legal theory in the collapse of Weimar: contemporary lessons?' *American Political Science Review*, 91 (1) 121–133.

Dyzenhaus, David (2019) 'Introduction.' In: Hermann Heller, *Sovereignty: A Contribution to the Theory of Public and International Law* (David Dyzenhaus, ed.). Oxford: Oxford University Press.

Edwards, Jason (2006) 'Critique and crisis today: Koselleck, Enlightenment and the concept of politics.' *Contemporary Political Theory*, 5, 428–446.

Faiclough, Norman (1995) *Critical Discourse Analysis: The Critical Study of Language*. London: Longman.

Febbrajo, Alberto and Giancarlo Corsi (eds) (2016) *Sociology of Constitutions: A Paradoxical Perspective*. London: Routledge.

Feldman, Stephen M. (1991) 'An interpretation of Max Weber's theory of law: metaphysics, economics, and the iron cage of constitutional law.' *Law and Social Inquiry*, 16 (2) 205–248.

Finlayson, Lorna (2017) 'With radicals like these, who needs conservatives? Doom, gloom, and realism in political theory.' *European Journal of Political Theory*, 16 (3) 264–282.

Fitzi, Gregor (2009) 'Sovereignty, legality and democracy: politics in the work of Max Weber.' *Max Weber Studies*, 9 (1–2) 33–49.

Flügel-Martinsen, Oliver, Franziska Martinsen, Stephen W. Sawyer and Daniel Schulz (eds) (2019) *Pierre Rosanvallon's Political Thought: Interdisciplinary Approaches*. Bielefeld: Bielefeld University Press.

Flynn, Bernard (2005) *The Philosophy of Claude Lefort: Interpreting the Political*. Evanston, IL: Northwestern University Press.

Føllesdal, Andreas, Johan Karlsson Schaffer and Geir Ulstein (eds) (2014) *The Legitimacy of International Human Rights Regimes*. Cambridge: Cambridge University Press.

Gallie, Walter B. (1956) 'Essentially contested concepts.' *Proceedings of the Aristotelian Society*, 56, 167–198.

Galston, William (2010) 'Realism in political theory.' *European Journal of Political Theory* 9 (4) 385–411.

Gammelgaard, Karen and Eirik Holmøyvik (eds) (2015) *Writing Democracy: The Norwegian Constitution 1814–2014*. New York: Berghahn.

Gauchet, Marcel (2009) 'Liberalism's lucid illusion' In: Helena Rosenblatt (ed.) *The Cambridge Companion to Constant*. Cambridge: Cambridge University Press.

Geenens, Raf and Stefan Sottiaux (2015) 'Sovereignty and direct democracy: lessons from Constant and the Belgian Constitution.' *European Constitutional Law Review*, 11 (2) 293–320.

Geuss, Raymond (2008) *Philosophy and Real Politics*. Princeton, NJ: Princeton University Press.

Geuss, Raymond (2010) *Politics and the Imagination*. Princeton, NJ: Princeton University Press.

Goldoni, Marco and Michael A. Wilkinson (2016) 'The material constitution.' *Law, Society Economy Working Papers*, no. 20. London: LSE Law Department.

Goldsworthy, Jeffrey Denys (1999) *The Sovereignty of Parliament: History and Philosophy*. Oxford: Oxford University Press.

Goldsworthy, Jeffrey (2010) *Parliamentary Sovereignty: Contemporary Debates*. Cambridge: Cambridge University Press.

Gray, John (1977) 'On the contestability of social and political concepts.' *Political Theory*, 5 (3) 332–348.

Gray, John (1978) 'On liberty, liberalism and essential contestability.' *British Journal of Political Science*, 8 (4) 385–402.

Gray, John (1995) *Enlightenment's Wake*. London: Routledge.

Greenhouse, Carol J. (2011) 'Durkheim and law: divided readings over division of labour.' *Annual Review of Law and Social Science*, 7, 165–185.

Grimm, Dieter (2005) 'The constitution in the process of denationalization.' *Constellations*, 12 (4) 445–584.

Grimm, Dieter (2009) *Sovereignty: The Origin and Future of a Political and Legal Concept*. New York: Columbia University Press.

Grimm, Dieter (2010) 'The achievement of constitutionalism and its prospects in a changed world.' In: Petra Dobner and Martin Loughlin (eds) *The Twilight of Constitutionalism?* Oxford: Oxford University Press.

Grimm, Dieter (2017) *The Constitution of European Democracy*. Oxford: Oxford University Press.

Guizot, Francois (1851/2002) *The History of the Origins of Representative Government in Europe*. Indianapolis, IN: Liberty Fund.

Guizot, Francois (1985) 'Philosophie politique: de la souveraineté.' In: *Histoire de la civilisation en Europe; [suivie de] Philosophie politique de la souveraineté: depuis la chute de l'Empire romain jusqu'à la Révolution française* (P. Rosanvallon, ed.). Paris: Hachette.

Habermas, Jürgen (1996) *Between Facts and Norms*. Cambridge, MA: The MIT Press.

Häkkinen, Teemu and Miina Kaarkoski (2018) 'Sovereignty versus influence: European unity and the conceptualization of sovereignty in British parliamentary debates 1945–2016.' *Contribution to the History of Concepts*, 13 (2) 54–78.

Hall, Edward (2017) 'How to do realistic political theory (and why you might want to).' *European Journal of Political Theory*, 16 (3) 283–303.

Heller, Hermann (1934a) 'Power, political.' *Encyclopaedia of the Social Sciences*. Vol. 12 (Edwin Seligman and Alvin Johnson, ed.). Michigan: Macmillan.

Heller, Hermann (1934b) *Staatslehre*. Leiden: Sijthoff.

Heller, Hermann (2019) *Sovereignty: A Contribution to the Theory of Public and International Law* (ed. and introduced by David Dyzenhaus). Oxford: Oxford University Press.

Hensel, Silke, Ulrike Bock, Katrin Dircksen and Hans-Ulrich Thamer(eds) (2012) *Constitutional Cultures: On the Concept and Representation of Constitutions in the Atlantic World*. Cambridge: Cambridge Scholars.

Hobbes, Thomas (1996) *Leviathan*. Cambridge: Cambridge University Press.

Hoffman, Stefan-Ludwig (ed.) (2011) *Human Rights in the Twentieth Century*. Cambridge: Cambridge University Press.

Horton, John (2010) 'Realism, liberal moralism and a political theory of *modus vivendi*.' *European Journal of Political Theory*, 9 (4) 431–448.

Howard, Dick (2010) *The Primacy of the Political*. New York: Columbia University Press.

Hübinger, Gangolf (2009) 'Max Weber's "Sociology of the State" and the science of politics in Germany.' *Max Weber Studies*, 9 (1–2) 17–32.

Ihalainen, Pasi (2010) *Agents of the People: Democracy and Popular Sovereignty in British and Swedish Parliamentary and Public Debates, 1734–1800*. Leiden: Brill.

Ihalainen, Pasi and Kari Palonen (2009) 'Parliamentary sources in the comparative study of conceptual history: methodological aspects of illustrations of a research proposal.' *Parliaments, Estates and Representation*, 29, 17–34.

Ihalainen, Paso, Cornelia Ilie and Kari Palonen (eds) (2016) *Parliament and Parliamentarism: A Comparative History of a European Concept*. New York: Berghahn.

Ilie, Cornelia (2009) 'Strategic uses of parliamentary forms of address: the case of the UK Parliament and the Swedish Riksdag.' *Journal of Pragmatics*, 42 (4) 885–911.

Ilie, Cornelia (2010) *European Parliaments under Scrutiny: Discourse Strategies and Interaction Practices*. Amsterdam: John Benjamins.

Ingram, James D. (2006) 'The politics of Claude Lefort's political: between liberalism and radical democracy.' *Thesis Eleven*, 87 (1) 33–50.

Iriye, A., P. Goedde, and W. I. Hitchcock (eds) (2012) *The Human Rights Revolution: An International History*. Oxford: Oxford University Press.

Jainchill, Andrew and Samuel Moyn (2004) 'French democracy between totalitarianism and solidarity: Pierre Rosanvallon and revisionist historiography.' *Journal of Modern History*, 76 (1) 107–154.

Jaume, Lucien (2013) *Tocqueville: The Aristocratic Sources of Liberty*. Princeton, NJ: Princeton University Press.

Jellinek, Georg (1900/1921) *Allgemeine Staatslehre*. Volume I. Berlin: Springer Verlag.

Kalmo, Hent and Quentin Skinner (eds) (2010) *Sovereignty in Fragments: The Past, Present and Future of a Contested Concept*. Cambridge: Cambridge University Press.

Kantorowicz, Ernst H. (1957) *The King's Two Bodies: A Study in Medieval Political Theology*. Princeton, NJ: Princeton University Press.

Kelly, Duncan (2003) *The State of the Political: Conceptions of Politics and the State in the Thought of Max Weber, Carl Schmitt and Franz Neumann*. Oxford: Oxford University Press.

Kelly, Duncan (2004) 'Revisiting the Rights of Man: Georg Jellinek on rights and the state.' *Law and History Review*, 22 (3) 493–529.

Kjaer, Poul F. (2009) *Constitutionalism in the Global Realm: A Sociological Approach*. London: Routledge.

Koselleck, Reinhart (1988) *Critique and Crisis: Enlightenment and the Pathogenesis of Modern Society*. Cambridge, MA: The MIT Press.

Koselleck, Reinhart (1996) 'A response to comments on the *Geschhichtliche Grundbegriffe*. In: Hartmut Lehmann and Melvin Richter (eds) *The Meaning of Historical Terms and Concepts: New Studies on* Begriffgeschichte. Washington, D. C.: German Historical Institute, Occasional paper no. 15.

Koselleck, Reinhart (2011) 'Introduction and prefaces to the Geschichtliche Grundbegriffe.' *Contributions to the History of Concepts*, 6 (1) 1–37.

Koselleck, Reinhart (2018) 'History, law, justice.' In: Reinhart Koselleck, *Sediments of Time: On Possible Histories*. Stanford, CA: Stanford University Press.

Krassner, Stephen D. (1999) *Sovereignty: Organized Hypocrisy*. Princeton, NJ: Princeton University Press.

Krause, Sharon R. (1999) 'The Politics of distinction and disobedience: honor and the defence of liberty in Montesquieu.' *Polity*, 31 (3) 469–499.

Krause, Sharon R. (2015) 'Freedom, sovereignty, and the general will in Montesquieu.' In: James Farr and David Lay Williams (eds) *The General Will: The Evolution of a Concept*. Cambridge: Cambridge University Press.

Kreijen, Gerard (2002) *State Sovereignty and International Governance*. Oxford: Oxford University Press.

Kreuder-Sonnen, Christian and Jonathan White (2021) 'Europe and the transnational politics of emergency.' *Journal of European Public Policy*, 29 (6) 953–965.

Kumm, Mattias (2008) 'Why Europeans will not embrace constitutional patriotism.' *International Journal of Constitutional Law*, 6 (1) 117–136.

Lange, Stefan (2003) *Niklas Luhmanns Theorie der Politik: Eine Abklärung der Staatsgesellschaft*. Wiesbaden: Westdeutscher Verlag.

Langford, Malcolm and Johan Karlsson Schaffer (2014) *The Nordic Human Rights Paradox: Moving beyond Exceptionalism*. Paper. Oslo: Norwegian Centre for Human Rights.

Langford, Malcolm and Johan Karlsson Schaffer (2019) *The Scandinavian Rights Revolution: Courts, Rights and Legal Mobilization since the 1970s*. Paper. Washington, D. C.: Law and Society Association.

Larsen, Signe Rehling (2021) *The Constitutional Theory of the Federation and the European Union*. Oxford: Oxford University Press.

Lefort, Claude (1986) *The Political Forms of Modern Society: Bureaucracy, Democracy, Totalitarianism* (John B. Thompson, ed.). Cambridge: Polity.

Lefort, Claude (1988) *Democracy and Political Theory*. Cambridge: Polity Press.

Levy, Daniel and Natan Sznaider (2006) 'Sovereignty transformed: a sociology of human rights.' *British Journal of Sociology*, 57 (4) 658–675.

Lindahl, Hans (2008) 'Constituent power and reflexive identity: towards an ontology of collective selfhood.' In: Martin Loughlin and Neil Walker (eds) *The Paradox of Constitutionalism: Constituent Power and Constitutional Form*. Oxford: Oxford University Press.

Lindseth, Peter L. (2004) 'The paradox of parliamentary supremacy: delegation, democracy, and dictatorship in Germany and France, 1920s–1950s.' *Yale Law Journal*, 113, 1341–1415.

Lindseth, Peter L. (2010) *Power and Legitimacy: Reconciling Europe and the Nation-State*. Oxford: Oxford University Press.

Loughlin, Martin (2003) *The Idea of Public Law*. Oxford: Oxford University Press.

Loughlin, Martin (2014a) 'Constitutional pluralism: an oxymoron?' *Global Constitutionalism*, 3 (1) 9–30.

Loughlin, Martin (2014b) 'The concept of constituent power.' *European Journal of Political Theory*, 13 (2) 218–237.

Loughlin, Martin (2015) 'The constitutional imagination.' *Modern Law Review*, 78 (1) 1–25.

Loughlin, Martin (2019) 'The contemporary crisis of constitutional democracy.' *Oxford Journal of Legal Studies*, 39 (2) 435–454.

Loughlin, Martin (2022) *Against Constitutionalism*. Cambridge, MA: Harvard University Press.

Loughlin, Martin and Neil Walker (eds) (2008) *The Paradox of Constitutionalism: Constituent Power and Constitutional Form*. Oxford: Oxford University Press.

Loughlin, Martin and Stephen Tierney (2018) 'The shibboleth of sovereignty.' *Modern Law Review*, 81 (6) 989–1016.

Lucchese, Filippo del (2017) 'Machiavelli and constituent power: the revolutionary foundation of modern political thought.' *European Journal of Political Theory*, 16 (1) 3–23.

Luhmann, Niklas (1969) *Legitimation durch Verfahren.* Neuwied: Suhrkamp.

Luhmann, Niklas (1973) 'Politische Verfassungen im Kontext des Gesellshaftssystems.' Parts 1 and 2. *Der Staat,* 12 (1) 1–22, 165–182.

Luhmann, Niklas (1988) 'The third question: the creative use of paradoxes in law and legal history.' *Journal of Law and Society,* 15 (2) 153–165.

Luhmann, Niklas (1990) *Political Theory in the Welfare State.* Berlin: de Gruyter.

Luhmann, Niklas (1991) 'Verfassung als evolutionäre Errungenschaft.' *Rechtshistorisches Journal,* 9, 176–220.

Luhmann, Niklas (2002) *Die Politik der Gesellschaft.* Frankfurt am Main: Suhrkamp.

Luhmann, Niklas (2004) *Law as a Social System.* Oxford: Oxford University Press.

Luhmann, Niklas (2010) *Politische Soziologie.* Frankfurt: Suhrkamp.

Luhmann, Niklas (2013) *Introduction to Systems Theory.* Cambridge: Polity.

Luhmann, Niklas (2014) *A Sociological Theory of Law* (Martin Albrow, ed.). London: Routledge.

Luhmann, Niklas (2022) 'The paradox of human rights and three forms for its unfolding.' *Journal of Law and Society,* 49 (3) 567–576.

Mac Amhlaigh, Cormac, Claudio Michelon and Neil Walker(eds) (2013) *After Public Law.* Oxford: Oxford University Press.

MacCormick, Neil (1999) *Questioning Sovereignty.* Oxford: Oxford University Press.

Madsen, Mikael Rask and Chris Thornhill (eds) (2014) *Law and the Formation of Modern Europe: Perspectives from the Historical Sociology of Law.* Cambridge: Cambridge University Press.

Madsen, Mikael R. and Gert Verschraegen (eds) (2013) *Making Human Rights Intelligible: Towards a Sociology of Human Rights.* Oxford: Hart Publishing.

Manin, Bernard (1997) *Principles of Representative Government.* Cambridge, MA: Harvard University Press.

Mansbridge, Jane (2003) 'Rethinking representation.' *American Political Science Review,* 97 (4) 515–528.

Masterson, M. P. (1972) 'Montesquieu's grand design: the political sociology of "Esprit de Lois".' *British Journal of Political Science,* 2 (3) 283–318.

Montesquieu, Charles (1977) *The Political Theory of Montesquieu* (Melvin Richter, ed.). Cambridge: Cambridge University Press.

Morgan, Edmund S. (1988) *Inventing the People: The Rise of Popular Sovereignty in England and America.* New York: Norton.

Morlok, Martin (2014) *Soziologie der Verfassung.* Munich: Beck.

Mouffe, Chantal (2005) *The Democratic Paradox.* London: Verso.

Moyn, Samuel (2005) 'Savage and modern liberty: Marcel Gauchet and the origins of New French Thought.' *European Journal of Political Theory,* 4 (2) 164–187.

Neuhann, Esther (2020) '*Constituent power: a history of what exactly?*' *VerfBlog,* 20 December, https://verfassungsblog.

Neves, Marcelo (2013) *Transconstitutionalism.* Oxford: Hart.

Newey, Glen (2001) *After Politics: The Rejection of Politics in Contemporary Liberal Philosophy.* New York: Palgrave.

Newey, Glen (2010) 'Two dogmas of liberalism.' *European Journal of Political Theory,* 9 (4) 449–465.

Newey, Glen (2012) 'Just politics.' *Critical Reviews of International Social and Political Philosophy*, 15 (2) 165–182.

Nicholls, Sophie (2019) 'Sovereignty and government in Jean Bodin's "Six Libres de la République".' *Journal of History of Ideas*, 80 (1) 47–66.

Nootens, Geniviéve (2015) 'Constituent power and the people-as-the-governed: about the "invisible" people of political and legal theory.' *Global Constitutionalism*, 4 (2) 137–156.

Oakeshott, Michael (1933) *Experience and its Modes*. Cambridge: Cambridge University Press.

Ochoa Espejo, Paulina (2011) *The Time of Popular Sovereignty: Process and the Democratic State*. University Park, PA: Pennsylvania State University Press.

Palonen, Kari (1997) 'Quentin Skinner's rhetoric of conceptual change.' *History of the Human Sciences*, 10 (2) 61–80.

Palonen, Kari (2004) 'Max Weber, parliamentarianism and the rhetorical culture of politics.' *Max Weber Studies*, 4, 273–292.

Palonen, Kari (2010) 'Max Weber's rhetoric of "Objectivity": The parliament as a paradigm for scholarly disputes.' *Max Weber Studies*, 10, 71–93.

Palonen, Kari (2012) 'Towards a history of parliamentary concepts.' *Parliaments, Estates and Representation*, 32 (2) 123–138.

Palonen, Kari (2014) *Politics and Conceptual Histories: Rhetorical and Temporal Perspectives*. Baden-Baden: Nomos Bloomsbury.

Palonen, Kari (2018) 'A comparison between three ideal types of parliamentary politics: representation, legislation and deliberation.' *Parliaments, Estates and Representation*, 38 (1) 6–20.

Pankakovski, Timo (2010) 'Conflict, context, concreteness: Koselleck and Schmitt on concepts.' *Political Theory*, 38 (6) 749–779.

Parsons, Talcott (1969) *Politics and Social Structure*. New York: The Free Press.

Peters, Anne (2009) 'Humanity as the A and O of sovereignty.' *European Journal of International Law* 20, 513–544.

Philp, Mark (2007) *Political Conduct*. Cambridge, MA: Harvard University Press.

Philp, Mark (2010) 'What is to be done? Political theory and political realism.' *European Journal of Political Theory*, 9 (4) 466–484.

Piketty, Thomas (2020) *Capital and Ideology*. Cambridge, MA: Belknap Harvard.

Pitkin, Hanna (2004) 'Representation and democracy: uneasy alliance.' *Scandinavian Political Studies*, 27 (3) 335–342.

Pocock, J. G. A. (2003) *The Machiavellian Moment: Florentine Political Thought and the Atlantic Republican Tradition*. Princeton, NJ: Princeton University Press.

Přibáň, Jiří (2009) 'The self-referential European polity, its legal context and systemic differentiation: theoretical reflections on the emergence of the EU's political and legal autopoiesis.' *European Law Journal*, 15 (4) 442–461.

Přibáň, Jiří (2012) 'Constitutionalism as fear of the political? A comparative analysis of Teubner's *Constitutional Fragments* and Thornhill's *A Sociology of Constitutions*.' *Journal of Law and Society*, 39 (3) 441–471.

Přibáň, Jiří (2015) 'Power in sovereignty and its self-legitimation: on the autopoietic semantics and contingency of popular sovereignty.' *International Journal of Law in Context*, 11 (4) 481–495.

Prinz, Janosch and Enzo Rossi (2017) 'Political realism as ideology critique.' *Critical Review of International Social and Political Philosophy*, 20 (3) 348–365.

Prosser, Tony (2018) 'Constitutions as communication.' *International Journal of Constitutinal Law*, 15 (4) 1039–1065.

Rask Madsen, Mikael and Gert Verschraegen (eds) (2013) *Making Human Rights Intelligible: Towards a Sociology of Human Rights*. Oxford: Hart Publishing.

Rasmussen, Terje (2003) *Luhmann: Kommunikasjon, medier, samfunn [Luhmann: Communication, media, society]*. Bergen: Fagbokforlaget.

Rasmussen, Terje (2015) *Offentlig parlamentarisme: Politisk strid og offentlig mening: 1945–2000 [Public Parliamentarianism: Political Conflict and Public Opinion: 1945–2000]*. Oslo: Pax Forlag.

Rasmussen, Terje (2017) 'Mediated frustration and self-legitimation.' In: Mauro Barisione and Asimina Michailidou (eds) *Rethinking Power and Legitimacy in the Digital Era*. London: Palgrave Macmillan.

Rasmussen, Terje (2022) *Political Legitimacy: Realism in Political Theory and Sociology*. London: Routledge.

Rasmussen, Terje (2024) *Suverenitet: Den uendelige debatten [Sovereignty: The Neverending Debate]*. Oslo: Cappelen Damm.

Rawlings, Richard, Peter Leyland and Alison Young (eds) (2013) *Sovereignty and the Law: Domestic, European, and International Perspectives*. Oxford: Oxford University Press.

Rosanvallon, Pierre (1995) 'The history of the word "democracy" in France.' *Journal of Democracy*, 6 (4) 140–153.

Rosanvallon, Pierre (2000) *La démocratie inachevée: Histoire de la souveraineté du peuple en France*. Paris: Gallimard.

Rosanvallon, Pierre (2002a) *Le peuple introuvable: Histoire de la représentation démocratique en France*. Paris: Gallimard.

Rosanvallon, Pierre (2002b) 'Political rationalism and democracy in France in the 18th and 19th centuries.' *Philosophy and Social Criticism*, 28 (6) 687–701.

Rosanvallon, Pierre (2003) *Pour une histoire conceptuelle du politique*. Leçon inaugurale faite au Collège de France le jeudi 28 mars 2002. Paris: Editions du Seuil.

Rosanvallon, Pierre (2006) *Democracy Past and Future* (Samuel Moyn, ed.). New York: Columbia University Press.

Rosanvallon, Pierre (2008) *Counter-democracy: Politics in an Age of Distrust*. Cambridge: Cambridge University Press.

Rosanvallon, Pierre (2011) *Democratic Legitimacy: Impartiality, Reflexivity, Proximity*. Princeton, NJ: Princeton University Press.

Rossi, Enzo (2010) 'Reality and imagination in political theory and practice: on Raymond Geuss' realism.' *European Journal of Political Theory*, 9 (4) 504–512.

Rossi, Enzo (2012) 'Justice, legitimacy and (normative) authority for political realists.' *Critical Review of International Social and Political Philosophy*, 15 (2) 149–164.

Rossi, Enzo (2013) 'Consensus, compromise, justice and legitimacy.' *Critical Review of International Social and Political Philosophy*, 16 (4) 557–572.

Rousseau, Jean-Jacques (1953) *Jean-Jacques Rousseau: Political Writings*. New York: Thomas Yelsen.

Rubinelli, Lucia (2018) 'Taming sovereignty: constituent power in nineteenth-century French political thought.' *History of European Ideas*, 44 (1) 60–74.

Rubinelli, Lucia (2019) 'How to think beyond sovereignty: on Sieyès and constituent power.' *European Journal of Political Theory*, 18 (1) 47–67.

Rubinelli, Lucia (2020) *Constituent Power: A History*. Cambridge: Cambridge University Press.

Sartori, Giovanni (1962) 'Constitutionalism: a preliminary discussion.' *American Political Science Review*, 56 (4) 853–864.

Saward, Michael (2008) 'Representation and democracy: revisions and possibilities.' *Sociology Compass*, 2 (3) 1000–1013.

Saward, Michael (2010) *The Representative Claim*. Oxford: Oxford University Press.

Scharpf, Fritz (1999) *Governing in Europe: Effective and Democratic?* Oxford: Oxford University Press.

Scheppele, Kim Lane (2017) 'The social lives of constitutions.' In: Paul Blokker and Chris Thornhill (eds) *Sociological Constitutionalism*. Cambridge: Cambridge University Press.

Schmitt, Carl (1922/2005) *Political Theology: Four Chapters on the Concept of Sovereignty*. Chicago: University of Chicago Press.

Schmitt, Carl (1932/1996) *The Concept of the Political*. Chicago: University of Chicago Press.

Schmitt, Carl (2008) *Political Theology II*. Cambridge: Polity Press.

Sciulli, David (1992) *Theory of Societal Constitutionalism*. Cambridge: Cambridge University Press.

Searle, John (1969) *Speech Acts: An Essay in the Philosophy of Language*. Cambridge: Cambridge University Press.

Sieyès, Emmanuel Joseph (2014) *The Essential Political Writings* (Oliver W. Lembcke and Florian Weber, eds). Hague: Brill.

Skinner, Quentin (1981/2019) *Machiavelli: A Very Short Introduction*. Oxford: Oxford University Press.

Skinner, Quentin (1999) 'Hobbes and the purely artificial person of the state.' *Journal of Political Philosophy*, 7 (1) 1–29.

Skinner, Quentin (2005) 'Hobbes on representation.' *European Journal of Philosophy* 13 (2) 155–184.

Skinner, Quentin (2018) *From Humanism to Hobbes: Studies in Rhetoric and Politics*. Cambridge: Cambridge University Press.

Sleat, Matt (2013) *Liberal Realism: A Realist Theory of Liberal Politics*. Manchester: Manchester University Press.

Soininen, S. and T. Turkka (2008) *The Parliamentary Style of Politics*. Helsinki: Finnish Political Science Foundation.

Somek, Alexander (2014) *The Cosmopolitan Constitution*. Oxford: Oxford University Press.

Somek, Alexander (2015) 'Delegation and authority: authoritarian liberalism today.' *European Law Journal*, 21 (3) 340–360.

Sottilotta, Cecilia Emma (2022) 'How not to manage crises in the European Union.' *International Affairs*, 98 (5) 1595–1613.

Spadafora, Andrew (2017) 'Georg Jellinek on values and objectivity in the legal and political sciences.' *Modern International History*, 14 (3) 747–776.

Stankiewicz, W. J. (ed.) (1969) *In Defence of Sovereignty*. New York: Oxford University Press.

Stanton, Tim (2016) 'Popular sovereignty in an age of mass democracy: politics, parliament and parties in Weber, Kelsen, Schmitt and beyond.' In: Quintin Skinner and Richard Bourke (eds) *Popular Sovereignty in Historical Perspective*. Cambridge: Cambridge University Press.

Stirk, Peter (2005) 'The Westphalian model, sovereignty and law in *fin-de-siècle* German international theory.' *International Relations*, 19 (2) 153–172.

Storberget, Knut (2017) '17- mai og alle de andre dagene' ('17 may and all the other days'). In: Andreas Føllesdal and Morten Ruud Geir Ulfstein (eds) *Menneskerettighetene og Norge: Rettsutvikling, rettsliggjøring og demokrati* (*Human Rights and Norway: Development of Law, Juridification and Democracy*). Oslo: Universitetsforlaget.

Swartz, David L. (2013) *The Political Sociology of Pierre Bourdieu*. Chicago: University of Chicago Press.

Teubner, Gunther (2012) *Constitutional Fragments: Societal Constitutionalism and Globalization*. Oxford: Oxford University Press.

Teubner, Gunther (2017) 'Societal constitutionalism: nine variations on a theme by David Sculli.' In: Paul Blokker and Chris Thornhill (eds) *Sociological Constitutionalism*. Cambridge: Cambridge University Press.

Thiem, Annika (2013) 'Schmittian shadows and contemporary theological-political constellations.' *Social Research*, 80 (1) 1–23.

Thornhill, Chris (2008) 'Towards a historical sociology of constitutional legitimacy.' *Theoretical Sociology*, 37 (2) 161–197.

Thornhill, Chris (2011) *A Sociology of Constitutions: Constitutions and State Legitimacy in Historical-Sociological Perspective*. Cambridge: Cambridge University Press.

Thornhill, Chris (2013a) 'State building, constitutional rights and the social construction of norms: outline for a sociology of constitutions.' In: Mikael Rask Madsen and Gert Verschraegen (eds) *Making Human Rights Intelligible: Towards a Sociology of Human Rights*. Oxford: Hart Publishing.

Thornhill, Christopher (2013b) 'A sociology of constituent power: the political code of transnational societal constitutions.' *Indiana Journal of Global Legal Studies*, 20 (2) 551–603.

Thornhill, Chris (2014) 'Legal revolutions and the sociology of law.' *Social and Legal Studies*, 23 (4) 491–516.

Thornhill, Chris (2016) 'The sociological origins of global law.' In: Alberto Febbrajo and Giancarlo Corsi (eds) *Sociology of Constitutions*. London: Routledge.

Thornhill, Chris (2017) 'The sociology of constitutions.' *Annual Review of Law and Social Science*, 13, 493–513.

Thornhill, Chris (2018) *The Sociology of Law and the Global Transformation of Democracy*. Cambridge: Cambridge University Press.

Thornhill, Chris (2021) *Democratic Crisis and Global Constitutional Law*. Cambridge: Cambridge University Press.

Thornhill, Chris and Samantha Ashenden (eds) (2010) *Legality and Legitimacy: Normative and Sociological Approaches*. Baden-Baden: Nomos.

Tilly, Charles (1997) 'Parliamentarization of popular contention in Great Britain, 1758–1834.' *Theory and Society*, 26 (2–3) 245–273.

Timmermans, Nora (2019) 'A positive or negative conception of sovereignty? Marcel Gauchet, Benjamin Constant and liberal democracy.' In: Bas Leijssenaar and Neil Walker (eds) *Sovereignty in Action*. Cambridge: Cambridge University Press.

Tocqueville, Alexis de (2017) *Democracy in America*. Vols. I and II. New York: Dover Publications.

Troper, Michel (2010) 'The survival of sovereignty.' In: Hent Kalmo and Quentin Skinner (eds) (2010) *Sovereignty in Fragments: The Past, Present and Future of a Contested Concept*. Cambridge: Cambridge University Press.

Tully, James (ed.) (1988) *Meaning and Context: Quentin Skinner and his Critics*. Cambridge: Polity.

Tuori, Kaarlo (2019) 'European constitutionalism' In: Roger Masterson and Robert Schütze (eds) *The Cambridge Companion to Comparative Constitutive Law*. Cambridge: Cambridge University Press.

Tuori, Kaarlo and Sankari Suvi (2010) *The Many Constitutions of Europe*. Farnham: Ashgate.

Urbinati, Nadia (2006) *Representative Democracy: Concept and Genealogy*. Chicago: Chicago University Press.

Urbinati, Nadia (2014) *Democracy Disfigured: Opinion, Truth, and the People*. Cambridge, MA: Harvard University Press.

Van Dijk, Teun (2003) 'Knowledge in parliamentary debates.' *Journal of Language and Politics*, 2 (1) 93–129.

Verschraegen, Gert (2011) 'Hybrid constitutionalism, fundamental rights and the state.' *Rechtsfilosofie & Rechtstheorie*, 40 (3) 216–229.

Vieira, Mónica Brito (ed.) (2017) *Reclaiming Representation: Contemporary Advances in the Theory of Political Representation*. London: Routledge.

Vincent, Steven K. (2015) 'Benjamin Constant and constitutionalism.' *Revista de Historia Constitucional*, 16, 19–46.

Volkenstein, Fabio (2019) 'Agents of popular sovereignty.' *Political Theory*, 47 (3) 1–25.

Vorländer, Hans (2017) 'Constitutions as symbolic orders: the cultural analysis of constitutionalism.' In: Paul Blokker and Chris Thornhill (eds) *Sociological Constitutionalism*. Cambridge: Cambridge University Press.

Waldron, Jeremy (1999) *Law and Disagreement*. Oxford: Oxford University Press.

Walker, Neil (2002) 'The idea of constitutional pluralism.' *Modern Law Review* 65, 317–359.

Walker, Neil (ed.) (2003) *Sovereignty in Transition*. Oxford: Hart.

Weber, Cynthia (1995) *Simulating Sovereignty: Intervention, the State, and Symbolic Exchange*. Cambridge: Cambridge University Press.

Weber, Max (2004a) *The Essential Weber: A Reader* (Sam Whimster, ed.). London: Routledge.

Weber, Max (2004b) *From Max Weber* (Hans H. Gerth and C. Wright Mills, eds). Cambridge: Cambridge University Press.

Weber, Max (2009) *Allgemeine Staatslehre und Politik (Staatssoziologie)* (G Hübinger, ed. with A. Terwey). MGW III/7. Tübingen: Mohr Siebeck.

Weber, Max (2010) *Political Writings* (Peter Lassman and Ronald Speirs, eds). Cambridge: Cambridge University Press.

Weber, Max (2013) *Economy and Society: An Outline of Interpretive Sociology.* Vols. I–II. Berkeley, CA: University of California Press.

Werner, Wouter G. and Jaap H. De Wilde (2011) 'The endurance of sovereignty.' *European Journal of International Relations*, 7 (3) 283–313.

Weymans, Wim (2005) 'Freedom through political representation: Lefort, Gauchet and Rosanvallon on the relationship between state and society.' *European Journal of Political Theory*, 4 (3) 263–282.

Williams, Bernard (2005) *In the Beginning Was the Deed: Realism and Moralism in Political Argument.* Princeton, NJ: Princeton University Press.

Williams, Bernard (2014) *Essays and Reviews 1959–2002.* Princeton, NJ: Princeton University Press.

Wodac, Ruth, Rudolf de Cillia, Martin Reisigl and Karin Liebhart (2009) *The Discursive Construction of National Identity.* Edinburgh: Edinburgh University Press.

Worthington, Glenn (1997) 'Oakeshott's claims of politics.' *Political Studies*, 45 (4) 727–738.

Index

Ackerman, Bruce 61, 65, 162, 178
Allan, James 172
Arendt, Hannah 80
Austin, John 18, 54

Beetham, David 26
Beetz, Pieter Jan 195
Bellamy, Richard 22, 186
Benjamin, Walter 126
Berlin, Isaiah 167
Bismarck, Otto von 25
Blackstone, William 104
Blokker, Paul 148
Bluntschli, Johann Caspar 20, 98
Bodin, Jean 2, 3, 39, 46, 67–71, 81, 96, 103, 106–107, 131, 133, 170, 195
Bourdieu, Pierre 13, 20, 45, 124, 145, 155–157, 162
Brunkhorst, Hauke 171
Brunner, Otto 36

Caldwell, Peter C. 96
Campbell, Tom K. 172
Castoriadis, Cornelius T. 45
Coleridge, Samuel Taylor 152
Collingwood, George Robin 3
Condorcet, Marquis de 110, 118, 120
Connolly, William 59, 60
Constant, Benjamin 83
Craiutu, Aurelian 88
Cromwell, Oliver 195

Dilthey, Wilhelm 57
Dobner, Petra 184
Dunn, John 59, 60

Durkheim, Emile 19, 45, 73, 75, 77–78, 84, 103, 110, 124–125, 147
Dworkin, Ronald 20

Elias, Norbert 20

Foucault, Michel 13
Freud, Sigmund 115

Gallie, Walter B. 59
Gauchet, Marcel 85
Geenens, Raf 83
Griffin, Stephen M. 150
Grimm, Dieter 16, 21–23, 66, 69, 178, 191–192
Grotius, Hugo 67
Geuss, Raymond 14, 157
Guizot, François 83, 86–88, 91, 110

Habermas, Jürgen 9, 20, 35, 43, 188
Heller, Hermann 105–109, 120, 140, 181, 184, 195
Hensel, Silke 148
Hintze, Otto 95
Hitler, Adolf 151
Hobbes, Thomas 1–3, 6, 10, 12, 31, 39, 46, 67–72, 77–78, 89, 124, 133, 146, 157–158, 179, 195–196
Holmes, Stephen 85
Husserl, Edmund 108

Ihalainen, Pasi 40, 53–56, 152

Jaume, Lucien 150
Jellinek, Georg 27, 66, 95–106, 115, 181, 195

Kant, Immanuel 168
Kantorowicz, Ernst H. 159
Kelly, Duncan 115
Kelsen, Hans 103, 106–111, 184
Koselleck, Reinhart 6–7, 12, 14,
    36–38, 53–55
Krause, Sharon R. 74

Laband, Paul 106
Larsen, Signe R. 189
Lefort, Claude 9, 12, 51, 85, 124–134,
    140–142, 147, 159–161, 165
Locke, John 12, 40, 71, 98, 168,
    180
Loughlin, Martin 5, 132, 141, 169–
    170, 179–181, 189, 195
Luhmann, Niklas 6, 9, 12–15, 19–24,
    30–45, 51–53, 61, 98, 113, 115,
    124–127, 140, 157, 166, 174, 178,
    197
Luther, Martin 74

Machiavelli, Niccolò 3, 6, 11, 14, 45,
    54, 62, 68–69, 72, 105, 124–125,
    196
Macron, Emmanuel 8, 18, 151, 195,
    198
Maistre, Joseph de 79, 87, 103
Malberg, Carrè de Raymond 80–81,
    95, 100–102, 115
Manin, Bernard 116
Mann, Michel 20
Mansbridge, Jane 116
Marx, Karl 19, 38, 90, 115
May, T. E. 152
Mill, John Stuart 152
Milton, John 195
Montesquieu, Charles 25, 40, 46, 68,
    72–78, 84, 114, 124, 137, 148,
    168, 180, 196
Morgan, Edmund S. 172
Mouffe, Chantal 6
Mussolini, Benito 151

Napoléon, Bonaparte 20, 82–84, 90,
    110
Neumann, Franz 75
Nietzsche, Friedrich 115

Oakeshott, Michael 132–133

Palonen, Kari 53–55, 62
Parsons, Talcott 14, 36, 38
Pitkin, Hanna 116, 117
Pocock, J. G. A. 62
Popper, Karl 111
Přibáň, Jiří 93
Proudhon, Pierre-Joseph 90, 116

Rawls, John 9, 20, 116, 188
Richter, Melvin 75
Rickert, Heinrich 57, 108
Robespierre, Maximilien de 110
Rosanvallon, Pierre 4, 9, 12–14, 76,
    109–114, 116, 119, 124, 128–129,
    134–135, 139, 147, 159, 171
Rossi, Enzo 195
Rousseau, Jean-Jaques 21, 46, 76–78,
    80–90, 95, 98, 100–104, 107, 111,
    113–114, 131, 145–147, 168, 170,
    180
Royer-Collard, Pierre-Paul 87
Rubinelli, Lucia 79, 103

Sartori, Giovanni 79, 103
Saussure, Ferdinand 159
Saward, Michael 116–117, 159–160
Schmitt, Carl 6, 9, 24, 36, 38, 80, 96,
    103–107, 124–126, 131, 140, 147,
    184
Schumpeter, Joseph 111
Skocpol, Theda 20
Sieyès, Joseph Emmanuel 21, 46, 55,
    68–69, 79–82, 86, 90, 102–103,
    110, 118, 131, 150, 198
Simmel, Georg 26, 108
Skinner, Quentin 2, 3, 7, 11–14, 37,
    51–55, 72
Somek, Alexander 184
Sottiaux, Stefan 83
Staël, Germaine de 83–84
Stirk, Peter 99

Teubner, Gunther 43, 171
Thatcher, Margaret 26
Thiem, Annika 105
Thornhill, Chris 42, 44, 169, 171,
    174–175
Tierney, Stephen 181
Tilly, Charles 20, 56
Tocqueville, Alexis de 89

Trump, Donald 150
Tuori, Kaarlo 191–192

Urbinati, Nadia 117, 159

Vincent, Steven K. 83
Vorländer, Hans 149, 152–154

Wahl, Rainer 24
Weber, Max 6, 9–16, 19, 21, 24–30,
    35, 41–42, 54–61, 73–75, 95–99,
    102–107, 117, 124, 140, 155–157,
    160
White, Jonathan 184
Williams, Bernard 14, 141

EU authorised representative for GPSR:
Easy Access System Europe, Mustamäe tee 50,
10621 Tallinn, Estonia
gpsr.requests@easproject.com

www.ingramcontent.com/pod-product-compliance
Lightning Source LLC
Chambersburg PA
CBHW052004270326
41929CB00015B/2779